Cabaret FAQ

Cabaret FAQ

All That's Left to Know About the Broadway and Cinema Classic

June Skinner Sawyers

APPLAUSE
THEATRE & CINEMA BOOKS
An Imprint of Hal Leonard LLC

Published in 2017 by Applause Theatre & Cinema Books
An Imprint of Hal Leonard LLC
7777 West Bluemound Road
Milwaukee, WI 53213

Trade Book Division Editorial Offices
33 Plymouth St., Montclair, NJ 07042

The FAQ series was conceived by Robert Rodriguez and developed with Stuart Shea.

Printed in the United States of America

Book design by Snow Creative

Library of Congress Cataloging-in-Publication Data
Names: Sawyers, June Skinner, 1957– author.
Title: Cabaret FAQ : all that's left to know about the Broadway and cinema
  classic / June Skinner Sawyers.
Description: Montclair, NJ : Applause Theatre & Cinema Books, 2017. | Series:
  The FAQ series | Includes bibliographical references and index.
Identifiers: LCCN 2017016614 | ISBN 9781495051449
Subjects: LCSH: Kander, John. Cabaret. | Isherwood, Christopher, 1904-1986.
  Goodbye to Berlin. | Van Druten, John, 1901-1957. I am a camera. | Ebb,
  Fred. | Cabaret (Motion picture : 1972) | Music-halls (Variety-theaters,
  cabarets, etc.)—Germany—History.
Classification: LCC ML410.K163 S39 2017 | DDC 792.6/42—dc23
LC record available at https://lccn.loc.gov/2017016614
www.applausebooks.com

www.applausebooks.com

To Rosemary Tirio, my wonderful English teacher
at Amundsen High School

Contents

Acknowledgments

I would like to thank Tim McGowan at Amundsen High School, Josh Fraenkel, Amanda Meyer and Holly Baker at Margie Korshak Inc., Michael Messina, Jeffrey Soto, Brian Black, Kevin Walsh, Frank Biletz, Rosemary Tirio, and, as always, Theresa Albini. An additional thank-you to Howard Reich of the *Chicago Tribune* and the members of the cabaret community nationwide, especially Beckie Menzie, Ann Hampton Callaway, Karen Mason, as well as Karen Kohler and Claudia Hommel. In addition, I offer my gratitude to the cast and crew of the Jones College Prep School production of *Cabaret*, especially Jack Siebert and Brad Lyons, and the cast and crew of the Roosevelt University production of *Cabaret*, especially Jane Lanier, Michael Lasswell, and Tim Stadler, and much appreciation to Marybeth Keating, Steven Thompson, and Lakia Young at Applause. Thanks also to Theresa Nugent, Cheryl Sauter, and Ann Dobbyn for accompanying me on one of my cabaret night-on-the-town adventures.

Introduction

So, life is disappointing? Forget it. In here, life is beautiful.

—*Emcee*

Those who ignore history are condemned to repeat it.

—*David Brooks*

There was a Cabaret and there was a Master-of-Ceremonies and there was a city called Berlin in a country called Germany. It was the end of the world . . . and I was dancing with Sally Bowles and we were both fast asleep. . . .

—*Cliff Bradshaw, Cabaret*

I saw the movie first. Reluctantly. To say I was a skeptic is an understatement.

The problem started at the 1973 Academy Awards. I was disappointed about all the awards that went to *Cabaret* that night rather than its chief rival and odds-on-favorite, *The Godfather.* True, Francis Ford Coppola's masterpiece would go on to grab the best picture Oscar, but *Cabaret* cleaned up most of the other big awards (eight all together), including best actress (I was rooting for Diana Ross in *Lady Sings the Blues*) and best director (poor Coppola was robbed, I thought).

Still, I knew I had to see it, eventually. And anyway, the director, Bob Fosse, attended the same high school I went to, Amundsen High, in Chicago. How could I not see it? So one Sunday afternoon I went over to my neighborhood theater, the Patio. The film had long finished playing the first-run theaters by then. I settled into my seat, almost daring the movie to prove me wrong.

It did.

I saw it once. Then again. And again. In fact, I went to the theater every week during its multiweek run.

I was smitten, and have been ever since. So when Liza Minnelli came to the Arie Crown Theater in May of that year, guess who was in the audience to see her?

And yet I was curious, not only about the movie itself but about its setting. I knew next to nothing about Weimar Germany aside from the obvious details picked up in high school history classes. I wanted to know not only more about the period but also the story, the backstory, of the movie. What about the stage version? I wanted to know more about that, too; listen to the original Broadway soundtrack; and, eventually, see an actual production for myself. And just who exactly was this Christopher Isherwood chap anyway?

First, I needed to get my hands on the original source material, Isherwood's *Berlin Stories*. But where? During those pre-Internet days, it was no easy feat. My high school library didn't have a copy, nor did my local library. And anyway I wanted my own copy for my own collection. I had to track it down. I made phone call after phone call to mainstream bookstores and small, independent bookstores alike. I felt like a detective on a literary trail that was going nowhere fast.

No luck. In fact, the trail was getting cold.

Christopher Isherwood's collection of stories *Goodbye to Berlin* was the source material for the musical and movie *Cabaret*.   *Author collection. Photo by Theresa Albini*

Until one day. . . . After many dead ends, I decided to contact Florence Shay, the owner of a fine used bookstore called Titles and located in Highland Park, a northern suburb of Chicago, to see if she could help me (I didn't know this at the time but she was the wife of the great street photographer Art Shay, who I would meet years later). Several weeks went by, or was it months? I don't remember now, but eventually I received a telephone call from her.

The elusive book had arrived.

I still have that copy on my shelf.

Cabaret was a different musical for a different time: a modern-day morality play for a difficult era. Even I knew that; I, who knew nothing about musicals nor cared to. It was a musical for people who didn't like musicals. In short, it was revolutionary, both onstage and on the big screen.

Like the best works of art, *Cabaret* has changed over the years just as we, the audience, has changed. A big part of its appeal, and durability, lies in its subversive edginess. It was ahead of its time. It was a new type of musical. Some called it a concept musical. It was hailed as a breakthrough in American musical theater.

What made it unique? What made it innovative?

First and foremost was its unusual subject matter: a musical set in the waning days of Germany's Weimar Republic and the relationships that exist between a brassy English singer who performs at a seedy Berlin cabaret and a diffident, introspective English novelist who gives English-language lessons to get by. But more than this, the cabaret served as a metaphor for the decadence of German society. In fact, *Cabaret* specifically associated the decadence of German culture to the collapse of the Weimar Republic and the rise of incipient Nazism.

Cabaret's journey to the stage and later the screen begins with a book, and a modest one. *Goodbye to Berlin* is a collection of linked stories by the English author Christopher Isherwood. This book will examine how the musical and movie that most of us know so well came to be, its significance, and its ongoing legacy. It also makes connections—sometimes directly, sometimes indirectly through association—between the musical and various other art forms, from art to popular song to the status of the modern cabaret.

But first we need to begin at the beginning. And for that we must begin elsewhere: in Paris. At the end of the nineteenth century.

Cabaret FAQ

The Roots of Cabaret

The First Cabarets

The first modern cabaret opened not in Germany but in Paris.

In 1878, Émile Goudeau (1849–1906) started a literary café in Montmartre that he called the Hydropathes, the precursor and role model of the more successful and better-known Chat Noir that he established three years later with his friend Rodolphe Salis. Goudeau's little group staged poetry and prose readings as well as songs. They also published a short-lived journal. During the 1880s, Goudeau published two bohemian books, a novel about the bohemian life, *La vache enrage*, and a memoir, *Ten Years of Bohemia*.

On November 18, 1881, the Chat Noir, or Black Cat, opened at 84 Boulevard Rochechouart in Montmartre, a rural area of Paris. Located in a small, dark former post building, it was modest in scale, consisting of two large rooms and separated by a curtain. The Chat Noir was popular from the beginning. It attracted poets, writers, dancers, singers, composers, painters, and playwrights, including Jane Avril, André Gill, Paul Verlaine, Henri Rivière, Claude Debussy, Erik Satie, Yvette Guilber, Émile Goudeau, Aristide Bruant, August Strindberg, and Henri de Toulouse-Lautrec.

Montmartre was known for its rustic charm—it was an area dotted with vineyards, dirt roads, and cheap cafés. Many of its cabarets were situated at the lower edge of the community along or near the boulevards Clichy and Rochechouart. The side streets, leading up to the hill, were populated by prostitutes, street people, pimps, con men, and thieves—what Lisa Appignanesi has called the rabble: the outcasts of society and all congregating among the quaint old buildings. By the 1890s, many artists and writers began to settle in the area, creating a volatile mixture of creativity and lawlessness and turning Montmarte into the center of bohemian life in Paris.

As a literary cabaret, Chat Noir combined elements of the literary salon (intellectual and political) and the café-concert, which consisted of songs and other forms of popular entertainment. It also served food and drinks.

More than this, it emphasized spontaneity and rude humor—traits that would later follow in Germany.

Chat Noir was known for its irreverence and social satire and set the tone for future cabarets. But what French, and later German, cabarets had in common was a sense of intimacy where people could talk and smoke, eat and drink. The cabaret was a meeting place for artists, but it was also an intimate revue. Today we would call it a third place, to use the term made famous by sociologist Ray Oldenburg, to refer to public gathering places that promoted democracy and civic dialogue.

The Chat Noir, located in the bohemian Montmarte district of Paris, is considered the first modern cabaret. In the late nineteenth century and early twentieth century, many artists had studios or worked in or around the area, including Pablo Picasso, Henri de Toulouse-Lautrec, Erik Satie, and many others.

Author collection

Montmartre stood apart from Paris in many ways, but perhaps its most distinctive feature was its quasi-rural, preindustrial character. Down its steep and winding streets, Montmartre was where art, cabaret, and anarchy not only reigned but coexisted. Montmartre, in fact, was the unofficial headquarters of the anarchist movement in 1890s Paris. Numerous anarchists published their newspapers and journals from here. Many well-known artists such as Camille Pisarro and Théophile Steinlen contributed images to the anarchist papers. The French even had a name to refer to middle-class people slumming in lower-class bohemia: "nostalgia for sordidness" or *nostalgie de la boue.*

In the French bistro or café tradition, French song, or *chanson*, was used as the medium of public communication, the broadsheet of its day, that reported current events and opinions. In essence, it functioned as the people's newspaper, a democratic tool that ridiculed authority and challenged hypocrisy; a rallying cry for ordinary people, especially in working-class Montmartre.

The café, or cabaret, eventually emerged into the café-concert, which became known as the music hall in other countries. The primary focus of the café was entertainment. In turn, the cabaret grew out of this café-concert tradition. In these kind of places, satire and protest songs formed "the ingredients that first went into the making of the cabaret," notes Lisa Appignanesi.

According to Harold B. Segel, the term "cabaret" was first recorded in French in the late thirteenth century to refer to a drinking establishment, a tavern, or a wine cellar.

The cabaret was a testing ground for young artists flexing their cultural muscles as well as a reflection of modern events and mores. A typical cabaret program at Chat Noir, for example, might have consisted of songs, monologues, sketches, poetry, and dance. Common themes would include elements that were rebellious, witty, satirical, and innovative, full of dissent and resistance.

What Is a Cabaret?

Cabaret is a type of entertainment that usually features a combination of music, song, dance, or drama of some sort. It might take place in a restaurant or a nightclub or a pub. The audience usually sits at a table. Typically, performances are introduced by a master of ceremonies. The material presented in cabarets, especially in Europe, can be subversive in nature. In the United States, the definition of what constitutes a cabaret can be quite broad. On the one hand, it could refer to an upscale nightclub act such as the elegant Café Carlyle in New York. On the other hand, the term might be used to indicate a strip club, a drag show, or a burlesque show, such as the Drifter or Bordel, both in Chicago.

Like a great bartender, a great cabaret singer is part philosopher, part poet, part storyteller, and part friend who also happens to sing of tragedy, loss, betrayal, love, dreams, and truth.

The physical elements of the cabaret might include the following:

- A small stage
- A small audience
- A social ambiance specific to the location
- A particular relationship between performer and spectator that could be, paradoxically, intimate and hostile
- The breaking down of the fourth wall

The root of the word "cabaret" comes from the French word meaning "wine cellar" or "tavern." But the word itself derives from the Middle Dutch "cabret," which essentially refers to a "small room."

Rodolphe Salis, the son of a wealthy brewer, is credited with being the creator of the modern cabaret. A cabaret was defined as a nightclub where customers sit at tables imbibing alcoholic drinks and enjoying a variety of performers on a stage who are introduced by a master of ceremonies who also interacts with the audience. Thus, a bar that featured entertainment was an innovative idea at the time.

Salis acted as the host and conférencier, that is, a master of ceremonies, who introduced the poets and songwriters, and improvised monologues as he addressed the audience with tongue-in-cheek deference.

During the early days of Chat Noir, Salis's artistic friends gathered in the club to chat, read, and perform their works for one another—much like people today gather in cafés and other gathering places. Then he came up with the idea of serving drinks and opening the club's doors to "a select public" once a week. He had a specific type of décor in mind too: medieval arms, old doors, wooden tables, a fireplace, rough Louis XIII chairs, and furniture castoffs. But one corner of the room was so dark and damp that no one wanted to go into it. To encourage customers—to make it special—he turned this part of the café into what he called the "Institute," where patrons were welcomed by waiters dressed in the traditional green scholarly robes of the French Academy. The Institute soon expanded into the room next door. In this way, he very shrewdly turned the idea of bohemia into theater.

Chat Noir presented dramatic readings of poetry or prose. Songs were also sung. During its early years, the program was unstructured, spontaneous. Poets and musicians performed. Chat Noir poked fun at politicians. Nothing was sacred, nothing was off-limits. Its clientele of eccentrics and misfits reflected the surrounding neighborhood. In addition to its artistic bent, it was also a hangout for prostitutes and petty criminals.

As its popularity increased, the Chat Noir attracted many famous visitors: Maupassant, Huysmans, Toulouse-Lautrec, Debussy, Émile Zola, Stéphane Mallarmé, Adolphe Willette, Henri Rivière, and Théophile Steinlen. Verlaine frequented the spot—his ex-brother-in-law, Charles de Sivry, was one of the pianists. Despite the cabaret's fame, the bohemian spirit was retained. Patrons exhibited their paintings, sketches, and drawings—the cabaret also functioned as an informal art gallery. Among the artists who Salis brought to the Chat Noir was a young, eccentric composer and pianist by the name of Erik Satie.

Erik Satie

Erik Satie was the ultimate bohemian. Satie (1866–1925) was a frequent visitor to the cabarets of Montmartre. Today he is best known perhaps for his whimsical piano works such as *Three Pieces in the Shape of a Pear* or his controversial ballet *Parade* (his collaboration with Pablo Picasso, who designed the drop curtain, costumes, and scenery while Jean Cocteau added the sounds of backfiring cars, typewriters, and machinery). Or perhaps his music is recognized from the soundtrack of the popular 1981 French film *Diva*. Either way, he lived a short distance from the Chat Noir, and began his career there. He began working as a piano accompanist at the Chat Noir in 1887, before he had a falling-out with owner Rodolphe Salis. He then went to another Montmarte cabaret, the Auberge du Clou, again playing the piano. But it was at the Chat Noir that he felt he could be himself. He grew his hair and beard and adopted a decidedly more bohemian appearance.

Eventually, Satie incorporated the popular music he heard in the Montmartre cabarets into his own singular creations. His music is considered the precursor to ambient music. Making a living as a cabaret pianist, he adapted more than one hundred compositions of popular music for piano or piano and voice. He later became involved in the Dadaist movement and contributed to the Dadaist magazine *391*.

Like the Hydropathes, the Chat Noir also published its own newspaper/ magazine, called *Le Chat Noir*, with Goudeau as its editor. In addition to news about goings-on at the cabaret, the paper eagerly promoted Montmartre itself as a community and as an artistic gathering place. Steinlen provided the graphic work. He created the famous Chat Noir poster: that of the black cat with the penetrating stare, which came to symbolize the cabaret. It also published satirical sketches, lyrics, poetry, and commentary.

Chat Noir was unique in many ways. One of its most distinctive features was its ribald atmosphere. People actually came to the cabaret to be insulted, to be mocked. Many of the songs and poems were parodies of middlebrow culture. Chat Noir performers depicted the lives of the people in the community, even going so far as adopting their speech rhythms and cadences in their work.

But things were changing. When the neighborhood became too rough even for Salis, the Chat Noir moved to new and larger digs in 1885 to 12, rue de Laval (now the rue Victor Massé). "The move itself was an enormous publicity stunt," writes Jerrold Seigel, "a loud and bizarre parade complete with costumes, music, and elaborate ceremonies for bringing pieces of furniture and decorations from the old hall to the new one."

The Chat Noir closed two years later in February 1897.

Despite its short run, the Chat Noir laid the groundwork for other cabarets, such as Cabaret des Quat'z' Arts, La Lune Rousse, and Les Pantins.

Le Mirliton

When Chat Noir closed in 1897, it was reborn as Le Mirliton ("the reed pipe"). Just as Chat Noir was run by the singular figure of Rodolphe Salis, Le Mirliton was under the helm of the indomitable Aristide Bruant. We know Aristide Bruant today largely through the work of Toulouse-Lautrec. That's him in the Toulouse-Lautrec posters: the swaggering image of a man wearing a broad-brimmed black hat, black velvet jacket, red shirt, and flowing red scarf. It perfectly captures his disdainful demeanor, his haughty pride. He was both a man of the people and a true artist. A songwriter at the Chat Noir and composer of the "Ballad of the Chat Noir," he introduced cabaret songs into the café-concert tradition.

> I seek my fortune
> At the Black Cat
> In the moonlight
> O Montmartre, in the evening.

Bruant was born in the Loiret in 1851, of a solid bourgeois family who had fallen on hard times. Apprenticed to a jewelry maker in Paris, he served in the French army during the Franco-Prussian War and a few years later returned to Paris to work as a clerk in a railway office. But his real life occurred after hours where he would hear the popular songs performed in the city's cafés. Before long he began to perform his own songs in public.

French cabaret singer and owner of Le Mirliton, Aristide Bruant, as captured by Henri de Toulouse-Lautrec in his "uniform": black velvet jacket and flowing red scarf.   *Author collection*

Like Edith Piaf, Bruant's songs have their roots in the argot of the Parisian working class; his rawness and simplicity and brutal honesty made him the best-known figure in the Montmartre cabarets and café world.

When Salis moved his cabaret to larger premises in 1885, Bruant took over the old Chat Noir location and ran it himself. He decorated it with paintings by Steinlen and Lautrec. It was not meant to be a replica of the Chat Noir. It had its own style and ambiance. Bruant installed a piano, tables, and chairs. The walls were hung with paintings, often by Bruant himself or by the cabaret's regulars such as Lautrec and Théophile Steinlen. Customers included journalists, artists, and the outcasts of Montmartre society as well as such notable patrons as Paul Verlaine, Anatole France, Sarah Bernhardt, and Jules Verne. Like the Chat Noir, he also published his own newspaper, which published poems, music, cartoons, and Bruant's own lyrics. He even published his own dictionary of modern Parisian slang but packaged for bourgeois consumption.

Bruant brought a brash and abrasive form of street poetry and socioeconomic criticism to the cabaret form that was colorful and brutal, cynical and lively. Although he got his start in the Parisian cafés-concerts—a favorite of the working class and where a particular style of French popular song flourished, the *chanson* (probably the best-known painting of the café-concert is Edouard Manet's 1879 *The Café-Concert*)—Bruant made his true home in the rough yet intimate confines of the cabaret. There was something special and slightly subversive about going to Le Mirliton. To gain entry customers had to knock at the door like a nineteenth-century French version of an American speakeasy. Once inside, patrons were subjected to a flurry of insults by Bruant—all part of the evening entertainment. Cabaret, after all, celebrated the notion of freedom and rebellion and promulgated a general disdain for the establishment. By welcoming, by relishing the opportunity to hear the verbal abuse, the audience was able to pretend that they too were nonconformists in their own right. The writer Raymond Rudorff described a typical Bruant scene:

> He fully believed in audience participation. Before reciting one of his songs, he would gaze disdainfully at his audience for a few moments and then announce the title of his next number. . . . After a dramatic pause, he would repeat [the title] and then exhort his listeners to join in: "As for you, herd of camels, try to bray together in tune, will you?" He would usually sing from ten or eleven at night until two in the morning, walking up and down or sometimes standing up on a table as he did so.

Le Mirliton was also a favorite of fashionable society, and they too enjoyed being insulted by Bruant. Like Salis before him, Bruant created a rabble-rousing ambiance along with the insults that the audience expected. Indeed, if a patron went away without being insulted they felt dissatisfied. Whether at the Chat Noir or Le Mirliton, the spirit of these Montmartre cabarets was called *fumisme* in French. Roughly speaking, it refers to a general disdain toward everything and everyone. Bruant loved to ridicule the hypocrisy of bourgeois culture. Add an ample dose of skepticism and you had the recipe for success for anyone seeking a taste of bohemia. In essence, it was theater as confrontation, a notion that subsequent generations of artists would entertain, from Bertolt Brecht to Alfred Jarry.

Patrons paid a high admission price to be publicly humiliated. "The innovation was nothing less than the inversion and erasure of the boundary between the spectators and the actor, between the entertainer and the consumers," observes Elena Cueto-Asín. It was this breaking of the fourth wall that would become such an important feature in Bertolt Brecht's work and in the German cabarets.

Bruant sang about the life of the people. His songs were so popular that they traveled beyond the walls of his Montmartre venue to form the foundation of the cabaret chanson tradition. They were sung and popularized by Yvette Guilbert, who carried the songs not in the cabarets (she did not perform in cabarets) but rather in famous clubs such as the Moulin Rouge, the Divan Japonais, and later in concert halls around the world.

Lapin Agile

There were other important cabarets. Lapin Agile was located on the Butte, an out-of-the-way, rural setting, at the tip of Montmartre. Around the turn of the century, the Lapin Agile was popular with local artists and writers as well as marginalized members of the community and students from the Latin Quarter—slumming bourgeoisie who wanted to see what the real "bohemia" looked like. The owner, Frédéric Gérard, a former fishmonger who kept a donkey as a mascot and played the guitar (apparently quite badly), gave free meals and drinks to struggling artists and poets.

In the early 1880s, André Gill took over at the Lapin Agile, modeling it after the Chat Noir. Gill (1840–1885) was a French caricaturist who had been connected to Goudeau's Hydropathes. He was much in demand as an artist. He drew caricature portraits of Sarah Bernhardt, Otto von Bismarck,

Émile Zola, Victor Hugo, Dickens, and Garibaldi, among others. His style was distinctive: large heads that sat on small bodies.

It was Gill who painted the still-famous sign of a black-hatted rabbit with red bowtie and red scarf around his belly precariously balancing a bottle of wine on his right arm while jumping out of a copper saucepan, the iconic Montmartre windmill in the background. From 1886 to 1903, the Lapin Agile was run by a former dancer by the name of Adèle, until she sold it to Aristide Bruant. But Bruant had little hands-on connection with Gill, preferring instead to let Gérard run it.

Lapin Agile might have been tiny—it was only one room—but it was a popular place. Its sardine-can size may actually have contributed to its success—all those patrons of many backgrounds consorting in one tight space created a combustible and intoxicating atmosphere. The clientele was diverse, and singular. Pablo Picasso was a regular; he even designed some of the club's decorations.

As an aside, the Lapin Agile was also known as the Cabaret des Assassins, a prophetic name of sorts since Gerard's son, Victor, was killed there one night in 1911. In fact, his untimely death sounded the death knell of the bohemian community of Montmartre as artists began abandoning the hills for safer parts of Paris; namely, Montparnasse.

Au Lapin Agile Cabaret, in the Montmarte district of Paris. The cabaret is known for its still-famous, and distinctive, sign: that of a rabbit balancing a bottle of wine and jumping out of a saucepan. *Photo by author*

Similar to Chat Noir and Le Mirliton, Lapin Agile was a meeting place for all kinds of artists and writers and painters. In addition to the aforementioned Picasso, they included Apollinaire, Max Jacob, Modigliani, Francis Carco, and Maurice Utrillo, among others. But it was also popular with various local eccentrics and petty criminals and students from the surrounding neighborhood. The bohemian life they lived offstage was reenacted every night on the cabaret stage. "The kinship of cabaret and the early twentieth-century avant-garde was a two-way dynamic: one created the other and was in turn influenced by it," writes Lisa Appignanesi.

In 1905, Picasso's painting *At the Lapin Agile* (1905) made it famous. Nearly ninety years later, in 1993, comedian, actor, and playwright Steve Martin wrote *Picasso at the Lapin Agile*, a fictional meeting between Picasso and Albert Einstein at the café.

The Lapin Agile, located at 22 Rue des Saules, still operates today, Tuesday to Sunday from 9:00 p.m. to 1:00 a.m.

Toulouse-Lautrec

The most famous artist associated with the French cabaret was undoubtedly Henri de Toulouse-Lautrec. He turned his artistic eye toward numerous Montmartre cabarets, cafés, and clubs, including the Moulin Rouge dance hall, and painted posters of the clubs' performers. But as Seigel points out, he actually started his career as an advertising illustrator in the clubs around Montmartre, including the Chat Noir, producing his first lithograph of Bruant in 1885. Lautrec also painted portraits of the popular dancers at the nearby Moulin Rouge and other nightclubs such as singer Yvette Guilbert, the dancer Louise Weber (who is credited with creating the Can Can, and is better known by her not-so-flattering sobriquet of La Goulue or "The Glutton"), and the dancer Jane Avril.

In 2016, the bio-musical *My Paris* by Charles Aznavour opened at the Long Wharf Theater in New Haven. Nearly twenty years earlier, Aznavour had written a West End musical in London, *Lautrec*, about the French artist and set it within the dance hall ambiance of the Moulin Rouge, but it had an unsuccessful run. For this version, Aznavour was joined by a stellar team of Broadway and Tony Award-winning veterans, including director-choreographer Kathleen Marshall and librettist Alfred Uhry. Moreover, Jason Robert Brown provided the English lyrics and musical arrangement.

Characters in the musical included the model Suzanne Valadon as well as cameos by figures made famous in Lautrec's paintings: the dancers La Goulue (Nikka Graff Lanzarone) and Jane Avril (Erica Sweaney); the chanteuse Yvette Guilbert (Kate Marilley); and the flamboyant nightclub owner Aristide Bruant

(Jamie Jackson). The Green Fairy, or absinthe, was embodied in physical form as a woman in white lit in lurid green and holding a bottle, beckoning patrons to imbibe. Lautrec was portrayed by Bobby Steggert.

From Paris, cabaret spread outward and found new life—and took on different and even more exciting forms in neighboring Germany.

The Birth of German Cabaret

The Weimar Republic

The Weimar Republic refers to the government of Germany that existed between the wars; that is, between Germany's defeat at the end of World War I in 1918 and Adolf Hitler's tumultuous rise to power in 1933. Despite or perhaps because of the chaotic atmosphere, Germany, and Berlin in particular, proved to be an exceptionally fertile ground for the arts: not just cabaret but also film, architecture, photography, fashion, and design. Weimar Germany embodied the essence of the modernist movement.

Berlin was considered the most American of the European capitals during the Weimar era. The city was often compared to Chicago. Chicago at the time had a reputation for being the crude exemplar of modern capitalism, the American capital of crass commerce, crackling with the raw energy of a fledgling metropolis with nothing to lose and everything to prove. The American novelist Albert Halper called Chicago "a raw, slangy city."

Those choice words could just as easily describe Berlin during the dozen-plus years of the Weimar Republic, a time of vast change in both the country and among the populace. Berlin was the licentious capital of the world. In 1930, more than two million people flooded into the city. Young men and women congregated in the bars, cafés, and private clubs, dancing to jazz and falling into bed with the first stranger they met. They were amoral and irreverent. They didn't care about the future; they lived for the present. Many were foreigners. In addition to Christopher Isherwood and W. H. Auden, they included the English poet Stephen Spender, the English painter Francis Bacon, the American novelist Paul Bowles, the Russian novelist Vladimir Nabokov, the American composer Aaron Copland, the Swedish actress Greta Garbo, and the American writer Djuna Barnes. But there were many more.

In Dire Straits

Weimar Germany was in dire straits, the result of an economic depression, a loss of trust in institutions, and the social and political humiliation heaped on the country as a result of the severe punishment represented by the Treaty of Versailles after Germany lost in World War I. The terms and reparations imposed by the treaty introduced punishing levels of inflation throughout Germany, and destroyed middle-class savings. Unemployment skyrocketed—at its worst, it exceeded 50 percent. The elites were blamed for being clueless and for not knowing how to fix the myriad problems. The invisible and forgotten were tired of being taken for granted. In essence, the people were ready for a strongman to rescue them from their plight; for someone to make them feel good about themselves, to make Germany great once again.

In Berlin, the population quadrupled between 1871 and 1919, as people swarmed into town, eager to start a new life and reinvent themselves. With the increase in the population came a concomitant jump in criminality, from petty crime to drug dealing to the rise of organized gangs. What's more, German youth, weary from war and intent to live in the moment, made it their mission to savor every experience since they could not take the future for granted. Instead they flocked to the city's many cabarets and nightclubs in search of cheap and preferably illicit thrills in an effort to forget the turmoil that reigned outside their doors.

Leave your troubles outside . . .

Adolf Hitler entered the public imagination in 1919, as a far-right agitator in Munich. A few years later, in 1923, his National Socialist German Workers' Party tried to overthrow the provincial government in the now-famous but unsuccessful Beer Hall Putsch. He served a short stint in jail. But after his release, he emerged stronger and more determined than ever to gain the power that had previously eluded him. The way to gain this power, he reasoned, and destroy the Weimar regime in the process was to do it through legal means; that is, the way to gain power was to appear reasonable, and persuasive: to appear to be on the side of the ordinary folk, the common man, the people, the *Volk*. The way to ingratiate himself to the people was to offer himself up as a kind of savior. All he had to do was to convince the people that he was the only man who could do it. "Hitler came to power," writes the American poet and literary critic Adam Kirsch, "because other, more respectable politicians thought they would be able to control him."

But as many have asked over the decades, including the German people themselves, how could the world have allowed it to happen? And always the unspoken fear: Could it happen again? Could it happen here, wherever "here" happens to be in the world?

Hitler rose through a dangerous combination of demagoguery, showmanship, and a brazen appeal to nativist instincts. He also happened to come to power through a confluence of circumstance, luck, and blindness on the part of his fellow politicians and the general public writ large. He was an egomaniac, a narcissist, and an undisciplined rogue, who was able to analyze and exploit situations to his advantage. He was also an insatiable liar who either could not tell the truth or did not know the difference between lies and the truth—but most likely he simply did not care and expected that his supporters felt the same way.

Hitler was an actor and showman at heart, who fed off the excitement and energy of the crowd at rallies. Indeed, he specialized in these large and theatrical events, many of the elements borrowed from the circus. He adapted the content of his speeches to appeal to the lowest common denominator. He fomented chaos by playing to the fears and prejudice of the mob, of what the American Founding Fathers called "the rabble." He presented himself as a leader who would restore law and order to a chaotic and immoral society. His propaganda could effectively be reduced to a few simple but powerful slogans, as effective as any 140-character tweet.

In short, Hitler appealed to emotion, not reason; to stereotypes and misstatements, not complicated truth; to falsehoods repeated over and over again until the line between fact and fiction becomes blurred. He used simple language and concise slogans to assail the opposition in order to simplify complex information. All nuance was thrown out the window. He created his own reality.

Within five months of assuming power, Hitler acted quickly and consolidated absolute power absolutely. The mainstream press was either suppressed or banned altogether. "Un-German" books were burned in public bonfires. He also imprisoned opponents, had his rivals murdered, and made himself the center of a cult of personality. In speeches, he spoke about Germany's destiny, or, in the lyrics of John Kander and Fred Ebb, how "tomorrow belongs to me."

It Can't Happen Here

In 1935, the American author Sinclair Lewis published his satirical novel *It Can't Happen Here*, a cautionary tale about the fragility of the American experiment in democracy and how, given the right set of circumstances and the right kind of strongman, fascism could indeed "happen" in America. It became a national best seller. Written during the Great Depression and published during the rise of Hitler and Mussolini in Europe, it combined political satire with the realistic rise of a president with the disarming name of Buzz Windrip who becomes a dictator for the benefit of the country: to protect it from welfare cheats, sexual immorality, crime, and the liberal press. His version of the Gestapo is given the patriotic name of the Minute Men. The charismatic Windrip is hailed as the "Savior of the Forgotten Men," a reference to 1 percent of the population controlling 47 percent of the wealth of the country.

Although not necessarily modeled after them, the character of Buzz Windrip is nevertheless reminiscent of several historic figures: Adolf Hitler, Louisiana senator Huey Long, and the strident radio priest Father Charles Coughlin. Nevertheless, following the American model, Windrip is more a combination of confidence man, flim-flam man, and master manipulator of human emotions than a real Nazi, a P. T. Barnum for the times.

And yet Lewis's concerns were real enough. The Nazi propaganda machine was already hard at work in America, denying the persecution and mass murder of Jews. In 1934, the magazine *Modern Monthly* featured a symposium with the ominous title "Will Fascism Come to America?" Years later, in 2013, American author Arnie Bernstein published *Swastika Nation*, a searing and true account of the German American Bund, a small but powerful national movement, led by the German-born Fritz Kuhn, that developed their own version of the SS and Hitler Youth and whose goal was nothing less than to install a fascist government in the United States "run by and for German Aryans and German Aryans alone." In 1935, according to Gary Scharnhorst, the Bund had a membership of about ten thousand members. Four years later, in 1939, a throng of Bund followers attended a huge rally in Madison Square Garden.

A stage adaptation of *It Can't Happen Here* was produced in 1936. In 2011, the play was performed by twenty or so theaters across the United States in honor of its seventy-fifth anniversary, and a new adaptation premiered at the Berkeley Repertory Theatre in September 2016 during the American presidential campaign of Hillary Clinton and Donald Trump.

After the "election" of Trump, the novel rose to the top of Amazon's Classic American Literature category. In an era of fake news, Orwellian alternative facts, and the unprecedented decision by *New York Times* to use footnotes to counteract the "facts" of the Trump administration, Lewis's novel was a chilling reminder of what happens when, against all odds and against all checks and balances, a demagogic populist rises to the presidency of the United States. Similarly, in January 2017, *1984*, George Orwell's classic novel about a dystopian future, surged in sales, rising to the top of the American best-seller lists. Sales increased for other authoritarian books too, including Aldous Huxley's novel *Brave New World* and Hannah Arendt's seminal nonfiction volume *The Origins of Totalitarianism*.

Sinclair Lewis's 1935 satirical novel *It Can't Happen Here* has surged up the best-seller charts since Donald Trump took office.
Author collection. Photo by Theresa Albini

There are other novels worth noting in the vein of *It Can't Happen Here*, including Herman Melville's *The Confidence-Man* (1857), Edward Dahlberg's *Those Who Perish* (1934), Nathanael West's *A Cool Million* (1934), Robert Penn Warren's *All the King's Men* (1946), Kurt Vonnegut's dystopian novel (and his first) *Player Piano* (1952), Margaret Atwood's *The Handmaid's Tale* (1985), and, more recently, Philip Roth's *The Plot Against America* (2004).

Berlin in the 1920s was amoral. Aimless. Lost. The Viennese author Stefan Zweig referred to it as the "Babylon of the world." Bars and honky-tonks "sprang up like mushrooms," he observed. "Along the entire Kurfürstendamm, powdered and rouged young men sauntered and they were not all professionals; every high school boy wanted to earn some money, and in the dimly lit bars one might see government officials and men of the world of finance tenderly courting drunken sailors without any shame."

Indeed, Berlin had a well-deserved reputation for decadence. The rise in prostitution after the war was especially marked, as it became a major feature of the city's underground economy and culture. As a result, tolerance for not only prostitution but also unconventional sexual behavior became more evident both on the stages of the cabaret and out on the street.

One of the most important artistic moments during the months leading up to the Weimar Republic was the founding of the November Group, in December 1918. The Group, which consisted of one hundred or so artists from various genres, held numerous exhibitions in Berlin until the Nazis took over. Its members included Walter Gropius, founder of Bauhaus, and Kurt Weill and Bertolt Brecht. The work of many of these artists as well as other composers, architects, playwright, filmmakers, artists, and sculptors would later be denounced as "degenerate art" by Hitler.

The Bauhaus Aesthetic

Weimar is now a tourist town located about fifty miles southwest of Leipzig, but it has an outsized cultural and historical significance in Germany. The Bauhaus started here. Founded in 1919 by German architect Walter Gropius, Bauhaus combined the fine arts, crafts, and design under one roof with the aim of creating what the Germans referred to as *Gesamtkunstwerk*, or total work of art. What's more, the emergence of the Bauhaus paralleled the development of the Weimar Republic, rising from the chaos and turmoil

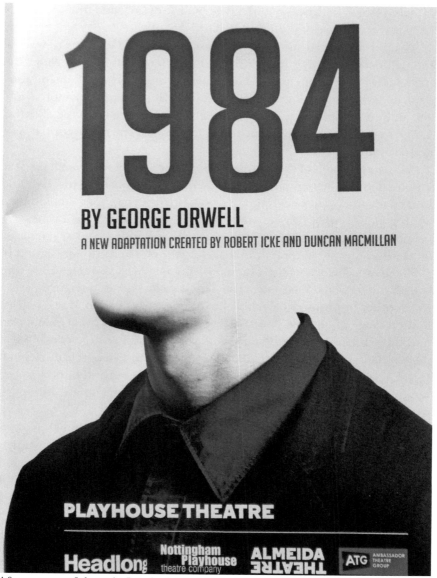

After a successful run in London's West End at the Playhouse Theatre, a new adaptation of George Orwell's classic 1949 dystopian novel *1984* by Robert Icke and Duncan Macmillan transferred in June 2017 to the Hudson Theatre in New York. It starred Tom Sturridge, Olivia Wilde in her Broadway debut, and Reed Birney.

Author collection. Photo by Theresa Albini.

of World War I, flourishing during the interwar years, and, finally, ending in 1933 with the rise of the Third Reich.

Gropius recruited some of the finest teachers in Germany to work at the Bauhaus, including Kandinsky, Klee, Albers, and Moholy-Nagy. But Bauhaus was more than just a school. It was a commune, a movement—and a spiritual movement at that—but most of all, it was a radical approach to art, an interdisciplinary approach designed to create a new type of living, a functional living environment and a shift toward constructivism. It integrated art and industry.

The student body at the Bauhaus was diverse and international. Like the hippies of the 1960s counterculture, Bauhaus students lived together and worked together. They held wild parties, wore their hair long, and donned androgynous clothing. Some would say they were ahead of their time.

In 1928, Gropius resigned his position at the Bauhaus and was replaced by Hannes Meyer, who reorganized the school. He in turn resigned in 1930. His successor was the pragmatist Ludwig Mies van der Rohe, who transformed the Bauhaus into a full-fledged school of architecture.

Another important teacher at the Bauhaus was Laszlo Moholy-Nagy. Moholy-Nagy joined the Bauhaus in 1923 at the age of twenty-eight and quickly became Gropius's most influential colleague. Prior to being hired at the Bauhaus, he was part of the Dada-Constructionist Congress in Weimar. In 1925, Bauhaus moved to the factory town of Dessau and built new and very modern headquarters, which housed everything from workshops to student accommodations.

A fierce nonconformist and restless experimenter, Moholy-Nagy was "connected" before it was cool. He was inspired by industrial cityscapes, which he considered symbols of progress. In the early 1920s, he began producing photomontages. The photomontage merged art and cultural commentary by cutting images from the illustrated press and pasting them together to make entirely new compositions. One of Moholy-Nagy's most effective photomontages was of the Tiller Girls (official title: "Slide"), famous English dancers who were very popular in Weimar Germany. Each dancer was matched in height and weight in such a way that led the German sociologist Siegfried Kracauer to see them as human equivalents of the factory assembly line. Moholy-Nagy also designed theatrical sets in Germany between 1929 and 1932, including for *The Merchant of Berlin*, directed by Erwin Piscator, a major figure in Weimar Germany, as abstract sequences of oblong rectangles set atop a circular, spinning stage.

"Slide (Rutschbahn)" (1923), a photomontage by the Hungarian painter and photographer László Moholy-Nagy of the Tiller Girls, an English revue that was popular in Berlin during the Weimar era. Moholy-Nagy was also a professor in the Bauhaus school.

Author collection

After the Nazi takeover in 1933, Moholy-Nagy moved to Amsterdam, then London. His work in London led him to Walter Paepcke, founder of the packaging company Container Group, which led him to Chicago. Paepcke invited Moholy-Nagy to Chicago in the summer of 1937 to become the founding director of the New Bauhaus with Walter Gropius as adviser. In 1949, it was integrated into the Illinois Institute of Technology (IIT), now called the Institute of Design. The offices of the New Bauhaus were located at 1905 S. Prairie Avenue, in the former Marshall Field mansion; the building was later converted to an aeronautics university before it was razed in 1955.

When the Nazis took over Dessau, Bauhaus moved again. In 1932, Mies established new quarters in an abandoned factory in Berlin, financing it with his own money. Within less than a year, though, the Gestapo shut the Bauhaus down for good as Hitler rose to power. Even after the Bauhaus closed, the Nazis continued to persecute its former members. Like the cabaret artists who stayed on in Germany, some died in the camps, but many escaped to Western Europe and the United States. The Harvard Graduate School of Design, for example, hired Gropius, while, as indicated, Moholy-Nagy founded Chicago's New Bauhaus. Mies moved to Chicago as well, changing the Chicago skyline and acting as the key figure of the International Style of modern architecture, which was known for its stripped-down, ornament-free aesthetics. Josef and Anni Albers established Black Mountain College in North Carolina, an incubator of the American avant-garde that helped launch the careers of John Cage, Merce Cunningham, Buckminster Fuller, Robert Rauschenberg, and Cy Twombly, among others. In 1938, the Museum of Modern Art sponsored a major exhibition on the Bauhaus.

Today, the former campus is known as the Bauhaus University. Bauhaus Walks are led by former and current students. Among the highlights of the walks are the stylized human figures by the German painter and sculptor Oskar Schlemmer: Schlemmer and the Bauhaus clearly influenced Fritz Lang's 1927 film *Metropolis*. Also here is Gropius's reconstructed office. Gropius donated objects to Weimar's State Art Collections, which forms the foundation of the ten-thousand-piece collection of the Bauhaus Museum at Theaterplatz. The Bauhaus Dessau Foundation hosts exhibitions, residencies, student exchanges and events, in addition to its permanent collection, the second-largest after Berlin.

Weimar and Post-Weimar Figures

The Weimar era featured an impressive number of renowned figures in the fields of architecture, literature, music, philosophy, theater and the cinema, and the visual arts. Many of these individuals would have a major influence, in both direct and indirect ways, on the various incarnations of *Cabaret*. The Weimar spirit is perhaps best exemplified in film by the Expressionist sets of *The Cabinet of Dr. Caligari*; the Bauhaus aesthetics of Walter Gropius; the disturbing art of George Grosz with his distortion of the human figure (and the human condition writ large); the equally brutal yet sympathetic portraits of various German misfits by Otto Dix; and the iconic image of that ultimate Berliner, Marlene Dietrich. Here is a partial list:

Architecture

Peter Behrens
(1868–1940)
Architect and designer

Bruno Taut
(1880–1938)
Architect and city planner

Walter Gropius
(1883–1969)
Architect; founder of Bauhaus
    School

Ludwig Mies van der Rohe
(1886–1969)
Architect

Dance

Mary Wigman
(1886–1973)
Dancer and choreographer

Literature

Bertolt Brecht
(1898–1956)
Playwright

Erich Kästner
(1899–1974)
Novelist and poet

Alfred Döblin
(1878–1957)
Novelist

Thomas Mann
(1875–1955)
Author

Christopher Isherwood
(1904–1986)
Writer

Ernst Toller
(1893–1939)
Playwright

Music

Alban Berg
(1885–1935)
Composer

Arnold Schoenberg
(1874–1951)
Composer

Paul Hindemith
(1895–1963)
Composer

Kurt Weill
(1900–1950)
Composer

Otto Klemperer
(1885–1973)
Conductor and composer

Philosophy

Theodor Adorno
(1903–1969)
Critical theorist

Martin Heidegger
(1889–1976)
Critical theorist

Walter Benjamin
(1892–1940)
Critical theorist

Max Horkheimer
(1895–1973)
Critical theorist

Martin Buber
(1878–1965)
Philosopher

Oswald Spengler
(1880–1936)
Philosopher and historian

Hans Freyer
(1887–1969)
Philosopher

Theater and Film

Marlene Dietrich
(1901–1992)
Actress

Erwin Piscator
(1893–1966)
Theater and film producer

Fritz Lang
(1890–1976)
Filmmaker

Max Reinhardt
(1873–1943)
Theater producer and director

Ernst Lubitsch
(1892–1947)
Filmmaker

Hans Richter
(1888–1976)
Filmmaker, actor, writer

Erika Mann
(1905–1969)
Theater producer, playwright,
    journalist, cabaret performer,
    actress

Leni Riefenstahl
(1902–2003)
Actress, filmmaker

F. W. Murnau
(1888–1931)
Filmmaker

Josef von Sternberg
(1894–1969)
Filmmaker

Pola Negri
(1897–1987)
Actress

Robert Wiene
(1873–1938)
Filmmaker

Visual arts

Max Beckmann
(1884–1950)
Painter, printmaker

Käthe Kollwitz
(1867–1945)
Printmaker, sculptor, and artist

Otto Dix
(1891–1969)
Painter and printmaker

Paul Klee
(1879–1940)
Painter

Max Ernst
(1891–1976)
Painter

Emil Nolde
(1867–1956)
Painter

George Grosz
(1893–1959)
Painter

Kurt Schwitters
(1887–1948)
Painter

John Heartfield
(1891–1968)
Photomontage

Hannah Höch
(1889–1978)
Photomontage
Painter

Erich Heckel
(1883–1970)
Painter and printmaker

German Expressionism

In the years prior to World War I, a group of German poets, writers, and artists met in the back rooms of cafés and bookshops performing and reading their own work. They were linked to such magazines as *Der Sturm* and *Die Aktion* as well as to the Blaue Reiter, Die Brücke, and New Secessionist movements.

They became known as the Expressionists.

The Expressionist movement peaked during the Weimar Republic era. It applied to architecture, dance, painting, sculpture, and cinema. Expressionism rejected traditional models of representation in favor of types and archetypes. It portrayed devastation and psychological anomie, running counter to whatever conventional society wrought. Both in theater and in cinema the Expressionist style consisted of sharp angles, odd juxtapositions, and ominous shadows. Stylized sets and particular camera angles emphasized fear and horror. Expressionist painters depicted grotesque and distorted figures. The style reflected the inner turmoil of German society during the Weimar era. Boris Aronson, who did the set design for the 1966 Broadway production of *Cabaret*, emulated this style at the Kit Kat Klub with its tilted mirrors, black box setting, and spiral staircase.

Among the earliest Expressionist films were *The Cabinet of Dr. Caligari* (1920), *Nosferatu* (1922), and *The Last Laugh* (1924). Later, horror films and film noir were influenced by Expressionism, especially the work of Fritz Lang, Billy Wilder, Otto Preminger, Alfred Hitchcock, Orson Welles, Carol Reed, and Michael Curtiz. But the film that had the greatest impact on cabaret was Josef von Sternberg's *The Blue Angel*.

The Blue Angel

Considered a masterpiece of German Expressionism, *The Blue Angel* (1930), directed and cowritten by Josef von Sternberg, was the first feature-length talkie in German and launched the international career of Marlene Dietrich. It was based on the novel *Professor Unrat* by Heinrich Mann.

The film begins with the appearance of a tidy, persnickety, and pompous professor by the name of Immanuel Rath (Emil Jannings) as he pours his tea while ignoring his housekeeper entirely. He tries to give his parrot a sugar cube, but, in a nice act of foreshadowing, we quickly learn that his beloved pet parrot is dead: not a good way to begin the day. During the entire scene, not a word is spoken between the professor and the housekeeper. In fact, the first spoken word is in the next scene when he tells his students to "sit

SPECIAL TWO DISC SET   KINO ON VIDEO

Marlene DIETRICH
Emil JANNINGS

Josef von STERNBERG's

The Blue Angel

DVD VIDEO

INCLUDES ORIGINAL GERMAN AND ENGLISH VERSIONS
• RARE ARCHIVAL MATERIAL •
NEWLY REMASTERED FROM THE 35MM NEGATIVE

Josef von Sternberg's *The Blue Angel* (1930) made an international star of Marlene Dietrich.   *Author collection* down." They're studying *Hamlet* but are more excited about a cabaret singer by the name of Lola Lola (Marlene Dietrich), who is performing in a seedy dive located by the waterfront called the Blue Angel. Like *Cabaret*'s Kit Kat Klub, the Blue Angel is a down-market club that offered low forms of entertainment: a small stage with mostly unattractive women (Dietrich, of course, being the exception), social and political parody, sexual innuendo, clowns, drag numbers, and animal acts. Although the Kit Kat Klub didn't use animals, it did feature a woman dressed as a gorilla and a wild scene involving the emcee and women wrestlers.

When we first see Dietrich, she is singing "Just a Man" on a tiny stage; the light is directed toward the audience. In a perfect casting nod, the great cabaret performer Rosa Valetti is one of the band members. An ominous clown, in another sign of foreshadowing, dances in between the magic and musical selections. "I love you," yells one of Lola's youthful admirers. "Nonsense," she responds, with equal parts detachment and disdain.

Rath visits her backstage in her dressing room. In a prank, one of his students, who had attended the show and is hiding from the professor, puts her knickers in his coat pocket. He returns it to her. Lola flirts with Rath, playfully blowing powder from her makeup in his face. "Poor baby. Did I hurt you?" she jokes. She is above it all. She needs no one. An admirer offers

A poster on the wall of Lola's dressing room at the Blue Angel nightclub coincidentally says "Mlle. Minelli's."

her a bottle of champagne; another presents a pineapple, a small detail that reminds this observer at least of the pineapple that the lovesick Herr Schultz gives to Fräulein Schneider in *Cabaret*. But she will have none of it. "Leave me alone," she responds. "Get out of here." Throughout his time with Lola, Professor Rath always attempts to protect her honor. But in the dressing room and onstage, chaos can—and often does—erupt at a moment's notice. The police show up, for example, when Rath slaps one of her admirers.

Back onstage she sings her signature song, "Falling in Love Again." The band members sit behind her, just as bored and jaded as she appears to be, and each holding a stein of beer. Valetti smokes and drinks from her stein. Meanwhile, the top-hatted emcee announces that Rath is the evening's guest of honor and that he is the professor of a local high school. She starts the song again, admonishing a band member to move, and sits on a beer barrel while singing directly to the professor while wearing her iconic costume of top hat, halter, and showing off her legs.

Rath doesn't go home that night. Instead, he sleeps off the alcohol in Lola's dressing room. Over breakfast with Lola, he adds three sugar cubes to his tea, prompting Lola to say, "My my. Sugar daddy."

"You can have this everyday," she tells him. By now completely smitten, he agrees, "Why not? I'm still a bachelor."

Back in class, his students are aware of his infatuation with Lola. They ridicule her and make a fool out of him, causing a commotion in class. The noise leads his colleagues to investigate the source of the raucousness. His superior shrugs, "I'm sorry, my friend, but you have left me no choice" and requests his resignation.

When Rath returns to Lola's dressing room with flowers, he learns she is ready to move on to the next town, on to the next gig. "Don't be sad. I'll be back next year," she says.

But unfazed, he offers her a ring and asks her to marry him, prompting her to laugh hysterically. "You are so sweet." They marry anyway. In the next scene, he looks disheveled as Lola sings onstage. He halfheartedly passes around photos of her to sell to customers but manages to sell only two postcards. "Cheap crowd," he complains.

He drinks too much. He smokes too much. Lola has lost all patience with him. "If you don't like it, you can go," she says. Finally, he announces that "I'm through. I can't stand it anymore" and walks out. As always, Lola is unfazed. He returns, sheepish, and puts her stockings on for her. He can't break the spell she has on him.

The years pass by. By 1929, Rath looks dreadful and dispirited. By now, he is acting the part of the clown onstage, and wearing an obscenely bulbous nose. We see him putting on his makeup. Now back at the Blue Angel, he steadfastly refuses to go onstage despite it being a sold-out show.

"What's wrong? Why the long face?" Lola asks. He ignores his third cue to go onstage. "I will not go on," he insists. When he finally does appear, the rowdy crowd breaks out in derisive laughter. He is humiliated.

The emcee and magician (Kurt Gerron) cracks an egg on the professor's head—not once but twice. Rath goes backstage to see Lola kissing someone else. He lets out an animal yelp, a rooster call, and tries to strangle her. In the next scene, it is clear he is defeated, spent; he is placed in a straightjacket, his hands and feet bound up so he won't hurt himself or

The Blue Angel was shot simultaneously in German and English at the Babelsberg Studio, outside Berlin, where *Metropolis* was shot a few years earlier.

anyone else. Back onstage, Lola sings "Falling in Love Again," wearing a black hat, polka dot dress, black stockings, and straddling a black chair—a darker version of the song, "Mein Herr," that Sally Bowles sings on the stage of the Kit Kat Klub. Rath leaves the club on the snow-filled streets to return to his old school, where he collapses at his desk. As the bell tolls, he dies, a broken man.

Musical Selections from *The Blue Angel*

The German composer Friedrich Hollaender wrote the music; Robert Liebmann penned the lyrics.

- "Falling in Love Again (Can't Help It)"
- "They Call Me Naughty Lola"
- "Those Charming Alarming Blond Women"
- "A Man, Just a Regular Man"

Lola Lola's performances have been parodied numerous times, most hilariously by Madeline Kahn as Lili von Shtupp in Mel Brooks's *Blazing Saddles*. Liza Minnelli's performance of "Mein Herr" in Cabaret—not to mention her similar outfit—also owe a great debt to Dietrich. Even the glam-rock sensibility of Queen is indebted to the persona of Dietrich: the cover of their 1974 second album, for example, *Queen II*, refers back to an iconic image of Dietrich, her hands cradling her upturned face. In 2017, Luc Besson's fantastical sci-fi adventure *Valerian and the City of a Thousand Planets*, the Barbadian singer Rihanna channeled the persona of both Dietrich and Minnelli as Bubble, a shapeshifting alien cabaret entertainer who wears a black bowler hat and skimpy black clothing and even drags a chair when she performs "Mein Herr"-style.

Movies Set in Berlin

Below is a sampling of movies set in Berlin, from the German Expressionism era to the present day.

1922

Dr. Mabuse the Gambler. First silent film about the character of Doctor Mabuse. Directed by Fritz Lang.

1924

The Last Laugh. Directed by F. W. Murnau.

1927

Berlin: Symphony of a Metropolis. Expressionist documentary. Directed by Walter Ruttmann.

Metropolis. The futuristic classic. Directed by Fritz Lang.

1930

People on Sunday. A look at ordinary life in 1930s Berlin. Screenplay by Billy Wilder and Curt Siodmak.

1931

M. The great Berlin thriller that started film noir with touches of late-stage Expressionism. Directed by Fritz Lang.

Berlin-Alexanderplatz. Adaptation of Alfred Döblin's novel. Directed by Phil Jutzi.

1933

The Testament of Dr. Mabuse. Berlin thriller. Directed by Fritz Lang.

1948

A Foreign Affair. Romantic comedy set in Berlin during the Allied occupation; costarring Jean Arthur and Marlene Dietrich. Directed by Billy Wilder.

1955

I Am a Camera. 1930s Weimar Berlin based on the work of Christopher Isherwood; starring Julie Harris and Laurence Harvey. Directed by Henry Cornelius.

1965

The Spy Who Came In from the Cold. Based on the classic spy novel by John Le Carré. Starring Richard Burton. Directed by Guy Hamilton.

1966

Funeral in Berlin. Another spy classic based on the novel by Len Deighton and starring Michael Caine. Directed by Guy Hamilton.

Torn Curtain. Hitchcock goes to East Berlin. Starring Paul Newman and Julie Andrews. Adapted screenplay by Northern Irish writer Brian Moore. Directed by Alfred Hitchcock.

1968

A Dandy in Aspic. Spy thriller set in East and West Berlin. Starring Laurence Harvey, Tom Courtenay, and Mia Farrow. Directed by Anthony Mann.

1972

Cabaret. But of course!

1976

Memories of Berlin: The Twilight of Weimar Culture. Documentary about Berlin's cultural scene during the Weimar years. Directed by Gary Conklin.

1977

Stroszek. Based on the life of Bruno Schleinstein, a West Berlin street performer and petty criminal. Directed by Werner Herzog.

The Serpent's Egg. An unemployed American-born Jew in 1920s Berlin is offered a job by a professor performing medical experiments. Starring Liv Ullmann and David Carradine. Written and directed by Ingmar Bergman.

1978

Just a Gigolo. A Prussian officer returns home to Berlin at the end of World War I. Unable to find employment, he works as a gigolo in a brothel. Starring David Bowie, Kim Novak, David Hemmings, Curt Jurgens, and . . . in her last film, the then-seventy-seven-year-old Marlene Dietrich, who was persuaded to come out of retirement for her two days of shooting. Directed by David Hemmings.

1979

The Marriage of Maria Braun. A woman tries to make a life for herself after surviving the despair of World War II. Directed by Rainer Werner Fassbinder.

1980

Berlin Alexanderplatz. Set in 1920s Berlin, adapted from the novel by Alfred Döblin. Made for German television. Directed by Rainer Werner Fassbinder.

1981

Christiane F.: We Children from Bahnhof Zoo. The West Berlin drug scene circa the 1970s. Directed by Uli Edel.

Lili Marleen. Set during the Third Reich; a German singer and a Swiss composer help a group of underground German Jews. Directed by Rainer Werner Fassbinder.

1987

Wings of Desire. An angel falls in love with a human in West Berlin—the Berlin Wall also features prominently in the plot. Famous for its gorgeous black-and-white photography (although it was also filmed in color). Includes concert footage by Nick Cave and the Bad Seeds. Inspired partly by the poetry of Rainer Maria Rilke; Austrian novelist/playwright Peter Handke wrote most of the dialogue. Directed by Wim Wenders.

1998

Run Lola Run. A drama set in post-reunification Berlin that features three alternate realties. Directed by Tom Tykwer.

2011

Christopher and His Kind. The dramatization of Christopher Isherwood's life in Weimar Berlin based on Isherwood's autobiographical writings. Starring Matt Smith. Directed by Geoffrey Sax.

2017

Atomic Blonde. Cold War thriller starring Charlize Theron as a British spy with a preference for (deadly) stiletto heels set in 1989 Berlin, days before the fall of the Berlin Wall. Co-starring James McAvoy, the film boasts a terrific soundtrack, including "99 Luftballons," "Under Pressure," "Blue Monday," and "Der Kommissar."

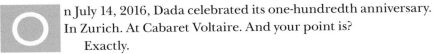

Cabaret Voltaire and Dada

The Big Bang of Modernism

On July 14, 2016, Dada celebrated its one-hundredth anniversary. In Zurich. At Cabaret Voltaire. And your point is?

Exactly.

On July 14, 1916, poet Hugo Ball announced the arrival of a new manifesto, and a new movement. Its name was Dada and its purpose was to "get rid of everything that smacks of journalism . . . everything nice and right." Dada was, in short, a protest, a violent smack in the face, against European civilization, against the world order. Any world order. Dada reflected the turmoil of the World War I era. It was anti-art as well as antiwar, anticapitalism, antiauthority. Essentially, it was paradoxical. Art v. anti-art, morality v. amorality, positive v. negative.

During the prewar years, Zurich, the birthplace of Dadaism, was already a refuge for artists, writers, and intellectuals of all sorts and varieties. Despite it being short-lived, Corinna da Fonseca-Wollheim has described Dada as being "the Big Bang of Modernism." Dada influenced all sorts of artistic movements in music, art, and dance from its beginnings to the present day.

A Declaration of Artistic Independence

Although most historians give July as the birthdate of Dada, actually the first Dada evening took place at the Cabaret Voltaire in Zurich on February 5, 1916; in the back hall of the Meierei café at Spiegelgasse 1.

Hugo Ball founded the Cabaret Voltaire as "a declaration of artistic independence," writes Dieter Mersch. Dadaists were appalled by the casualties of World War I, and the war's false promises ("the war to end all wars").

Ball issued a press release, asking artists to "report for duty with suggestions and contributions without regard to a particular direction."

> Cabaret Voltaire. Under this name a group of young artists and writers has been formed whose aim is to create a centre for artistic entertainment. The idea of the cabaret will be that guest artists will come and give musical performances and readings at the daily meetings . . .

It was a call to action, an early-twentieth-century version of social media.

Jerrold Seigel sees echoes of the old Chat Noir in the spirit of Cabaret Voltaire. Like the Chat Noir, it was spontaneous and provocative. The Dadaists said or did "whatever came to mind at any moment." They embodied the spirit of *fumisme*, the same spirit, suggests Seigel, that had animated the original Chat Noir.

The Enigmatic Hugo Ball

If one person should be considered the "founder" of Dada—and with Dada, quotation marks are often necessary—it is the tall, slightly pockmarked writer and producer from Germany named Hugo Ball. In 1910, Ball had moved to Berlin after studying at universities in Munich and Heidelberg, ostensibly to become an actor and to work with theater director Max Reinhardt. Disillusioned with the atrocities during World War I, he decided to move to neutral Switzerland with the cabaret performer and poet Emmy Hennings, whom he would later marry. Ball's diary *Die Flucht aus der Zeit* (*The Flight from Time*) is considered one of the founding documents of the Dadaist movement. Ball was both an idealist and a skeptic. He searched for meaning in what he considered an absurdist, meaningless world.

Ball began creating a particular point of view, a manifesto that came to be known as the Dada Manifesto, which had "as its sole purpose to draw attention, across the barriers of war and nationalism, to the few independent spirits who live for other ideals."

Cabaret Voltaire was a combination of nightclub and art salon. The cabaret's patrons were largely emigrants, random patrons, and, according to Ball, "drunken students and intellectuals not unwilling to express their antagonism in an occasional fist fight."

The first night at Cabaret Voltaire consisted of a reading from the cabaret's namesake, Voltaire. Hennings sang the Parisian cabaret ballads of Aristide Bruant. There were readings by Jean Arp from Alfred Jarry's *Ubu Roi*; also a bit of Paul Verlaine, Arthur Rimbaud, and Charles Baudelaire, exhibitions of paintings by Arp and Marcel Janco; and mime and some shaggy dog stories.

From Babble to Hobbyhorses

The word "Dada" first appeared in print at the Cabaret Voltaire on June 15, 1916. But the first Dada soiree took place a month later, on July 14, 1916, at the Waag guild hall in Zurich. Cabaret programs consisted of variety shows that featured music, chansons, exhibitions, and a series of song cycles performed by Hennings. Something to please everyone or no one because it didn't matter. Or, as Tristan Tzara once said, "I'm not even interested in knowing if anyone existed before me."

What did Dada mean? Various explanations have emerged: the babble of a child, perhaps, or a toy, a kind of lily-white soap, French for hobbyhorse, or even a hair tonic popular at the time. Others say it meant Daddy. Still others dismissed it as a nonsense word. Wrote Ball, "What we call Dada is foolery, foolery extracted from the emptiness in which all the higher problems are wrapped . . . a game played with the shabby remnants . . . a public execution of false morality."

Total Work of Art

Dada was whatever you wanted it to mean. But however you described it, Dada rebelled against the establishment, defied all notions of conformity, redefined what it meant to create art, and shocked the members of the bourgeoisie. It was a series of happenings in a cabaret setting. The performers were part of the ongoing spectacle.

Dada had no program per se, although Tzara did edit and design the periodical also called *Dada*. Order was no different than disorder, order no different than chaos. The manifesto was clear: Dada meant nothing. But it was also a variation of the Bauhaus notion of *Gesamtkunstwerk* (total work of art) and something that painter Wassily Kandinsky had promulgated: the union of all art and its effect on everyday life. Ball, in particular, sought to achieve total art by connecting readings and lectures to dance and performances to music and poetry.

Ball recited his phonetic poem "Karawane" ("Caravan") at Cabaret Voltaire on June 23, 1916. The text consisted of a made-up language drawing on various languages, including French, German, Italian, Spanish, and Latin; a Dadaesque *Finnegans Wake*. It was his most famous performance.

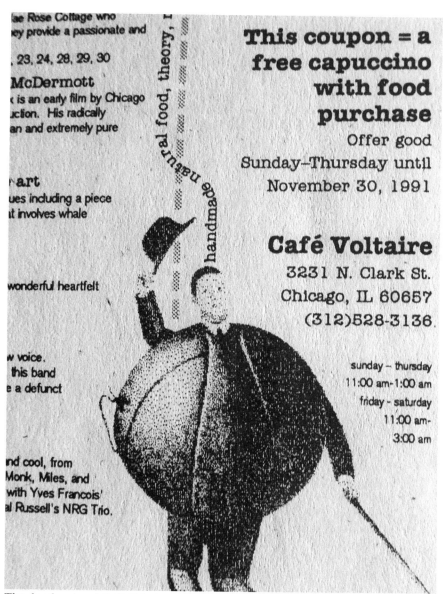

ae Rose Cottage who
ey provide a passionate and

, 23, 24, 28, 29, 30

McDermott
c is an early film by Chicago
uction. His radically
an and extremely pure

art
ues including a piece
it involves whale

wonderful heartfelt

w voice.
this band
e a defunct

nd cool, from
Monk, Miles, and
with Yves Francois'
al Russell's NRG Trio.

natural food, theory, handmade

This coupon = a free capuccino with food purchase

Offer good
Sunday–Thursday until
November 30, 1991

Café Voltaire

3231 N. Clark St.
Chicago, IL 60657
(312)528-3136

sunday – thursday
11:00 am-1:00 am
friday - saturday
11:00 am-
3:00 am

The dearly missed Café Voltaire at 3231 N. Clark Street in Chicago had a restaurant upstairs and underground performances in its basement cabaret. Inspired by Cabaret Voltaire in Zurich, it featured "handmade natural food, theory, manifestoes, poems, pictures, music, performance, coffee." The artists at the cabaret included the band Dead Reckoning, which performed songs about women in Weimar "and what they cut with their kitchen knives."   *Author collection. Photo by Theresa Albini*

He wore a costume—a "special costume" he called it—designed by Janco and himself. In his diary, Ball described the costume:

> My legs were encased in a tight-fitting cylindrical pillar or shiny blue cardboard which reached to my hips so that I looked like an obelisk. Above this I wore a huge cardboard coat-collar, scarlet inside and gold outside, which was fastened to my neck in such a way that I could flap it like a pair of wings by moving my elbows. I also wore a high, cylindrical, blue and white striped witch-doctor's hat.

Ball set up music stands on three sides of a platform on which he placed his manuscript consisting of abstract poems. Since "an obelisk cannot walk," Tzara carried Ball to the platform. Suitably attired, he then chanted a phonetic poem of dubious meaning, spoken in a string of gibberish lines that completely baffled the audience. Then they erupted in laughter and broke out in applause.

This was the epitome of Ball's Dada moment.

Karawane

jolifanto bambla ô falli bambla
grossiga m'pfa habla horem
égiga goramen
higo bloiko russula huju
hollaka hollala
anlogo bung
blago bung
blago bung
blago fataka
ü üü ü
schampa wulla wussa ólobo
hej tatta gôrem
eschige zunbada
wulubu ssubudu uluw ssubudu
tumba ba– umf
kusagauma
ba - umf

Dadaists held soirees, multimedia events; they performed songs and music; they danced. They engaged in farce . . . they just made a lot of plain noise. Dadaists wanted to create a new type of art, something that the world had never experienced before. They used new means of expressing themselves: through photomontage, collage, typography, poetry, and film. They created conceptual art, readymades, happenings, performance art, kinetic art, film. In particular, photomontage and collage were essential aspects of Dadaism.

Dada allowed artists to escape from the madness of the times. Dadaists, especially Ball, owed their intellectual debt to Friedrich Nietzsche (cabaret artists, in general, appreciated Nietzsche's provocative philosophy and his Dionysian call for his fellow citizens to "rejuvenate themselves and their culture"). Dadaists had a deep distrust of rationalism, preferring instead to rely on satire, insults, and nonsense; similar in tone to the barbs flung in the Montmartre cabarets and, later, in the German cabarets.

- Dadaists created something out of nothing.
- Dadaists were against anything that existed.
- Dadaists advocated contradictions.
- Dadaists were against principles.
- Dadaists encouraged laughter—laughter was liberating; laughter was the essence of freedom.
- Dadaists welcomed the absurd.
- Dadaists relished anarchism and chaos.

But not everyone was happy with the goings-on at Voltaire, including the actual proprietor. Booted out from the space, Cabaret Voltaire resurfaced at the newly named Galerie Dada in March 1917. By May, though, the gallery, too, closed. But during that short and fruitful time, the gallery exhibited work of Dada, Cubist, Expressionist, and Futurist art and organized half a dozen art soirees, including lectures on Paul Klee and Wassily Kandinsky.

The final large Dada soiree took place on April 9, 1919, at the Kaufleuten guild hall in Zurich. Some fifteen hundred guests showed up. But by then, Dada had spread to New York, Barcelona, Hanover, Cologne, Amsterdam, Prague, Paris, and Berlin.

The Berlin Dadaists were perhaps the most aggressive, certainly the most political, artists.

Berlin Dada

It was in Berlin that Dada found its political power. George Grosz, John Heartfield (born Johann Herzfelde), Raoul Hausmann, Hannah Höch, Walter Mehring, and Richard Huelsenbeck founded the Berlin Club Dada. Their first soiree was held on April 12, 1918.

Dada took distinctly different forms in Berlin. The Berlin Dadaists were anti-everything, as were all Dadaists, but their brand had a particularly savage political edge. The Berlin Dadaists published periodicals, mani-festos, posters, and other printed material as well as made ingenious uses of photographic collages and photomontage. During its short life, the Berlin Club Dada organized a dozen public readings and in 1920 held the First International Dada Fair. Perhaps one of the most disturbing images

Founded in 1985, the Chicago Cabaret Ensemble presented cabaret at various venues around town. Many of the programs featured German themes such as "Weimar," which was written and directed by Warren Leming.   *Author collection. Photo by Theresa Albini*

associated with the Club is that of the stuffed effigy of a German officer with a pig's head that hung from a ceiling. One Berlin Dadaist, Johannes Baader, proclaimed, "Dada is the cabaret of the world, just as . . . the world is the cabaret DADA."

Berlin Dada, notes Peter Jelavich, "emphasized montage in both the visual arts and literature. Its collages, photomontages, and free-verse lyrics consisted of snippets" drawn from advertising, newspapers, handbills, posters, postcards, and telegrams.

Among the best known of the Berlin Dada figures was the artist George Grosz. He appeared in whiteface on cabaret stages (shades of the Emcee in *Cabaret*), reciting his provocative and aggressive poetry. Other Dada members included John Heartfield, the inventor of the photomontage; Raoul Hausmann, artist, poet, and philosopher; and poet Walter Mehring. They staged Dada evenings and demonstrations. Between 1918 and 1920, they laid the foundations for other German artistic institutions such as Erwin Piscator's Epic Theatre and the Bauhaus' Theatre Workshop.

But the German Dadaists were not satisfied with staging their presentations in the cabarets. They brought their very German brand of Dada out into the streets. Dada, after all, was the cabaret of the world and the world was their very own cabaret.

Dada in Other Cities

Independent from Zurich, New York City was also having its Dada moment. The instigator behind the American version was photographer Alfred Stieglitz. Years earlier, in 1905, he had opened the Photo Secession Gallery on Fifth Avenue. Over the years, he held exhibitions by Rodin, Matisse, and Lautrec. A group of American painters, most of whom had studied in Paris, joined Stieglitz's inner circle, including Alfred Maurer, Charles Demuth, Arthur Dove, Joseph Stella, Marsden Hartley, and John Marin.

Stieglitz's gatherings set the scene for the biggest artistic event in modern New York history: the opening in February 1913 of the Armory Show, an international exhibit of modern art. It presented an entirely new conception of art, and what art could be. The biggest hit of the show was Marcel Duchamp's *Nude Descending a Staircase*. Like Hugo Ball, Duchamp also acknowledged the essential absurdity of life. His work reflected this nihilistic point of view. And he too rejected art for art's sake. To be more precise, he rejected art period. This philosophy led to the logical creation of what he called readymades: ordinary items masquerading as art. They became works of art because he said they were.

It was sheer Dada.

Dada Offshoots

Dada may have been a short-lived movement, but its legacy is enduring and far-reaching. Dadaists pushed the boundaries of art in dance, theater, printmaking, music, and sculpture. It paved the way for later art movements such as Surrealism, Fluxus, Pop Art, performance art, and concept art. Its influence can be found in readymades, the Happenings of the 1960s, even poetry slams. Its heroes have included Alan Kaprow, Andy Warhol, and Yoko Ono. Dada has lived on in the music of John Cage, the choreography of Merce Cunningham, and in the art of Robert Rauschenberg, Jasper Johns, Frank Stella, and Andy Warhol. The logical extension of Dada was punk. Like Dada, punk claimed no tradition. It had no past, no future—it lived only for the present. Punk is a type of anarchy reminiscent of Dada. Just like Dada was anti-art, punk was anti-rock, even anti-music. In the mid-1970s, to show its connection to the spirit of Dada, an English band called itself Cabaret Voltaire.

David Byrne, the Scots-born lead singer of Talking Heads, is a Dadaist at heart. Byrne set Hugo Ball's poem "Gadji beri bimba" to music with "I Zimbra," the second single from *Fear of Music*. Other avant-garde musicians and bands owed a debt to Dada: Frank Zappa, Captain Beefheart, Devo, and Pere Ubu, which was inspired by Frenchman Alfred Jarry's proto-Dadaist play, *Ubu Roi*, among others. Other Dadaists, at least in spirit, include John Cage (his best Dada moment was his piece *4.33*, which consisted of complete silence); Marcel Duchamp's readymades; Francis Picabia's *La Nourrice Americaine* (*The American Nurse*) is basically three notes repeated ad infinitum; Erik Satie's *Vexations* was meant to be played more than eight hundred times without a break. Baroness Elsa von Freytag-Loringhoven, one of the twentieth century's first performance artists, was a proto-Dadaist. Her best Dada moment? Her entire life.

The spirit and name of Cabaret Voltaire lived on in Chicago in the 1980s and 1990s. Café Voltaire presented live music, theater (from a one-man *Moby Dick* to Dylan Thomas's *Under Milkwood*), comic revues, poetry, films, and performance art seven nights a week in the basement of its Lakeview location. Its motto was "Give of yourself. Provoke a response." The venue even printed images of the Dada past in its promotional material, including the likeness of Hugo Ball wearing his famous costume.

There were other cabaret groups in Chicago during the 1980s. The Chicago Cabaret Ensemble, for example, was founded in 1985 by writer and producer Warren Leming. Among their programs was an adaptation of Rainer Werner Fassbinder's 1972 film *The Bitter Tears of Petra von Kant*, but they also presented music programs and solo shows. Like their German counterparts, the ensemble's productions were often tied to social and political issues. The Chicago Poetry Ensemble combined poetry and story-telling with performance and a touch of burlesque—one of its members, Marc Smith, is considered the founder of the poetry slam, a competition in which poets read or recite original work—and presented their work at clubs around town.

4

Early German Cabarets

French Yet German

The German cabaret inherited some of its best performers from the Dada movement. What's more, several significant factors contributed to the birth of the German cabaret, but perhaps none were as important as the influence and cross-fertilization from Montmartre.

Near the turn of the twentieth century, Berlin pubs developed into cabarets based on the French model. In October 1901, German artist Max Tilke reportedly opened the first cabaret in Berlin, the Hungry Pegasus (Zum hungrigen Pegasus). Tilke, who also sang and played guitar, had frequented the cabarets in Paris. He acted as the conferencier, or emcee. The performances took place in the back room of an Italian restaurant. The audience consisted of a coterie of artists, writers, society folk, civil servants, and journalists; in other words, mostly middle-class people who pretended to be bohemians. Today we would call it slumming.

These early cabarets were known as pub-cabarets, or *Kneipenbrettl*. They presented sketches and songs. Many were created in direct response to the popularity of American vaudeville and variety shows, usually held inside restaurants or pubs and recalled the raucous tavern scenes depicted in the German film *The Blue Angel*. Another name attached to them was *tingel-tangels*, taken from the verb *tingeln*, meaning the clinking of coins onto a plate that was passed around.

According to German law, circa 1904, a tingel-tangel refers to a

> commercial presentations at a fixed place of operation, consisting of musical performances, especially vocal music, declamations, dances, shorter musicals and similar works, devoid of any higher artistic or scholarly interest, and which are capable, through either their content or their manner of presentation, of arousing the lower instincts, in particular the sexual lust of the audience.

At the opposite end of the entertainment spectrum were the large commercial establishments; most distinguished was the Wintergarten in Berlin that booked such major figures as Yvette Guilbert and Lillian Russell. Cabarets fell somewhere in the middle ground between the tingel-tangel and the concert setting.

Meanwhile, in Munich, a group calling themselves the Eleven Executioners formed a cabaret whose specialty was attacking the legal system and, in particular, social hypocrisy—anything to shock the people out of their complacency. Among the members was the dramatist and poet Frank Wedekind. In 1891, he had written *Spring Awakening* but because of its frankly erotic nature—the sexual stirrings of adolescent youth—it was not produced until a few years later, in 1906. (In late 2006, an alternative rock version, with music by Duncan Sheik and lyrics by Steven Sater, opened at the Eugene O'Neill Theatre on Broadway. It went on to win a Tony for best musical.)

He brought back to Germany the subversive, anti-authoritarian spirit of those Montmartre cabarets. And also like the French cabarets, he established a newspaper, the illustrated satirical weekly *Simplicissimus*, which attacked hypocrisy, morality, and authority.

Wedekind also wrote satirical songs. Like Aristide Bruant, he had a singular stage presence. He too would treat the audience with contempt, singing his own songs with raw emotion in a voice that was brittle, nasal, and defiantly untrained—an early-twentieth-century German version of Bob Dylan. Both his stage persona and his songs were abrasive and brutal. Later, Bertolt Brecht would imitate Wedekind's style, a style that would also become the hallmark of the German cabaret.

Subversive Entertainment

Another important figure, the poet Ernst von Wolzogen, opened the Überbrettl in Berlin, which combined elements of the variety show with satire and ample doses of lyricism and eroticism. On opening night, he presented a pantomime Pierrot play, a shadow play, poems, songs, and a portion of Arthur Schnitzler's operetta play, the *Anatol* cycle—all of which captured the spirit of the times. (A variation of a shadow play appears in the film version of *Cabaret* with the Kit Kat Klub's version of *Arabian Nights*, as a cellist plays "Willkommen.")

In 1901, Max Reinhardt, then a young actor, with a group of fellow intellectuals and artists, did a benefit performance for the German poet

Christian Morgenstern. The performance consisted of parodies interspersed with satirical comments. It was such a success that the group decided to do weekly performances. They named themselves Schall und Rauch or Sound and Smoke. Several months later, the group became the Kleine Theatre, one of Germany's early experimental theaters. German cabaret thus increasingly became known for its satirizing elements.

An entertainment district developed in Berlin's Friedrichstadt district, along the Friedrichstrasse between Unter den Linden and Leipzigerstrasse. Most of the cabarets and pub-cabarets were located here. Not coincidentally, this part of Berlin at the time also happened to be the red-light district.

Berlin soon emerged as Germany's first cosmopolitan center. In the post-World War I era, a new permissiveness set in. The German capital attracted artists but also its fair share of drug addicts, outcasts, misfits, and outsiders—similar to the potent mix that helped produce the cabaret scene in Montmartre. Russians fleeing the Revolution came here. Theaters sprang up almost overnight, cabarets flourished, and the exotic sound of jazz arrived from America.

But satire was not forgotten entirely. A new generation of intellectuals and artists used the cabaret stage as a medium for exploring, satirizing, and criticizing German society. Songs, poems, sketches, and monologues were their chosen vehicles.

Specifically, in the mid-twenties, the Germany cabaret spawned the cabaret satirical revue, mostly consisting of acts and sketches, parodies and catchy music. Bars with sleazy entertainment often dubbed themselves cabarets, to the horror of the cabaret purists. Indeed, in order to avoid this linguistic confusion, the German language now differentiates between *Cabaret* and *Kabarett*. The words were used interchangeably through the Weimar era, but since the 1950s, *Cabaret* has referred to a strip show, while *Kabarett* is reserved for social criticism or political satire.

Chicago Tribune music critic John von Rhein has described *Kabarett*, or Kabaret, as "nightclubs drenched with smoke and sex, where biting political and social protest was set to the heady rhythms of American jazz." It was a world, he notes, where "leftist intellectuals and Dada-esque artists mingled with refugees and revolutionaries, profiteers and pimps." Like modern cabaret performers, the great cabaret artists of Weimar Germany made an indelible mark on their songs, making them new and fresh with each rendition.

Another kind of cabaret in Berlin between the wars were known as dive cabarets, or *Amüsierkabarett*, which, as its name indicates, exclusively emphasized their entertainment value. The more serious cabaret, which trafficked in satirical songs and revues, were known simply as *Kabarett*. The artists in these Kabaretts used the stage as an outlet for dissent and provocation. The often cheerful music masked the quite sexually frank and politically inflammatory lyrics.

With their defiant tone and subject matter, many of the songs are especially relevant in today's post-news and alternative facts landscape; topics such as the abuse of power, out-of-control capitalism, and alienation were usually dispensed with a wickedly mordant wit and suffused with an uncommonly intelligent sense of wordplay. It was in these venues that Marlene Dietrich got her start, as did many composers and writers: Kurt Tucholsky, Walter Mehring, Mischa Spoliansky, Rudolf Nelson, among others. More than a few of the cabaret singers were considered sexually subversive themselves—even by decadent Weimar Germany standards. Dietrich may be the best-known example, but the lesbian cabaret entertainer Claire Waldoff once performed a Friedrich Hollaender song, "Raus mit den Mannern!" ("Chuck Out the Men!") that advocated ridding the German Reichstag of its male members.

> Chuck all the men out of the Reichstag . . .
> We women have had it up to here

Tongue in cheek or not, it sent an incendiary message to the broader mainstream society.

Although Bertolt Brecht and Kurt Weill did not write for the cabaret per se, Peter Jelavich maintains they were part of a wider culture of satirical and cynical songwriting that found expression on the cabaret stage.

A typical cabaret consisted of a small stage. Audiences sat around tables with direct eye-to-eye contact between performers and audience (think of the physical setup of the revamped 1998 *Cabaret* production on Broadway). A show might feature short (five- or ten-minute) numbers, usually songs, dance, puppet shows, and short films. Topical issues might touch on sex, fashion, culture, and, lastly, politics (if at all). Either way, the presentations were linked by the presence of an emcee, a master of ceremonies. Indeed, the emcee was the cord that tied everything together.

Jelavich mentions two other popular genres within the Berlin cabaret milieu: the revue and agitprop. The former performed on large stages with a plotline; the latter, which flourished in the later years of the Weimar Republic, focused on political issues. "Predictably, the Nazi era saw the most radical changes in the cabaret landscape. Entertainers who were

Jewish . . . fled the cabarets, and the country as well, leaving insipid variety-show programs in their wake," he notes.

Among the most important figures on the Berlin cabaret scene were the following (in no particular order):

Kurt Tucholsky: 1890–1935

Journalist, satirist, and writer. Tucholsky was considered one of the most important journalists of the Weimar Republic and a fierce social critic. He contributed many lyrics to cabaret songs in the post-World War I era. He believed popular entertainment should be a form of high art. He wrote chansons, satirical stories, and parodies and was considered the premier satirist of the Weimar era. He was also the editor of the German left-wing weekly *Die Weltbühne*, which covered politics and culture. A prescient artist, he warned against the authoritarian tendencies of Hitler under National Socialism. When the Nazis took power, his books not only were censored and listed as Degenerate Art but also they were burned. Tucholsky himself was stripped of his German citizenship. In 1935, he reportedly committed suicide by overdosing on sleeping pills.

Rosa Valetti: 1878–1937

German actress, cabaret singer, and subversive extraordinaire. A veteran of Berlin's cabaret scene, Valetti founded her own cabaret, Café Grössenwahn (Café Megalomania), on the Kurfürstendamm in late 1920. The café became one of the most popular cabarets in Weimar Berlin—it was among the most political cabarets and became known for its trenchant sketch comedy and political songs. Modeled after Bruant's Le Mirliton, the club showcased Valetti performing some of Bruant's songs on opening night. Most of the songs, though, were about Berlin's own misfits and outcasts—a never-ending flow of material. After it shut down, she opened other cabarets. In 1928, she snared the role of Mrs. Peachum in the original cast of Brecht's and Weill's *The Threepenny Opera* at Berlin's Theater am Schiffbauerdamm.

Valetti began acting in the fledgling German movie industry in 1911. But her most famous cinematic role—a small one—was in *The Blue Angel*, opposite another star of the German cabaret, Kurt Gerron—that's her stern visage and stony presence on the stage next to Marlene Dietrich. She also appeared in Fritz Lang's classic *M* (1931), appropriately, as the proprietor of an underground café.

Valetti strongly believed that cabaret could be—should be—an outlet for political criticism and an agent of social change. Following the rise of Hitler, she went into exile, first in Vienna, then in Prague, and, finally, in Palestine.

Walter Mehring: 1896–1981

Considered the most scathing of the German cabaret chanson writers, Mehring harbored a deep suspicion of authority. He wrote bawdy songs and lyrics of modern city life while revealing its urban absurdities and injustices. He was also one of the leading figures of Berlin Dada. Several of his lyrics were set to music and performed at Max Reinhardt's Sound and Smoke. A pacifist, in 1933, he fled to France and then, in 1940, to the United States, where he worked briefly in Hollywood.

Anita Berber: 1899–1928

If any one person could epitomize Weimar excess, it would have to be the German dancer and actress Anita Berber, who wore her hair in a fashionable short, bright red bob. Her performances—and persona—broke cultural boundaries not only because of her use of full nudity but also because of her androgyny, alcohol abuse, and overt drug addiction. The 1925 painting by Otto Dix *The Dancer Anita Berber* captures her essence. She wears a long red gown, her right hand on one hip, the other hand in a claw-like pose. Bright red lipstick, a small belly protruding from her gown, and raccoon eyes amid pasty white skin completes the disturbing portrait.

Claire Waldoff: 1844–1957

Known by her sobriquet "the Berliner," Waldoff was one of the most popular entertainers on the Berlin cabaret circuit well into the 1930s. Waldoff was an everywoman and appealed to the ordinary man and woman of the street. Her appearance conformed to that image. Her performance style was also unique and in sharp contrast to the stylishly dressed divas of the upper-class cabarets. She specialized in portrayals of lower-status Berliners. A lesbian, she had a stocky build, bushy hair, dressed simply, and sang in a guttural voice. When performing she stood absolutely still, with her arms hanging down and her hands neatly folded in front of her. Her demeanor, if not her character, evokes the Sally Bowles of *I Am a Camera*. An iconic figure and the prototype of the ordinary Berliner.

Trude Hesterberg: 1892–1967

An operetta singer, Hesterberg attended Max Reinhardt's acting school. She opened her own cabaret, the Wild Stage, in the basement of the Theater des Westens in 1921, and hired the best cabaret talent in town. The Theater des Westens was the first cabaret to perform the songs of Erich Kästner, who, contends Peter Jelavich, would "write some of the best cabaret lyrics in the waning years of the Weimer Republic." Brecht performed his songs at the Wild Stage in early 1922, the only time, adds Jelavich, that Brecht did so in a Berlin cabaret. One of the songs he sang there was the macabre "The Ballad of the Dead Soldier," which condemns the government. In the song, the German army, desperate for recruits, "revives" the dead soldier by dousing him with schnapps, covers the smell of death with incense, and sends him back to the front.

Friedrich Hollaender: 1896–1976

Film composer and author, Hollaender wrote music for Max Reinhardt's productions and was a major figure on the Berlin cabaret scene. Along with Kurt Tucholsky, Walter Mehring, and Mischa Spoliansky, he worked at Reinhardt's Sound and Smoke—and provided the music to songs performed there—and with Trude Hesterberg at the Theater des Westens, where he established the Tingel-Tangel Theater cabaret in 1931. In addition, he was also a composer and lyricist at Rosa Valetti's Megalomania Café. His music was frequently performed by Weintraub's Syncopaters, considered the best German jazz band of its day.

But he is best known for writing the film score for *The Blue Angel*, including Marlene Dietrich's signature song, "Falling in Love Again" (Can't Help It)." He left Nazi Germany in 1933, immigrating to the United States the following year. In America, he composed scores for more than a hundred films, including *Destry Rides Again* (1939), with Dietrich; *A Foreign Affair* (1948), also with Dietrich; *The 5,000 Fingers of Dr. T* (1953); and *Sabrina* (1954). Dietrich made many of his songs famous, such as "Black Market," "Illusions," "Ruins of Berlin"—all of which appear in *A Foreign Affair*.

Erich Kästner: 1899–1974

One of *Die Weltbühne*'s most popular contributors and one of the leading figures of the New Objectivity movement, Kästner wrote chansons that became staples of Berlin's cabarets as well as numerous children's books.

He also published poetry, articles, and reviews and a column in Berlin's many periodicals. The Nazis burned the pacifist Kästner's books as being "contrary to the German spirit."

Kurt Gerron: 1897–1944

Actor and film director, Gerron worked for director Max Reinhardt in the early 1920s, and appeared in silent films before he began directing short films. He originated the role of Tiger Brown in the 1928 production of Brecht's and Weill's *The Threepenny Opera*. His best-known role was opposite Marlene Dietrich in *The Blue Angel* as the magician and emcee Kiepert.

After the Nazis assumed power, Gerron left Germany, eventually settling in Amsterdam. But when Germany occupied the Netherlands, Gerron was sent to the infamous Theresienstadt concentration camp. At Theresienstadt, he presented the cabaret revue *Karussell,* in which he reprised the role of Mack the Knife. In 1944, the Nazis coerced him into directing a Nazi propaganda film depicting the "humane" conditions at the camp. After filming ended, Gerron and members of his Ghetto Swingers jazz band were transported to Auschwitz, where he and his wife perished in the gas chambers.

Rudolf Nelson (born Rudolf Lewysohn): 1878–1960

Nelson founded numerous cabarets in Berlin and wrote many songs in a variety of musical styles, including ragtime, the cakewalk, and the two-step but also in the style of Central European popular tunes that were about daily life in Berlin. The topics of his cabaret songs were often sex and extramarital affairs. One of the cabarets he opened was the Chat Noir, in honor of the famous French cabaret, located on the corner of Friedrichstrasse and Unter den Linden. Nelson also operated the Theater am Kurfürstendamm, which started as a cabaret but moved on to presenting revues.

Golden Age of the Weimar Revue

In the 1920s, the "Americanization of popular entertainment," to use Peter Jelavich's phrase, took place in Berlin. Melodies onstage were dominated by popular dances such as the fox trot, the shimmy, and the Charleston. The time frame, between 1924 and 1929, was considered the golden age of the Weimar revue, according to Jelavich. There could be up to sixty different

Kit Kat Klub boys and girls, *Cabaret* national tour, 2016.   *Courtesy Margie Korshak, Inc.*

scenes or numbers in an evening. Two revues in particular were especially popular among German audiences: the Chocolate Kiddies troupe, which featured the music of Duke Ellington, and the singular presence of dancer and singer and all-around entertainer, Josephine Baker. Also popular in the revues was the kick line where ten to twenty girls performed perfectly coordinated dance steps. The most famous of these female troupes was the Tiller Girls, from England. "The precision of the Girls evoked images not only of machinery but of the military as well," notes Jelavich, which also recalls the goosestep kick line of the Emcee and the Kit Kat Girls in *Cabaret*.

The final years of the Weimar period saw a brief revival of political cabaret. During these years on the cabaret stage, Hitler was often dismissed as a buffoon and a bully. Political cabarets tried to revive the spirit of the early 1920s by performing the songs of Kurt Tucholsky and Walter Mehring. Still, cabaret artists—as well as German society writ large—failed to take Hitler seriously until it was too late. Most of the population felt he had little chance of succeeding.

The takeover by the Nazis in 1933 virtually destroyed the cabaret in Germany since most of the entertainers were liberal or Jewish, or both.

Instead, the Nazis called for a "positive cabaret" that would celebrate Nazism and mock its enemies: the antithesis of cabaret. But even this experiment didn't last long. In December 1937, Joseph Goebbels, the Minister of Propaganda, issued a decree banning political themes altogether. Any cabarets that did survive turned into vaudeville theaters. Moreover, most of the prominent cabaret artists had already fled Germany; almost all were Jewish, including Kurt Gerron, Valeska Gert, Paul Graetz, Friedrich Hollaender, Walter Mehring, Paul Morgan, Rudolf Nelson, Kurt Robitschek, and others. Some, like Paul Nikolaus, committed suicide, as did Tucholsky.

As Jelavich showed, cabaret acquired its edge from its ability to challenge the status quo, to attack conformity, as well as its immediacy and topicality. It sought to persuade people to reexamine their preconceived notions. It assailed political figures, established institutions, and symbols of authority, much like improvisational comedy revues and television shows such as Second City and *Saturday Night Live* do today.

The Emcee

The rouge cheeks. The white mask. The grotesque grin. Ever since Joel Grey and later Alan Cumming came on the scene as the emcee of the Kit Kat Klub, the image has been set: that of the leering, voyeuristic host who watches over the stage like an eagle-eyed sentinel.

Whether referred to as the conferencier, the compere, or the *ansager*, the emcee has played a significant role in the history of cabarets. Aristide Bruant at Le Mirliton was arguably the first emcee of note in entertainment history. Flamboyant and charming, he insulted patrons with abandon—and they came back night after night to hear the abuse. The official function of the emcee was to interact with the audience and introduce the performers. But he was much more than that— he symbolized the power of the cabaret and the hold it had on German society.

Paul Nikolaus, the emcee of the most successful cabaret of the late Weimar period, the Kabarett der Komiker, told political jokes as he presided over a venue that combined elements of vaudeville and theater, including mock operettas (such as *Quo Vadis*), which ridiculed Hitler's Beer Hall Putsch. Kabarett der Komiker was in fact the showpiece for Berlin cabaret stars Rosa Valetti and Paul Graetz, as well as international stars such as Yvette Guilbert.

On the other hand, the Emcee at Roosevelt University's college production appeared in a leather kilt. Director and choreographer Jane Lanier told me she wanted him to look attractive to members of both sexes. "In Berlin, anything goes," she says. "I wanted everyone to be attracted to him." Director Sam

Mendes once suggested that his emcee had more in common with Alex, the charming but antisocial lead character in *A Clockwork Orange*, than Joel Grey.

Thus, the idea of using the emcee as a unifying theme as portrayed in the musical *Cabaret* had historical roots. But the physical manifestation of the emcee in *Cabaret* comes from a specific time and place. In 1951, director Hal Prince remembered watching a performer in a nightclub called Maxim's in Stuttgart. "There was a dwarf MC, hair parted in the middle and lacquered down with brilliantine, his mouth made into a bright-red cupid's bow, who wore heavy false eyelashes and sang, danced, goosed, tickled, and pawed four lumpen Valkyres waving diaphanous butterfly wings," he wrote in his memoir, *Contradictions*. According to James Leve, John Kander saw a similar entertainer while at the Tivoli Gardens in Copenhagen, where Marlene Dietrich happened to be performing. Significantly, the emcee announced each act in three languages, as the Emcee also would do in *Cabaret*.

The emcee is still a big part of many cabaret shows. Petterino's Monday Night Live! in Chicago, for example, features an impromptu musical showcase of local cabaret talent. Some singers are there to promote upcoming shows (several cast members of a forthcoming production of *Priscilla, Queen of the Desert* were there the night I attended the show). The number of performers at these Monday night cabarets vary from a dozen to just short of twenty. Co-emcee Denise McGowan Tracy offers a sunny Midwestern take on the cynical German version: whereas *Cabaret*'s emcee is darkly cynical and sexually androgynous, Tracy is gregarious, chatty, and effervescent. She began the evening with a cheerful rendition of Debbie Reynolds's "Good Morning"—Reynolds had just died a few weeks earlier—but also offered gentle ribbing of Donald Trump.

Max Reinhardt: 1873–1943

Among the most prominent figures on the German cabaret scene was the theater and film director/producer Max Reinhardt. Born Maximilian Goldmann in Baden near Vienna, Reinhardt grew up in Vienna and acted in various theaters in his native Austria when he caught the attention of the critic Otto Brahm in Salzburg. He then joined the Deutsches Theater ensemble in Berlin under Brahm's direction, where he became known for his acting. Increasingly frustrated with the theater's realism, he argued that theater should present a different view, a view separate from the ordinary world. He preached naturalism.

Reinhardt did some acting outside the Deutsches Theater, but his biggest step was establishing the Schall und Rauch (Sound and Smoke) in

Joel Grey as the Emcee in the motion picture production of *Cabaret*.   *Photofest*

Berlin, a cabaret that emerged from the weekly social gatherings held at the Café Monopol. The members of the gathering formed their own club, which they called the Spectacles (Die Brille). The group parodied current theater productions. They eventually changed their name to the more forceful Schall und Rauch. The first performance under that name took place at the Kunstlerhaus in the Bellevuestrasse in early 1901. In a pre-Dadaist touch, Reinhardt along with Friedrich Kayssler and Martin Zickel introduced the program clad in Pierrot outfits. Sound and Smoke opened its own theater in October 1903 in the Hotel Arnim located in Berlin's Friedrichstrasse neighborhood. Reinhardt hired Peter Behrens to design a small theater in the space. At the time, Behrens contributed to the Jugendstil exhibition at the Darmstadt Artists' Colony.

By this time, Schall und Rauch was less cabaret than a new repertory of serious full-length drama. And yet Reinhardt did not abandon his cabaret roots altogether. The Schall und Rauch's repertory still drew on visual and musical elements, pantomime and sound. Reinhardt strongly believed that theater should encourage both play *and* experimentation.

Reinhardt went on to adopt more ambitious theatrical experiments. He presented theater-in-the-round productions of classical plays on arena stages and in circus halls, and held open-air productions of mystery plays. He used innovative techniques in stage design, music, and choreography.

German poet, playwright, and theatrical director Bertolt Brecht.   *Ullstein bild/Lebrecht Music & Arts*

During 1915–1918, Reinhardt worked as a director of the Volksbühne theater. In 1920, he established the Salzburg Festival with Richard Strauss and Hugo von Hofmannsthal, including an annual production of the morality play *Everyman*. By 1930, he ran numerous theaters throughout Berlin.

With conditions in Germany deteriorating, Reinhardt migrated first to Britain and then to the United States, where he found work in the American theater and film industries. He produced a popular theatrical version of *A Midsummer Night's Dream* in 1927 on Broadway; a film version, featuring James Cagney, Mickey Rooney, Joe E. Brown, and Olivia de Havilland, was released in 1935. He also opened the Reinhardt School of the Theatre in Los Angeles, on Sunset Boulevard. In 1940, Reinhardt became a naturalized citizen.

Reinhardt died in New York in 1943. His papers are housed at Binghamton University (SUNY), in the Max Reinhardt Archives and Library). The collection contains over 240,000 papers, personal letters, and documents; over 14,000 photographs and negatives, including costume and set designs; films of some of his productions; and a portion of his personal library.

Other Reinhardt works on Broadway included *The Miracle* (1924) as co-playwright and director; *The Merchant of Yonkers* (1938), based on Thornton Wilder's play; and *Sons and Soldiers* (1943), as producer and director.

Bertolt Brecht and Kurt Weill

Bertolt Brecht and Kurt Weill were among the most successful artistic collaborators in German and American theater. Brecht, a poet, playwright, and theater director, and Weill, a composer, created some of the finest theatrical work of the twentieth century. Their influence had a profound effect on drama and musical theater, from *Cabaret* to the discordant films of Lars von Trier, as well as the work of individual artists.

Bertolt Brecht

Bertolt Brecht (1898–1956) was born in Bavaria. He studied drama at Munich University with Arthur Kutscher, who introduced him to the work of the cabaret performer Frank Wedekind. Brecht was especially influenced by the great Munich comedian/clown Karl Valentin, who he compared to Charlie Chaplin. Valentin performed short sketches, much of it political in nature. In the early 1920s, Brecht wrote the script for a short slapstick film, *Mysteries of a Barbershop*, which starred Valentin, before turning his hand to playwrighting. Early on in his career, Brecht wrote and performed his own songs in Berlin's cabarets, accompanying himself on the guitar. In 1922, he even opened his own cabaret, the short-lived Die Rote Zibebe (the Red Grape), which featured the dancer Valeska Gert and Valentin. Brecht lived in the Wilmersdorf neighborhood of Berlin, within walking distance of some of the Weimar era's best writers and painters, including Heinrich Mann, Walter Benjamin, Kurt Tucholsky, Erich Kästner, George Grosz, and Alfred Döblin.

Brechtian Legacy

Many playwrights and directors (both theater and film) were influenced by Bertolt Brecht and his singular vision for the stage. A small sampling would include the following:

Lindsay Anderson
(1923–1994)
English filmmaker

Robert Bolt
(1924–1995)
English screenwriter

Peter Brook
(1925–)
English theater director

Caryl Churchill
(1938–)
English playwright

Rainer Werner Fassbinder
(1945–1982)
German filmmaker

Dario Fo
(1926–2016)
Italian Futurist, actor, play-
    wright, and director

Jean-Luc Godard
(1930–)
French filmmaker

Tony Kushner
(1956–)
American playwright
    and screenwriter

Joseph Losey
(1909–1984)
American filmmaker

Lars von Trier
(1956–)
Danish filmmaker

Joan Littlewood
(1914–2002)
English theater director;
    "mother of modern
    theater"

Brecht's early plays included *Baal, Drums in the Night,* and *In the Jungle.* With Lion Feuchtwanger, he adapted Christopher Marlowe's *Edward II* in 1924. It was around this time that his conception of "epic theatre" began to develop. By then his work had caught the eye of Max Reinhardt, who hired him as an assistant dramaturge for his Deutsches Theater in Berlin. Like Aristide Bruant in Montmartre, in works such as *Baal* and even *The Threepenny Opera,* Brecht was inspired by the German street ballads and speech patterns from his native Augsburg. "As far as he was concerned, cabaret was the only form of existing theater that was worthwhile," writes Pamela Katz. He attended cabarets in Munich and also performed in Karl Valentin's Laughing Cellar.

Increasingly, though, Brecht emphasized collaboration with various friends and colleagues. His work became part of the Neue Sachlichkeit (New Objectivity), a post-Expressionist movement in Germany that stressed collectivity over individual achievement. Studying Marxism and socialism, he wrote several agitprop plays. In 1927, he joined the collective of Erwin Piscator's Proletarian Theater, a documentary theatrical company. Piscator wanted theater to reach the working masses. He believed that theater should be the home of revolutionary ideas. He developed some of the techniques that Brecht would later call epic theatre.

As indicated, epic theatre was influenced by the New Objectivity movement, then popular in Germany. Proponents of this movement used a cool, detached style to satirize and comment on contemporary society. Essentially, the movement was a reaction against the excesses of Expressionism and a form of artistic democracy meant to honor everyday people. It was looked upon by Brecht, and others, as a "useful" art.

Brecht collaborated with Piscator on several important productions, including *The Good Soldier Schweik.* From Piscator he learned the value of staging and design, especially the use of projections as well as songs that commented on the action. For *Schweik,* George Grosz did the background projections. Among its more controversial images was the image of Jesus on the cross wearing a gas mask.

In the late 1920s, Brecht began collaborating with the German composer Kurt Weill. They began to develop Brecht's *Mahagonny* project. *Rise and Fall of the City of Mahagonny* was a loose narrative involving an imaginary boom town set nowhere in particular although the production had touches of the Klondike and Gold Rush-era San Francisco (Charlie Chaplin's film *The Gold Rush* had just been released in Germany in 1926 and had been hugely influential on Brecht). The town, which Ronald Sanders called a "fool's-paradise of a city," was a violent place populated by poker players and prostitutes and flowing with whiskey. For Brecht, America during the Gold Rush era represented the epitome of capitalism, a land of greed and avarice.

Piscator used cinematic projections as part of his epic theatre vision. Brecht expanded on this with highly artificial sets and backdrops. He also adopted an artificial acting style that was closer in tone to cabaret than theater. Brecht synthesized the ideas of both Piscator and the Russian director and theatrical producer Vsevolod Meyerhold, advocating the role of theater as an outlet for political ideas.

As someone who advocated the New Objectivity movement, Brecht believed the audience should be an active part of the program, not just a passive observer. His use of a narrator who breaks through the fourth wall to comment on events echoes *Cabaret*'s Emcee. When Alan Cumming in Sam

Threepenny Cast Members

Many famous actors and actresses have been in the cast of *The Threepenny Opera* over the decades. Here are cast members of some of the more prominent revivals:

1954–1955: Off-Broadway production, Theater de Lys, New York. Featured Lotte Lenya as Jenny, Edward Asner as Mr. Peachum, Charlotte Rae as Mrs. Peachum, Bea Arthur as Lucy Brown, Jerry Orbach as Mack the Knife, as well as John Astin and Jerry Stiller.

1976–1977: Joe Papp's New York Shakespeare Festival at the Vivian Beaumont Theater at Lincoln Center. Featured Raul Julia as Macheath, Blair Brown as Lucy Brown, and Ellen Greene as Jenny.

1986: National Theatre, London. Featured Tim Curry as Macheath.

1989: Broadway. Featured Sting as Macheath, Georgia Brown as Mrs. Peachum, Maureen McGovern as Polly, Kim Criswell as Lucy Brown, KT Sullivan as Suky Tawdry.

2006: Broadway, Roundabout Theatre Company. Featured Alan Cumming as Macheath, Nellie McKay as Polly, Cyndi Lauper as Jenny, Jim Dale as Mr. Peachum, Ana Gesteyer as Mrs. Peachum.

Mendes's revival spoke directly to the audience, when he danced with audience members, he was directly continuing the Brechtian tradition.

Brecht felt epic theatre should provoke self-reflection. It should be an avenue for the recognition of social injustice. This in turn would encourage observers—the audience—to go one step farther by effecting change in the outside world. Theater, he concluded, should be a *representation* of reality rather than a depiction of reality itself. Thus, Brecht employed vcarious techniques—the actor's direct address to the audience, harsh stage lighting, use of songs to interrupt the action, and speaking stage directions out loud—to bring the audience's attention to what was happening onstage; that is, to help the audience realize that what occurred onstage was not reality but merely a theatrical version of it.

The Threepenny Opera

In 1928, Brecht adapted John Gay's *The Beggar's Opera*. Brecht's lyrics were set to Kurt Weill's music and retitled *The Threepenny Opera* (*Die Dreigroschenoper*). A huge success in 1920s Berlin, it ridiculed pompous behavior and the hypocrisy of conventional morality imposed by established religion in the face of working-class poverty and hunger. In 1728, John Gay had parodied Handel's operas that were then fashionable in London by using simple, traditional English ballads. His "opera" was intended to be a critique of capitalism. Brecht's twentieth-century update also exposed modern society as corrupt and morally bankrupt.

The plot of Brecht's *Threepenny* follows the basic outline of Gay's *Beggar*. Set in Victorian London, the hero (or anti-hero) Macheath, or Mackie Messer, also known as Mack the Knife, is considered London's most notorious criminal, which Gay reportedly based on a historical figure, a thief by the name of Jack Sheppard. The German title, *Die Moritat von Mackie Messer*, refers to a medieval murder ballad performed by strolling minstrels, which explains why it is sung not by Macheath but by a street singer following in the German *moritat* tradition.

Macheath marries Polly Peachum, much to the displeasure of her father. Using his influence—an old friend, Tiger Brown, the chief of police—manages to get Macheath arrested. He is sentenced to the hangman's noose. But in a parody of the happy ending, Macheath cheats death moments before his execution. In fact, a messenger from the queen pardons Macheath and grants him the title of baron.

The original cast of *The Threepenny Opera* featured Harald Paulsen as Macheath; Erich Ponto as Mr. Peachum, who controls the fate of all the beggars in London and conspires to have Macheath hanged; Rosa Valetti as Mrs. Peachum; Roma Bahn as Polly Peachum, the Peachums' daughter, who agrees to marry Macheath despite only knowing him five days; Kurt Gerron as Tiger Brown, the London police chief and Macheath's best friend from their days in the army; Kate Kuhl as Lucy Brown, Tiger Brown's daughter, who claims to be married to Macheath; and Lotte Lenya as Jenny, a prostitute once involved with Macheath who turns him over to the police. Gerron also played the role of a street singer in the opening scene, performing "Mack the Knife."

Threepenny was a combination of theater and song, with touches of opera, jazz, and cabaret. The highlight of the production was "Pirate Jenny." As embodied by Lotte Lenya, it was part revenge fantasy and part wish fulfillment. The character of Polly explains the origin of the song. She once saw a girl washing glasses in a cheap Soho dive. Angered by the condescension of the clientele, the girl sings about the day when a pirate ship "with eight sails and fifty cannons" will appear in the harbor and destroy the entire town except for the seedy hotel where she lives. Then a hundred pirates will disembark, take prisoners, and ask the girl which patrons should be killed.

All of them!

Then the ship will sail away with her on it.

Another song on the topic of elusive love, "Barbara Song"—unable to find a sweetheart among the nice young men of her town, she falls instead for a cad—echoes the Berlin cabaret sound. "One can easily imagine it being sung by a Marlene Dietrich and or Greta Keller," notes Ronald Sanders. Although not as successful, their next collaboration, *Happy End,* featured some of Brecht and Weill's best-known songs, including "Bilbao Song" and "Surabaya Johnny."

Brecht left Nazi Germany in early 1933. After brief spells in Prague, Zurich, and Paris, he moved to Denmark. With war imminent, he moved to Sweden and then Finland before immigrating to the United States in 1941. During the war years, he wrote some of his best-known and anti-fascist plays, including *Puntila and His Hired Hand, Life of Galileo, Mother Courage and Her Children, The Good Person of Szechwan, The Resistible Rise of Arturo Ui, The Caucasian Chalk Circle,* and *Fear and Misery of the Third Reich.*

Brecht also wrote or cowrote numerous screenplays. During the Red Scare, he was blacklisted by Hollywood and interrogated by the House

Un-American Activities Committee. Although a committed Marxist, he was never a member of the Communist Party.

Brecht died in August 1956 of a heart attack. He was fifty-eight.

Kurt Weill

Kurt Weill (1900–1950) grew up in Dessau, Germany, the son of a cantor. He studied composition with Engelbert Humperdinck at the Berliner Hochschule fur Musik and attended philosophy lectures by Ernst Carrirer and later studied at the Preßische Akademie der Künste in Berlin.

In 1922, he joined the Novembergruppe, a group of left-leaning Berlin artists that included Hanns Eisler and Stefan Wolpe. Two years later, the conductor Fritz Busch introduced him to the dramatist Georg Kaiser. He would write several one-act operas with Kaiser. It was Kaiser's home in Grünheide where Weill first met his future wife, Karoline Blamauer, better known to the world as Lotte Lenya.

Weill may be best known for his collaborations with Bertolt Brecht, especially *The Threepenny Opera*, but he also wrote gorgeous ballads for Broadway with the American lyricists Maxwell Anderson, Ira Gershwin, and Ogden Nash. Among his many works, he also wrote a radio cantata called *The Ballad of Magna Carta* that featured music in the style of English folk songs and Scottish ballads with prose passages.

Weill fled Nazi Germany in early 1933. He went to Paris, where he had worked with Brecht on the ballet *The Seven Deadly Sins* in 1928. Weill's score was very much influenced by the jazz and German dance music popular at the time.

In April 1933, *Threepenny* premiered on Broadway in an English translation. Although it closed after only thirteen performances, it enjoyed a successful off-Broadway revival in 1954 in a translation by Marc Blitzstein at the Theatre de Lys in Greenwich Village. Blitzstein had studied with Austrian composer Arnold Schoenberg in Berlin years earlier, where he had seen the original production of *Threepenny* (his political play with music, *The Cradle Will Rock*, was influenced by it). Originally scheduled for a three-week run, it ran for seven years. Lotte Lenya reprised her role as Jenny, which she originated in Germany. Its success led to a Brecht and Weill revival in America, a revival that lives on to this day.

In 1935, Weill moved to New York. He began to adopt an American composing style. He and his wife rented a house during the summer of 1936 in Connecticut, the summer home of the Group Theatre, where he composed the musical *Johnny Johnson* with lyrics by Paul Green. In 1939, he wrote the music for *Railroads on Parade*, which celebrated the American railroad. He worked with writers Maxwell Anderson and Ira Gershwin; wrote the film score for Fritz Lang's *You and Me* (1938); composed *Street Scene*, a series of short operas inspired by American folk music and based on a play by Elmer Rice, with lyrics by Langston Hughes; and composed *Lost in the Stars* (1949),

German composer Kurt Weill, best known for his collaboration with Bertolt Brecht, including *The Threepenny Opera.*   *Kurt Weill Foundation/Lebrecht Music & Arts*

with lyrics by Maxwell Anderson, a musical based on Alan Paton's South African novel *Cry, the Beloved Country*.

Weill died in April 1950 in New York.

In 1985, Hal Willner produced *Lost in the Stars: The Music of Kurt Weill*, a tribute album that featured interpretations of Weill songs by Todd Rundgren, Ella Fitzgerald, Tom Waits, Sting, and Lou Reed. For many years Weill's hometown of Dessau, Germany, had ignored his accomplishments. Not anymore. Every March the Kurt Weill Festival takes place there. The town is also home to a Weill society and a Kurt Weill Center at the Bauhaus.

Brecht and Weill Compositions

A sampling of works by Brecht and Weill:

The Threepenny Opera (1928). Play with music. Text by Brecht. Music by Kurt Weill. Adapted from Elisabeth Hauptmann's translation of John Gay's *The Beggar's Opera*. Includes "Moritat of Mackie Messer," "Pirate Jenny," "Barbara Song," "Ballad of Sexual Dependency," "Tango Ballad."

"Mack the Knife" was a top ten hit by Bobby Darin in 1959. "Pirate Jenny" has been recorded numerous times, including under the title of "The Black Freighter" by the English folk band Steeleye Span. But probably the most unusual inspiration is Bob Dylan's "When the Ship Comes In." Dylan had seen a theatrical collage called *Brecht on Brecht* in Greenwich Village (John Kander reportedly also saw the revue). He came away impressed by the lyricism of Brecht's work, but one song in particular lingered in his memory, "Pirate Jenny." Somehow Brecht and Weill's revenge fantasy song morphed into "When the Ship Comes In."

"It's a nasty song, sung by an evil fiend, and when she's done singing, there's not a word to say. It leaves you breathless," Dylan wrote in *Chronicles*. Dylan "took the song apart," studying its structure in order to uncover why it had such an intoxicating effect on him and how he himself could one day write songs just as good and just as powerful. In particular, he admired its free verse association and its "disregard for the known certainty of melodic patterns." He admired too the "raw intensity" of the *Threepenny* songs, their toughness, their essential weirdness. They reminded him of folk songs and yet were different because they were "sophisticated." By specifically using "Pirate Jenny" as a prototype, as a musical foundation, he eventually was able to create his version of what he heard that night in Greenwich Village or listened over and over again to the original off-Broadway cast album of *The Threepenny Opera*. If he hadn't attended the theater that night, he insists that he would not have been able to write "When the Ship Comes In" or "It's Alright Ma (I'm Only Bleeding)," "Mr. Tambourine Man," "A Hard Rain's A-Gonna Fall," "Visions of Johanna," and, indeed, the entire album of his remarkable *Blonde on Blonde*.

Happy End (1929). Musical comedy by Kurt Weill, Bertolt Brecht, and Elisabeth Hauptmann. Includes "Surabaya Johnny," "Bilbao Song," and "Sailors' Song."

Rise and Fall of the City of Mahagonny (1930). Opera. Music by Kurt Weill, text by Bertolt Brecht. Includes "Alabama Song."

Knickerbocker Holiday (1938). Musical comedy with book and lyrics by Maxwell Anderson. Includes "September Song."

Lady in the Dark (1941). Musical play. Text by Moses Hart, lyrics by Ira Gershwin. Music by Kurt Weill. Includes "My Ship."

One Touch of Venus (1943). Musical. Music by Kurt Weill, lyrics by Ogden Nash, book by S. J. Perelman and Ogden Nash based on the novella *The Tinted Venus* by Thomas Anstey Guthrie and loosely inspired by the Pygmalion tale. Includes "I'm a Stranger Here Myself," "Speak Low."

Street Scene (1946). American opera based on Elmer Rice's play. Music by Kurt Weill, lyrics by Langston Hughes, book by Elmer Rice.

Lost in the Stars (1949). Musical. Based on Alan Paton's novel *Cry, the Beloved Country*. Book and lyrics by Maxwell Anderson, music by Kurt Weill. Includes title song.

Tribute and Other Recordings

Lost in the Stars: The Music of Kurt Weill (A&M Records, 1985). Produced by Hal Willner. Featuring Carla Bley, Marianne Faithfull, Lou Reed, Tom Waits, John Zorn, and others.

September Songs: The Music of Kurt Weill (Sony Music, 1997). Produced by Hal Willner. Featuring Nick Cave, Elvis Costello, PJ Harvey, and others.

Ute Lemper Sings Kurt Weill (Decca, 1990). Includes "Alabama Song" and "I'm a Stranger Here Myself."

Speak Low—Songs by Kurt Weill (Deutsche Grammophon, 1995). Anne Sofie von Otter. Conducted by John Eliot Gardiner.

Lotte Lenya Sings Kurt Weill's The Seven Deadly Sins & Berlin Theatre Songs (Sony, 1997). Includes "Mack the Knife," "Barbara Song," "Alabama Song," "Bilbao Song," "Pirate Jenny."

The Seven Deadly Sins (1998). Marianne Faithfull. (RCA Victor Europe, 2004). Includes "Alabama Song," "The Ballad of Sexual Dependency," "Pirate Jenny."

This Is New (Umvd, 2002). Dee Dee Bridgewater. Includes "Lost in the Stars," "Bilbao Song," "My Ship," "Alabama Song," "September Song."

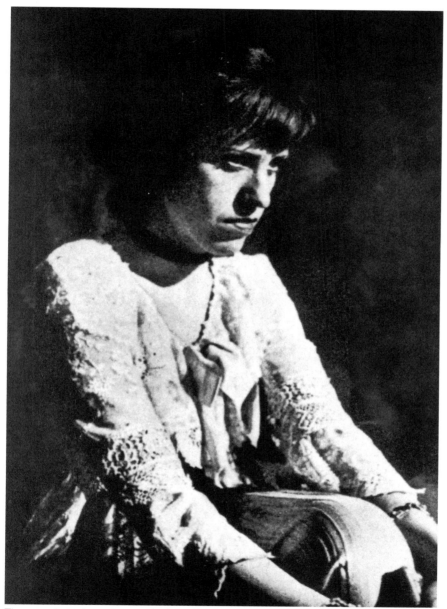

The young Lotte Lenya in a production of Brecht and Weill's *The Threepenny Opera*.

Photofest

Mad Jenny and the Society Band's production of "Mad Jenny's Love und Greed," at New York's Pangea in 2016, featured songs from Weimar Berlin by Mischa Spoliansky, Brecht and Weill, Brecht and Eisler, and Claire Waldoff. It featured Maria Dessena on accordion and piano, Ric Becker on trombone, Marty Isenberg on bass, and the Russian-born contortionist and dancer Miss Ekaterina as a special guest. The "Mad Jenny" of the title is Jenny Lee Mitchell.

Author collection. Photo by Theresa Albini

"Alabama Song" was originally published as a poem and appeared in Brecht's *Home Devotions* (*Hauspostille*) in 1927, then was set to music by Weill for the play *Little Mahagonny* (1927) and later in the Brecht and Weill opera *Rise and Fall of the City of Mahagonny*. It has been recorded numerous times, most notably by the Doors in 1966 as "Alabama Song (Whisky Bar)" from their eponymous album and as a single by David Bowie in 1980, with "Space Oddity" on the B-side.

Brecht's early songs placed him directly in the cabaret tradition. "One imagines his impact was akin to the young Bob Dylan's," writes Lisa Appignanesi. Along with his collaborator Kurt Weill, he used the cabaret as a model. In particular, he used the short sketches of the cabaret-revue as well as their satirical content in works such as *The Resistible Rise of Arturo Ui*. Many of the actors who appeared in Brecht's plays had their roots on the cabaret stage.

And yet, German cabaret did not travel well once outside German borders. Kurt Robitschek tried to recreate the Kadeko in New York, only to fail. Valeska Gert opened the Beggar's Bar in Greenwich Village in 1938, but that too met with little success. Hollaender chose to go West, to Los Angeles, attempting a California version of the Tingel-Tangel on Santa Monica Boulevard. Although unsuccessful, he did manage to write music for the movies in Hollywood.

But as for the city itself, cabaret and Berlin were meant for each other. The wit of Berlin was subversive and caustic. It captured the essence of the character of Berlin: the residents' reputation for pushiness; their sharp tongue; and their overall questioning, and disdain, of authority. Performers such as Claire Waldoff and Paul Graetz spoke or sang in a strong Berlin dialect. Berlin was a city of cynical skeptics with a unique identity.

Cabaret was the perfect form to express the city's uncommon character.

5

Goodbye to Berlin

Back to the Source

"I am a camera . . . quite passive, recording, not thinking."

—*Christopher Isherwood, Goodbye to Berlin*

Christopher Isherwood, the writer, could capture the essence of a character in a flitting gesture, a moment in time. Far from being a passive observer, Isherwood in story after story used his own life as a model for his work. He fictionalized the people that he met and the situations that he experienced. Isherwood was a prolific novelist, memoirist, journalist, and generally a scribbler extraordinaire, but invariably, it is nevertheless true that the hero of his stories was himself, or, more accurately, an alter ego that he also called "Christopher Isherwood." Photography had always appealed to him. As a boy, he had received a Box Brownie camera from his father. As a writer, he turned his knack for observation into selecting and arranging the action in his stories to create an unconventional, but compelling, narrative, with the camera as a metaphor, as a mechanism to explore the Germany that he came to know.

William Bradshaw was the name of the character in *Mr. Norris Changes Trains*, one of Isherwood's novels that is sometimes included in *Goodbye to Berlin* collections. "William Bradshaw" also happens to be Isherwood's middle names. The name "Christopher Isherwood" also appears in Isherwood's novel *Prater Violet* and in his memoir and subsequent film version *Christopher and His Kind*. Isherwood used himself as a character, even in his nonfiction. In the various Berlin stories, he uses the literary device of the neutral observer to comment on the environment and people around him. All through his time in Berlin, he kept a detailed diary, a habit he would continue even up to his death.

In the late 1920s, Christopher Isherwood spent some time in Berlin with poet W. H. Auden, his friend and occasional lover.

Photofest

"My name is Christopher Isherwood"

Christopher William Bradshaw Isherwood was born on August 26, 1904, at his parents' home of Wybersleigh Hall near the village of High Lane in Cheshire, England. His father, Frank Isherwood, was killed at the Battle of Ypres in Belgium during World War I, in which hundreds of thousands Allied soldiers died. After his father's death, Isherwood's mother, Kathleen, never remarried. Isherwood himself had an estranged relationship with his mother, rebelling against everything that she stood for.

Isherwood attended Repton School, a boarding school in Derbyshire, but he expressed more interest in boys than actual study ("the younger and blonder the better," Hilton Als writes). He met his friend, and object of sexual interest, Edward Upton, there. Not one to follow tradition or custom, he was expelled from Cambridge University in 1925, after his first year. He also briefly studied medicine at King's College in London. Three years later, in 1928, Isherwood published his first novel, *All the Conspirators*, another piece of semiautobiographical fiction, which sold less than three hundred copies. By then, he had grown weary, and plainly bored, with provincial England. Berlin, on the other hand, was an entirely different story.

Isherwood first went to Berlin in the spring of 1929, following his friend, and sometime lover, the poet W. H. Auden. According to Jonathan Fryer, he originally intended to stay for ten days. He stayed until 1933. To Isherwood, Berlin meant freedom. "In Berlin," notes Als, "the laws against Isherwood and company's sexual predilections were much easier to defy than in England."

When he first arrived in Berlin, Isherwood rented a room on Nollendorfstrabe, which he described as a "shabby, solemn street of monumental houses and bankrupt middle-class families in the west of the city." In *Cabaret*, Herr Schultz, proprietor of the "finest fruit market," lives in the same area.

Isherwood spent his mornings writing in a café on the Winterfeldtplatz. He was a bit of an eavesdropper himself, writing down snippets of conversation that he overheard. In the afternoon he taught English; in the evening, along with Auden, he would frequent the city's many nightclubs or, with the English poet Stephen Spender, go to the cinema. Among his favorite movies at the time were *Diary of a Lost Girl* starring Louise Brooks, Fritz Lang's German thriller *M*, and Marlene Dietrich in *The Blue Angel*.

Meanwhile, always taking copious notes, he began working on a novel that he intended to be a magnum opus about Berlin. The working title was *In the Winter*, and then *The Lost*, written in diary form. The *Lost* of the title referred to the mass of Germans who had lost their moral compass; about the doomed victims of Hitler; moral outcasts such as Sally Bowles, Otto Nowak, and Mr. Norris; and, writ large, the moral and economic bankruptcy of the world.

In 1931, Isherwood met Jean Ross. They became fast friends. Sometimes he allowed Ross to stay in his room on the Nollendorfstrabe whenever "she was in need, or in love, or pregnant," writes Rory MacLean.

Most everyone that Isherwood met was turned into a piece of fiction. "Through his autobiographical fiction," contends MacLean, "Isherwood's Berlin became a literary construct. He transformed ordinary people into extraordinary characters who exuded a new kind of mythical ethos for the city."

The character of Natalia Landauer, for example, was based on Stephen Spender's girlfriend, Gisa Soleweitschick, who MacLean describes as the "erudite, chaste, eighteen-year-old daughter of a Lithuanian banker." Soleweitschick and her family lived in a large apartment in the Wilmersdorf neighborhood.

According to MacLean, Soleweitschick enjoyed long walks discussing art (with a capital "a"). In his story "The Landauers," Isherwood describes her as having "dark fluffy hair; far too much of it—it made her face, with its sparkling eyes, appear too long and narrow. She reminded me of a young fox." Like the character portrayed in John Van Druten's *I Am a Camera* and the film version of *Cabaret*, her English is formal, stilted. It is the English of a student still learning the language. In the family sitting room, she shows Isherwood her collection of recordings, photographs, and books: "You like Mozart? Yes? Oh, I also! Vairy much. . . . You are fond of Heine? Say quite truthfully, please?" Although Soleweitschick and Jean Ross never met in real life, through the magic of fiction, Isherwood brought them together on the page, and later in the films *I Am a Camera* and *Cabaret* (but not on the Broadway stage).

Another character that appears in the film adaptations is based on an American named John Blomshield, who was passing through town. He is transformed into the crass Clive in *I Am a Camera*, but in Bob Fosse's *Cabaret* he re-emerges as the rich German baron-playboy Maximilian von Heune.

Isherwood also re-created the scruffy dives and transvestite clubs that he and Auden frequented. Among his favorites were the Cosy Corner at 7 Zossenerstrasse, in the working-class area of Hallesches Tor, which catered to all tastes and persuasions, "from powdered 'aunties' in pearls to blue-eyed lads with smooth thighs and very short *Lederhosen*," says MacLean. Although both homosexuality and prostitution were officially outlawed in Germany, Berlin remained, in Auden's estimation, a "bugger's daydream"—and, like late-nineteenth-century Montmarte, a great place for slumming.

Isherwood lived in various Berlin neighborhoods: in a slum tenement in Hallesches Tor, a nearby slum of Kottbusser Tor, and to the then more respectable Nollendorfplatz, near Berlin's main entertainment area, at 17 Nollendorfstrasse in the Schöneberg area, a middle-class neighborhood. This was where he rented a room in a flat belonging to Fräulein Meta Thurau, who was then in her mid-fifties. Built in 1905, her apartment was located at the top two floors of a five-story building. Double doors led to smaller rooms. Isherwood would write that she reminded him of a character out of a Beatrix Potter story: Mrs. Tiggywinkle, the female hedgehog. They hit it off; she endearingly called Isherwood "Herr Issyvoo." He, of course, immortalized her as Fräulein Schroeder, his Berlin landlady in *Goodbye to Berlin* (the name was changed to Fräulein Schneider in *I Am a Camera* and *Cabaret*). She slept on a daybed in the living room while her tenants entertained their guests in the bedrooms. Fräulein Thurau's tenants were, for the most part, unreliable and morally dubious—perfect material for a writer and familiar to anyone who has seen *Cabaret* in its many incarnations: Fräulein Kost, a prostitute; Fräulein Mayr, an unemployed Nazi sympathizer; and Bobby, a bartender and male prostitute. In a few quick paragraphs, Isherwood captures their essence on the page.

Christopher Isherwood's Berlin

> From my window, the deep solemn massive street. Cellar-shops where the lamps burn all day, under the shadow of top-heavy balconied facades, dirty plaster frontages embossed with scroll-work and heraldic devices.
>
> —*Christopher Isherwood, "A Berlin Diary (Autumn 1930)"*
> *in* Goodbye to Berlin

Christopher Isherwood lived in various locations throughout his stay in Berlin. Here is a list of them:

A room next to the former Institute for Sexual Research in the Tiergarten district;

In October 1930, he moved into an attic flat that he shared with the Wolffe family at Hallesches Tor. He had a romantic relationship with the Wolffes' son, Walter;

In November 1930, he moved to the Admiralstrasse, an apartment in the rather seedy at the time Kottbusser Tor;

In December 1930, he moved into Fräulein Thurau's boardinghouse at Nollendorfstrasse 17 in the Schöneberg district; where he lived for two and a half years, in a building with a pale yellow facade. (A plaque commemorating Isherwood's residence here is located next to the ornate front door.) This is the famous flat that he fictionalized in *The Last of Mr. Norris* (in Britain it was called *Mr Norris Changes Trains*) and *Goodbye to Berlin*. And this too is the flat where Jean Ross, the model for Sally Bowles, also lived. The street was bombed during World War II. Across the street is a speakeasy-style cocktail bar with the bluesy name Stagger Lee (Nollendorfstrasse 27), and around the corner is a 1920s-era café that includes live music and is appropriately named Sally Bowles Café & Bar (Eisenacher Strasse 2). It offers *A Cabaret Story: Berlin's Live Historical Revue*, an English-language show dedicated to performing the Berlin-style cabaret of the Weimar Republic.

Both then and now, the Schöneberg district was a center of gay life. Isherwood's flat was a short walk from several popular clubs, including the Eldorado Club, which was known for its transvestite shows. Marlene Dietrich and Friedrich Hollaender were said to frequent the place.

Other Isherwood sites include

The Cosy Corner, one of Berlin's many "boy bars" and a frequent haunt of Isherwood, is the model for the Alexander Casino in *Goodbye to Berlin*; it was located on Zossenerstrasse 7.

Another Isherwood favorite was the Kleist Casino in Kleitstrasse, a short walk from Fräulein Thurau's boardinghouse. It reportedly was in business until 2002; now it is a gay bar called the Bull Bar.

See Brendan Nash's "Isherwood's Neighborhood" tours (www.10777tours.com or Brendan@10777tours.com).

Fräulein Schneider's Boardinghouse

Fräulein Kost is described as "a blonde florid girl with large silly blue eyes." Fräulein Mayr is a music hall *jodlerin*, or yodeler ("one of the best"), who speaks in an "aggressive" Bavarian dialect. She possesses "a bull-dog jaw, enormous arms, and coarse string-coloured hair." Bobby, who has dropped his Teutonic moniker because Anglo-Saxon names were popular on the Berlin cabaret scene at the time, mixed drinks at a bar called the Troika. He is pale with "sleek black hair." He walks around the flat in shirt-sleeves, "wearing a hair-net."

Fräulein Schneider rented out the rooms to a diverse group of characters. Isherwood's fellow lodgers also included Gisa Soleweitschick. Spender introduced her to Isherwood. Born in Shanghai of Irish parentage, the gay Gerald Hamilton was the model for the character of Mr. Norris. Isherwood met Hamilton when the latter was working as the Berlin sales rep for the *Times* of London.

Another friend, Archie Campbell, introduced Isherwood to an American artist friend, John Blomshield, who became Clive in *Goodbye*.

Goodbye to Berlin

Christopher Isherwood's semiautobiographical *Goodbye to Berlin* (1939) is an episodic collection of linked stories—sketches of a society on the eve of destruction—that takes place in Weimar Berlin from late 1930, just as Hitler is assuming power, to early 1933. Isherwood describes the collection as "a roughly continuous narrative." "Sally Bowles" was published as a separate novella in 1937 but later included in *Goodbye to Berlin*. The stories consist of, in the order of their appearance:

"A Berlin Diary (Autumn 1930)"

"Sally Bowles"

"On Ruegen Island (Summer 1931)"

"The Nowaks"

"The Landauers"

"A Berlin Diary (Winter 1932–1933)"

The main characters include:

* Fräulein Schroeder, the landlady where the Isherwood character lives
* the "divinely decadent" Sally Bowles, an English singer who performs at a local cabaret
* Natalia Landauer, a young Jewish women and heiress of her family's department store
* Peter and Otto, a gay couple
  and
* "Christopher Isherwood," the author's alter ego

He had married a wealthy woman but was about to get a divorce when he met Isherwood. He had an entire suite at the plush Adlon Hotel, "where he seemed to live off champagne," quips Jonathan Fryer. Spender arranged a date with Ross and Blomshield at a local dance hall. It was a short-lived fling. They met one time only before his sudden return to the United States, an anecdote that made its way into *I Am a Camera* and *Cabaret*.

In Isherwood's fiction, Sally became pregnant by Klaus Linke, but in reality, Ross became pregnant by the very real Peter van Eyck. When Hitler came to power, van Eyck, like many other Germans, moved to Los Angeles. He later became famous for starring in the film version of John Le Carré's novel *The Spy Who Came In from the Cold*. Sally had an abortion, as did Ross.

For five months, Isherwood lived next door to the Institut für Sexualwissenschaft, housed in an imposing mansion. Founded in 1919 by Magnus Hirschfeld, it was considered a pioneering institute for the study of the burgeoning field of sexology. It contained a considerable library as well as a clinic and research center. Hirschfeld (1868–1935) was a German Jewish physician and sexologist who was among the first to advocate for gay and transgender rights. The institute even housed a Museum of Sex, an educational resource open to the public. Hirschfeld's work was serious—he campaigned to decriminalize homosexuality. His work was supported by the painter George Grosz and the Austrian playwright and novelist Stefan Zweig, among other Berlin residents of note. In addition to Isherwood, a number of other important figures rented or stayed for free in the institute's rooms, including literary critic Walter Benjamin, actress and dancer Anita Berber, and the philosopher Ernst Bloch.

Darryl Pinckney's Berlin

The African American writer Darryl Pinckney loves *Cabaret*. I know that for a fact. He told me so one rainy and chilly Chicago afternoon when he was in town to give a talk, along with the marvelous Margo Jefferson, at the city's Humanities Festival. He even confessed that he saw the film thirteen times. In his novel *Black Deutschland*, Jed is a young African American expatriate who goes to Berlin to follow in the footsteps of Christopher Isherwood. In a reference to Brian Roberts, Isherwood's alter ego in *Cabaret*, Jed says, "I got up, as discreet as Michael York as Brian in *Cabaret*, and went out onto the front terrace to smoke again." Like Isherwood, he goes to Berlin to reinvent himself.

In the novel, Jed is a young, gay, black man—newly sober—who flees his hometown of Chicago to live out his fantasies in Berlin, the capital of modernism and decadence and, as the American author Adam Haslett once described it, "the unofficial capital of the Cold War." The time is the 1980s, but Jed is inspired by the stories he has read of the black American expatriate experience but also has visions of Isherwood's Berlin running through his head. "Berlin meant boys," Isherwood famously said, and that's how Pinckney begins his tale. But he goes further. "Berlin," writes Jed, "meant white boys who wanted to atone for Germany's crimes by loving a black boy like me." Other *Cabaret*-like references are here too: Dietrich, Brecht, and Sally Bowles herself.

Jed is an outsider passing through his hometown of Chicago. Berlin, on the other hand, is the city of his "rebirth," a city that would succeed in putting him back together again. He is in love with Weimar culture. The Berlin that makes him swoon is not the bourgeois Berlin of his cousin and her husband and four children and a nanny from Stratford-upon-Avon no less but rather Isherwood's Berlin: the porn theaters, the "loud" beer bars "tucked under the S-Bahn tracks."

"I did live in Berlin," he told Eugene Holley Jr. in *Publishers Weekly*. "People in New York in the '70s were discovering Weimar and were discovering the culture, politics, and romance of that time. It was a period of great vitality in the arts, and of political disintegration."

One could easily imagine young Jed—or young Darryl Pinckney himself—patronizing Isherwood's Cosy Corner and relishing every decadent minute of it. Jed's Cosy Corner is the ChiChi, ostensibly a gay bar although "anybody and everybody could be found there." People went there to forget their troubles, or to get into new kinds of trouble. It didn't matter in the end because, notes Jed, "the real business of everyone there was to drink." Not Jed, though. In his sobriety, he drank cola and water "with gas, no ice."

And like the Cosy Corner, there was nothing particularly glamorous about ChiChi:

> The place looked like the inside of a shoebox of secrets. It was so swathed and coated and coded, no one ever knew what time it was outside. Nights passed unseen. . . . Small round red tables were placed under the windows and along the remaining wall space. You took a seat and maybe someone interesting would join you.

Pinckney closes *Black Deutschland* with another nod to Isherwood. During his last days in Berlin, Jed notes that Isherwood visited his old haunts before the police shut them down. Back in Chicago, Jed carries Isherwood's Berlin novel "around with me. I'd skip class for the day," he says, "and go from the bar on North Wells Street [in Old Town] to the bar on Woodlawn [in Hyde Park], lost in the daydream of being the rootless stranger in Berlin who seduced tough German boys."

The Party Is Over

Toward the end of his time in Berlin, Isherwood witnessed firsthand the city as it changed under the heavy shadow of incipient Nazism. As Claud Cockburn once said, "In Berlin you felt that the deluge was always just round the corner." The young men Isherwood saw frolicking at the Cosy Corner were now wearing Nazi uniforms, or as Rory MacLean notes, like the Emcee in *Cabaret*, "Berlin's pretty boys had become its doomed men." When Hitler assumed power, the boy bars were closed.

Book Jackets and Poster Art—Avati and Morrow

James Avati and Tom Morrow were artists who enjoyed distinguished careers in their own field: the former as a pre-eminent paperback book cover artist, the latter as the designer of numerous iconic theater posters.

Avati (1912–2005), an American illustrator who specialized in paperback covers, has been called the Father of Paperback Book Covers. His style is instantly recognizable: provocative, sensuous, rough. Today we would call it pulp, but that doesn't do his work justice. His efforts were a combination of gritty realism and naturalist painting with echoes of Edward Hopper; the polar opposite of Norman Rockwell. His biggest client was the New American Library, and its imprints Signet and Mentor, which published affordable paperback reprints of literary classics as well as popular fiction and nonfiction ("Good reading for the Millions" and "Rich Reading at Low Prices" were their slogans).

The Signet cover of *Goodbye to Berlin* (1952) reveals a come-hither Sally Bowles sitting on a sofa, cigarette in hand, one leg crossed over the other. She seems to be looking at someone else outside the frame. The tagline sums up the cheeky atmosphere: "Bohemian Life in a Wicked City." On May 4, 1952, Avati showed the original painting and the book cover to Julie Harris backstage at the Empire Theater, where the actress was playing the role of Sally Bowles in *I Am a Camera*.

Avati's other book covers include James T. Farrell's *Young Lonigan*, J. D. Salinger's *The Catcher in the Rye*, Willard Motley's *We Fished All Night*, Mickey Spillane's *The Big Kill*, Erskine Caldwell's *God's Little Acre*, Ralph Ellison's *Invisible Man*, Richard Wright's *Black Boy* and *Native Son*, and *Moulin Rouge*, a novelization of Henri de Toulouse-Lautrec's life.

Tom Morrow (1928–1994) designed many posters for Broadway plays and musicals from the 1950s to the 1980s. A graduate of the Parsons School of Design in Greenwich Village, he began his career as a book illustrator before moving on,

Pulp meets Weimar. Artist James Avati's sultry 1952 Signet paperback cover of Isherwood's *Goodbye to Berlin*.   *Author collection. Photo by Theresa Albini*

in the mid-1950s, to designing Broadway theater advertisements. During his long career, he designed images for posters, Playbills, sheet music, and record covers of original cast albums. Among his best work is the poster of the original 1966 Broadway production of *Cabaret* that depicts a crowded nightclub scene with the image of a blonde woman in a short red dress blowing a saxophone prominently placed in the foreground.

Morrow's other Broadway posters included *Auntie Mame* (1955), *Candide* (1956), *The Unsinkable Molly Brown* (1960), *She Loves Me* (1963), *Fiddler on the Roof* (1964), *Zorba* (1968), *George M!* (1968), and *Grind* (1985).

In 1999, Morrow's work was the subject of a one-man exhibition at the gallery of the off-Broadway York Theatre in New York.

Isherwood in America

In 1939, on the eve of World War II, Isherwood and his friend and traveling companion Auden sailed for the United States. During this visit, the novelist George Davis, who was also fiction editor of *Harper's Bazaar*, introduced Isherwood and Auden to Kurt Weill and his wife Lotte Lenya in New York.

Later that year, Isherwood, now on his own, moved to Los Angeles when the city, writes Brian Finney, was still "small, sleepy, spread out like a garden

Isherwood in LA

Christopher Isherwood lived a peripatetic life in Los Angeles, flitting from house to house, on his own and later with his longtime companion, Don Bachardy. Here is a list of some of his residences.

- 7136 Sycamore Trail in the Hollywood Hills
- 303 South Amalfi Drive in Santa Monica Canyon
- 8826 Harratt Street in West Hollywood
- 137 Entrada Drive in Santa Monica Canyon
- 333 East Rustic Road in Santa Monica Canyon
- 31152 Monterey Street in South Laguna
- 1326 Olive Drive in West Hollywood
- 364 Mesa Road in Santa Monica
- 322 East Rustic Road in Santa Monica Canyon
- 145 Adelaide Drive in Santa Monica

Isherwood and Hollywood

A sample listing of other Isherwood projects in Hollywood:

Max Reinhardt's son Gottfried, who was a producer at MGM, hired Isherwood to write the dialogue for a screenplay of James Hilton's *Rage in Heaven*;

Collaborated with Aldous Huxley on a film adaptation of *Lady Chatterley's Lover*;

Wrote an adaptation of Somerset Maugham's *Up at the Villa* for Max Reinhardt's son Wolfgang;

Contributed scenes to an adaptation of the Wilkie Collins novel *The Woman in White*;

Worked on Dylan Thomas's script of Robert Louis Stevenson's story "The Beach of Falesa" for Richard Burton;

Worked on a film treatment of *The Hour Before Dawn* by Somerset Maugham;

Worked with Lesser Samuels on a modern ghost story, *The Vacant Room*;

Wrote *The Wayfarer*, a movie about Buddha;

Proposed adaptations of Anthony Burgess's *A Clockwork Orange* and Morris West's *The Shoes of the Fisherman*;

Wrote a "Christmas Spectacular" for ABC about the origins of "Silent Night"; most of what he wrote was cut from the final film;

Wrote a stage adaptation of George Bernard Shaw's *The Adventures of the Black Girl in Her Search for God* for a Los Angeles theater company;

Wrote an adaptation of *The Mummy*, which they called *The Lady from the Land of the Dead*;

In 1975, NBC commissioned Isherwood and Don Bachardy to write an adaptation of F. Scott Fitzgerald's *The Beautiful and the Damned*. Perry King got the lead role. But NBC got cold feet; the film was never made. It was the last screenplay Isherwood wrote.

The original *Cabaret* album cover with a distinctive design by Tom Morrow.

suburb, dotted with orange groves and almost virgin hills." During his many years in the City of Angels, he cultivated a coterie of famous friends. His inner circle included Aldous Huxley and his wife Maria (Huxley would later introduce Isherwood to Vedanta philosophy); writer Anita Loos; playwright Tennessee Williams; such German and Austrian émigrés as Berthold Viertel, Thomas and Heinrich Mann, Max Reinhardt, as well as members of Hollywood royalty, Greta Garbo and Charlie Chaplin. Williams and Isherwood would frequently go out for dinner together on the Santa Monica pier. Later, in 1950, Isherwood escorted Dylan Thomas around Hollywood when the Welsh poet was on one of his American tours.

Isherwood, the college dropout, taught or lectured at various colleges and universities in the Los Angeles area for many years. He taught courses on twentieth-century British literature at Los Angeles State College. He was Regents Professor of English at Santa Barbara, a post previously held by Huxley, which consisted of spending two days a week taking seminars and delivering lectures; he was a lecturer at UCLA's University Extension program and a visiting professor at University of California at Riverside; a visiting professor in the English Department of California State College; and a visiting professor at the University of California at Santa Barbara.

Isherwood worked extensively for the Hollywood studio system, writing script after script, many of which were never produced. He also wrote dialogue and served as a script doctor and collaborated with other writers. Often his works went uncredited.

Isherwood and Bachardy were asked to write the "definitive" adaptation of Shelley's *Frankenstein* for television. The project was eventually made with Leonard Whiting (Romeo in Franco Zeffirelli's *Romeo and Juliet*) in the title role and Michael Sarrazin as the Creature. Other cast members included David McCallum, James Mason, and Jane Seymour as well as John Gielgud, Margaret Leighton, Ralph Richardson, Michael Wilding, and Agnes Moorehead in smaller roles. When Isherwood saw the final result, he was crestfallen. "Our poor Frankenstein is butchered," he wrote.

In one of the coincidences associated with *Cabaret*, in March 1964, Tony Richardson, father of Natasha Richardson, who would play Sally Bowles in Sam Mendes's acclaimed revival in 1998, asked Isherwood to collaborate with Terry Southern on an adaptation of Evelyn Waugh's *The Loved One*. When it went into production, not much remained of Isherwood's original script. But he did appear in the movie as a mourner at the funeral of the character played by John Gielgud. He also agreed to write a screen adaptation for Richardson of Carson McCullers's novel *Reflections in a Golden Eye*, but the film was never made with Isherwood's script; instead, John Huston later acquired the rights and hired another writer to adapt the novel.

Isherwood's other major works include the autobiographical *Lions and Shadows* (1938); *Prater Violet* (1945); *The World in the Evening* (1954); *Down There on a Visit* (1962); *An Approach to Vedanta* (1969); *A Single Man* (1964), which was made into a feature film starring Colin Firth in 2009; *Kathleen and Frank* (1971); and *My Guru and His Disciple* (1980).

Christopher and His Kind

In 1976, Isherwood published his memoir *Christopher and His Kind*. It was adapted into a television film by the BBC in 2010, starring Matt Smith as

Isherwood and Imogene Poots as Sally Bowles. Isherwood used real names and real events from his life in the memoir and in the subsequent movie.

The movie begins in Los Angeles, in 1976. An older Isherwood sits at his desk, typing his memoirs. The camera pans to titles on his bookshelf, including *Mr Norris Changes Trains* and *Sally Bowles.*

The next scene is a flashback to Berlin, circa 1931, as Isherwood is about to leave England for Germany. On the train he meets a ner'er-do-well, Gerald Hamilton (Toby Jones). He suggests that Isherwood take a room at a boardinghouse where he lives. Once in the city, Isherwood meets his fellow English ex-pat, and friend, Wystan Auden (who would become famous, of course, as W. H. Auden). Auden takes Isherwood to the Cosy Corner, an underground cavern and one of the many seedy gay clubs in Berlin. Isherwood described it as "plain and homely and unpretentious. Its only decorations were a few photographs of boxers and racing cyclists, pinned up above the bar. It was heated by a big old-fashioned iron stove." Because of the stifling heat, the boys stripped and sat around with their shirts "unbuttoned to the navel and their sleeves rolled up to their armpits."

At the boardinghouse, Isherwood meets his landlady, Fräulein Thurau. Also there is Jean Ross, an aspiring English actress who has been in Berlin a scant three months—just like Liza Minnelli's Sally Bowles in Fosse's *Cabaret*—and sings at an underground cabaret. Also like Minnelli's Sally, she name-drops Max Reinhardt, who promised her a role in a movie. Ross sing-talks her way through the show. She has presence and style and plenty of attitude.

Meanwhile, Isherwood begins a tempestuous affair with Caspar, one of the so-called rent boys who hang out at the Cosy Corner. Like *Cabaret*'s Brian Roberts, Isherwood makes his living by giving English lessons. One of his students is Wilfrid Landauer, the wealthy Jewish owner of the German department store. Aware of the turmoil in Germany, Landauer encourages Isherwood to take a political stance, but he politely demurs.

One day while sitting at his favorite outdoor café, Isherwood becomes instantly smitten with a street sweeper, Heinz Neddermayer. His mother takes a liking for Christopher but Heinz's brother, Gerhardt, a Nazi sympathizer (Hitler, he says, "wants to make us proud again") does not. When the mother enters a sanatorium for tuberculosis, Gerhardt tells Heinz that Christopher and Jean are not welcome in his house.

Bobby Gilbert, an American steel heir, courts Jean, promising to take her to Hollywood. But he makes a sudden departure from Berlin, not only abandoning her but also leaving her pregnant. She pawns her jewelry to pay for the abortion. "I only belong to myself," she sings. She too leaves Berlin. The situation in Germany is worsening—violence is on the upswing, and the Nazis are burning the books of Oscar Wilde and Thomas Mann. Given the escalating turmoil, Isherwood and Heinz also decide to leave Berlin.

The only one who stays behind is Fräulein Thurau. "Where else would we go?" she asks. "You get used to everything." Her world-weary comment echoes what Fräulein Schneider sings in "What Would You Do?" in *Cabaret*: whether Nazis or Communists, Fräulein Schneider will survive. "For, in the end," she asks Cliff Bradshaw, "what other choice have I?"

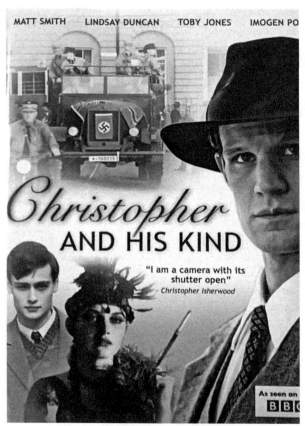

The 2011 BBC film *Christopher and His Kind*, based on Christopher Isherwood's autobiography of the same name, starred Matt Smith (who later gained fame as Dr. Who) as Isherwood. Other cast members included Toby Jones, Douglas Booth, and Imogen Poots as Jean Ross, the role model for the fictional Sally Bowles.

Author collection

Several years later, back in England, Isherwood and Ross meet each other in a chance encounter at an outdoor café. She is now working for the *Daily Worker* newspaper. She carries with her a copy of *Sally Bowles*, which she shows to Isherwood. They reminiscence about the old days. "Do you ever miss Berlin?" he asks. "No, I miss everything," she replies. Ross tells Isherwood that Heinz was arrested and sent to prison.

In 1952, Isherwood returns to Berlin for the first time since he left in the 1930s to conduct research for the *Observer* newspaper. He reunites with Heinz, now a married man with a son who lives in East Berlin. In one of the most poignant moments in the film, Isherwood returns to his old boardinghouse to see Fräulein Thurau. Her building is located in the American sector of the city. Clearly touched by his visit, she gives him a dolphin clock that was in his old room as a reminder, a souvenir of better times, before the world was engulfed in madness.

The closing titles note that in 1953, Isherwood met his long-time companion, Don Bachardy. They remained lovers until Isherwood's death.

Christopher and His Kind (2011)

Directed by Geoffrey Sax; adapted by Kevin Elyot.
Cast: Matt Smith as Christopher Isherwood; Toby Jones as Gerald Hamilton; Imogen Poots as Jean Ross; Pip Carter as W. H. Auden; Douglas Booth as Heinz Neddermeyer; Alexander Dreymon as Caspar; Tom Wlaschiha as Gerhardt Neddermeyer; Issy Van Randwyck as Fräulein Thurau; Iddo Goldberg as Wilfrid Landauer; Lindsay Duncan as Kathleen Isherwood; Perry Millward as Richard Isherwood.

Christopher Isherwood died on January 4, 1986, in Santa Monica, California.

6

"A Most Strange and Extraordinary Person"

The Real Sally Bowles

> She had a small dark head and a finely arched nose. Her plumage was
> black silk with white collar and cuffs. Her fingernails were painted
> emerald green.
>
> —*Rory MacLean describing Jean Ross*

W e all know her, or think we do. We certainly know her persona:
the devil-may-care attitude of a life lived on the edge. We definitely know her unique look (the emerald green nail polish)
and distinctive breakfast (prairie oysters). "Divine decadence," she called
it. The heart, the star, of the many incarnations of *Cabaret* is one person:
Sally Bowles.

Christopher Isherwood created one of the most famous characters in
modern literature. She first appeared in Isherwood's novella *Sally Bowles*,
which was originally published by the Hogarth Press in 1937. She then
appeared when Isherwood's stories were repackaged as *Goodbye to Berlin* in
1939. She is also the featured character in John Van Druten's 1951 stage play
I Am a Camera and in the 1955 film of the same name, as well as in the 1966
musical stage adaptation *Cabaret* and the 1972 Academy Award-winning
film musical.

In Isherwood's novel, Sally is English, the daughter of a Lancashire
mill owner who also happens to be an heiress. She sings at a bohemian
club in Berlin called the Lady Windermere. The Sally of both the novel
and the Van Druten adaptations is a middling singer but an effective one,
writes Isherwood, because of "her startling appearance and her air of not
caring a curse what people thought of her." Her goal is to be an actress.

Failing that, she would be pleased with a sugar daddy, someone to take care of her and allow her to live the life she has grown accustomed to. When both aspirations fall through, she leaves Berlin behind. The last we hear from her is when she sends a postcard to the Isherwood character from Rome.

Arrivederci. Auf wiedersehen . . .

The fictional Sally is usually English; but once, and only once, she was an American. But no matter what the nationality, the core of the character remains the same: flighty, decadent, and seductive. Sally has been portrayed by Julie Harris, Jill Haworth, Natasha Richardson, Michelle Williams, Emma Stone, Sienna Miller, among others, and, most famously of course, by Liza Minnelli. But once upon a time there really was a Sally Bowles. Her name? Jean Ross.

Before describing the real Sally Bowles, there is the question of the surname. Why did Isherwood choose Bowles? In his memoir, *Christopher and His Kind*, Isherwood acknowledges he borrowed the name from the American author Paul Bowles. Bowles would later become famous as the author of the 1949 novel *The Sheltering Sky*, which was adapted in 1990 into a movie by Bernardo Bertolucci and starred Debra Winger and John Malkovich. Isherwood had met Bowles in Berlin. The Englishman liked the sound of Bowles's name—"and the looks of its owner"—and borrowed his surname for the character of Sally.

Both Ends Burning

Born in Alexandria in 1911, Jean Ross was brought up in Egypt, the daughter of a Scottish cotton merchant. She was working as a nightclub singer in Berlin in 1931—she came to Berlin with a girlfriend to find work—when Christopher Isherwood first set his eyes on her. She was only nineteen years old, and a dropout from the Royal Academy of Dramatic Art (RADA) in London. Despite her outgoing demeanor, she was essentially shy—especially with strangers—and used her boastful tales of sexual contest as a compensatory measure.

And yet she always had a flair for the dramatic. While growing up in Egypt, she, writes Rory MacLean, "put on plays for her parents." Sometimes she was a Barbary pirate; other times, the leader of a harem. Whatever role she chose to play, she was never a victim: she was always the heroine of the tales. When she returned to England as a teen, she was just as headstrong.

Although she was clever, she was forced to repeat her studies, remaining at school for another year. In an act of nonconformity, she told a fellow classmate that she was pregnant. It wasn't true, but she was sent off to the sanatorium just the same. And when, later, the school learned she was in fact lying, she was quickly banished altogether.

Ross's flamboyant personality led to her enrollment at RADA. Unable to secure much work in London, she moved to Berlin, where she was told there was plenty of work for actresses. Work was one thing, but what really appealed to her was the volatile politics of the German capital. Unlike the apolitical Sally Bowles, Jean Ross was very political.

She arrived in Berlin with a girlfriend, just like her alter ego and Isherwood's creation, Sally Bowles. She sang badly and spoke poor German. Both the fictional Sally (in *I Am a Camera* and the musical) and the very real Jean were nineteen years old. Their personalities were similar. Both told fibs, exaggerating their stories for effect. And they both tried their hardest to shock people.

"I'm most terribly tired," Sally says to Isherwood's alter ego in *Goodbye to Berlin*. "I've got a marvellous new lover." And then asks, "Do I shock you when I talk like that, Christopher darling?"

"Not in the least," he replies to a disappointed Sally.

Ross had presence and plenty of personality and could put across a song even if she couldn't really carry a tune in the conventional sense. "Like Dietrich," writes Isherwood's biographer Peter Parker, "Ross's singing voice was fashionably low-pitched." She also performed in Max Reinhardt's production of Offenbach's *The Tales of Hoffmann*; the same Max Reinhardt that Sally herself courts in the film version of *Cabaret*.

Ross shared lodgings with Isherwood in Berlin. They maintained an apparently chaste brother-and-sister relationship and remained friends until her death in England in 1973, ironically, one year after the release of the film *Cabaret*, which catapulted her cinematic alter ego, Liza Minnelli, into superstardom.

Isherwood describes Ross as having a "long, thin handsome face" with an "aristocratic nose, glossy dark hair" and "large brown eyes." In the Berlin stories, Sally is English, the daughter of a Lancashire mill owner and an heiress. The fictional Sally is an aspiring actress who sings, badly as it turns out, at a local Berlin club just off the Tauentzienstrasse called the Lady Windermere (named after the famous character in Oscar Wilde's four-act comedy *Lady Windermere's Fan*). The atmosphere has a bit of a speakeasy flavor to it with a Teutonic edge: members of the orchestra

German postcard of the film *Cabaret*.   *Author collection. Photo by Theresa Albini*

don traditional Bavarian costumes as they drink and cavort on stage. Despite Sally's vocal inadequacies, Isherwood makes clear that she has presence even though her stage persona is far from conventional ("her hands hanging down at her sides") and an attitude ("her air of not caring a curse") that makes her strangely appealing. Take me or leave me, she seems to be saying.

Isherwood met Ross two days before he watched her perform at the Berlin nightclub. He and Stephen Spender were living in Berlin, at a friend's flat, when Ross popped in to use the telephone. She was a mere nineteen years of age at the time, a dropout, or so she said, from the Royal Academy of Dramatic Art. Despite her youth, or perhaps because of it, she feigned an air of nonchalant bohemianism to cover, some think, her essential shyness. According to Rory MacLean, she was even known to pull a diaphragm out of her handbag "with smoke-stained fingers" in order to shock complete strangers. Was it a stunt to compensate for her natural reticence? Isherwood, for one, was immune to her more outrageous behavior, dismissing her antics as those of a naughty schoolgirl even though he quickly found himself taking an immense liking to her. People swarmed to Jean Ross, much like her fictional counterpart.

By all accounts, Ross was a rebel, a free spirit, and much like her fictional alter ego she did things her own way, damn the consequences. Like Sally, she boasted about having many lovers, to the extent that Isherwood himself thought she might be exaggerating, although he seemed to have changed his mind. "Now I am not so certain," he later said. Ross at one point went so far as to refer to herself as a precursor to the countercultural hippies during the eighteen months she spent in Weimar Berlin. "Chris's story was quite, quite different from what really happened. But we were all utterly against the bourgeois standards of our parents' generation. That's what took us to Berlin. The climate was there."

Isherwood began writing "Sally Bowles" in 1933 and continued to revise it over the years before completing his first draft in June 1936. Later that year, he submitted it for publication to John Lehmann, editor of the literary magazine *New Writing*. Although Lehmann liked the piece, he thought it too long. Worse, he was concerned that the subject matter was too risqué for the times—Sally has an abortion during the course of the story—and that Ross herself might consider a lawsuit.

During her eighteen months in Weimar Berlin, Ross learned German and was fluent enough to work as a screenwriter in the British film industry with German directors who fled the horror of Nazi Germany. In 1934, she married fellow journalist Claud Cockburn; they divorced in 1940, but both were active against fascism. A lifelong Communist, Ross also wrote under the pseudonym "Peter Porcupine." She wrote about the Spanish Civil War for the *Daily Express* and the *Daily Worker*. She even wrote film criticism for the *Daily Worker*.

Then there was the issue of the abortion. "Only Jean stalled," said Isherwood. Ultimately, Ross did grant permission for Isherwood to use her story in his fictional tales. Isherwood's publisher, John Lehmann at Hogarth Press, requested Ross' approval to avoid any chance of a lawsuit. Lehmann was concerned about censorship, too; in fact, he was "nervous whether our printers—in the climate of those days—would pass it." At one point, Lehmann even suggested that Isherwood drop the whole abortion plot device altogether. Isherwood refused. "It seems to me," he wrote back in response, "that Sally, without the abortion sequence, would just be a silly little capricious bitch. Besides, what would the whole thing lead up to?" Isherwood maintained that the whole idea of "Sally Bowles"—and the stories of *Goodbye to Berlin* by extension—was "to show that even the greatest disasters leave a person like Sally Bowles essentially unchanged." *Sally Bowles* appeared in 1937 as a stand-alone novella before later appearing in Isherwood's collection *Goodbye to Berlin*.

Ross never did much like Isherwood's *Goodbye to Berlin* even though she remained friends with the author until she died. In fact, according to her daughter, Sarah Caudwell, she was "hurt" by Isherwood's portrait of her. The fictional Sally was, in her mind, too crude and too shallow for her taste. Ross, after all, was no apolitical naïf. In fact, she became a journalist who wrote from an antifascist perspective and later protested against nuclear weapons and the war in Vietnam. If she were alive today, she would probably be a guest on *Charlie Rose* or participate in the Occupy Wall Street and Black Lives Matter street protests. She most certainly would have been an avid opponent of the policies of the Trump administration. But following the Broadway success of *Cabaret*, no one wanted to hear about her journalistic exploits. Instead, she complained, all they were interested in was what it was like in Berlin in the 1930s—the spectacle of it—and how many men she slept with, not about "the unemployment or the poverty or the Nazis marching through the streets. . . ."

Clearly, she was no vamp or femme fatale. Of course, Jean Ross was not Sally Bowles, just a fictional approximation of her as imagined by an Englishman writing in Berlin as the world was coming to an end.

Jean Ross died in Richmond on Thames, Surrey, in 1973, at the age of sixty-two.

Sallys in a Nutshell

The character of Sally Bowles has been played by many different actresses over the decades:

The first Sally was Julie Harris in *I Am a Camera*. Harris appeared in the 1951 stage adaptation of *Goodbye to Berlin*. She received the 1952 Tony Award for best performance by a leading actress in a play. Isherwood described Harris's Sally as "more essentially Sally Bowles than the Sally of my book, and much more like Sally than the real girl who long ago gave me the idea for my character." When Harris left the stage production, Barbara Baxley took over. Harris reprised the role in the 1955 film adaptation of *I Am a Camera*.

Other noteworthy Sallys include the following:

Jill Haworth in the original 1966 Broadway production of *Cabaret*. Subsequent Sallys during its long run included Penny Fuller, Anita Gillette, and Melissa Hart;

Cabaret made its West End debut in 1968 with Judi Dench as Sally. Subsequent West End revivals featured Kelly Hunter in 1986, Toyah Willcox in 1987, Jane Horrocks in 1993, and Anna Maxwell Martin in 2006. Samantha Barks played the role during the 2008–2009 UK national tour;

Liza Minnelli portrayed an Americanized Sally in Bob Fosse's 1972 film adaptation of the musical;

Alyson Reed played Sally in the 1987 Broadway revival;

Natasha Richardson played Sally in Sam Mendes's critically acclaimed 1998 revival for which she won the 1998 Tony. Other Sallys during this run were Jennifer Jason Leigh, Susan Egan, Joely Fisher, Gina Gershon, Deborah Gibson, Teri Hatcher, Melina Kanakaredes, Jane Leeves, Molly Ringwald, Brooke Shields, and Lea Thompson;

Imogen Poots played the real-life Ross in the 2011 BBC television film adaptation of *Christopher and His Kind*;

The 2014 Broadway revival starred Michelle Williams as Sally and later Emma Stone and Sienna Miller. Calling Stone's Broadway debut "scin-tillating," Ben Brantley loved her "dance-till-you-drop energy" and "gin-soaked desperation." He added, "she's a Sally you're unlikely to forget." But he was even more impressed with Sienna Miller's performance, which he called "a revelation . . . the most realistic Sally since Natasha Richardson." This Sally, writes Brantley, is "a pragmatist, with a calloused core."

7

I Am a Camera

Meet Julie Harris

The story of how Christopher Isherwood's *Goodbye to Berlin* transformed itself into a play (John Van Druten's *I Am a Camera*), then a cinematic adaptation of Van Druten's play, and then, finally, the musical *Cabaret* is a convoluted tale, but the character of Sally Bowles is the starting point.

It begins with an American novelist and playwright with the unlikely name of Speed Lamkin. Like many before and since, Lamkin found the character of Sally Bowles charming. Lamkin's play *Comes a Day* had a short run on Broadway in 1958. Already a friend of Isherwood, he took it upon himself to adapt Isherwood's novella with Gus Field, a young screenwriter. (Keith Garebian surmises that Isherwood and Field met at MGM when they were both working for the studio.) The script was called, appropriately enough, *Sally Bowles*.

Isherwood's friend, the English playwright, novelist, and former actress Dodie Smith and her manager/husband Alec Beesley read the script but found it wanting. So they came up with their own plan. While visiting playwright John Van Druten at his ranch in Southern California, Beesley asked Van Druten bluntly, "Why not make a play out of Sally Bowles?" Van Druten also knew Isherwood, and by this time he had experienced a measure of success in the theater: three of his light comedies were produced on Broadway (*Voice of the Turtle* in 1943, *I Remember Mama* in 1944, and, the best known perhaps, *Bell, Book, and Candle* in 1950). Although initially reluctant, he was not one to turn down a challenge. He quickly wrote a first draft, reading it aloud to Isherwood himself and the American actor and theater producer Walter Starcke in late May 1951. The script combined elements of Isherwood's "Sally Bowles," "The Landauers," and "A Berlin Diary (Autumn 1930)." But he made several notable changes. He invented the character of Sally's insufferable mother, for example; created the Fritz-Natasha subplot;

and gave Fräulein Schneider rather pronounced anti-Semitic traits, making her a largely unsympathetic character.

Isherwood had some reservations—he disliked the treatment of the Christopher character, nor did he like the portrayal of his Berlin landlady (this was when he asked that her name be changed from Schroeder to Schneider to protect her identity). But he especially had a problem with Sally. He felt Van Druten made her appear too cute and too naughty—her edge was gone. In the introduction to the play, Van Druten admitted that adapting Isherwood's material into a play "was not easy." First, there was the "unpleasantness" of Sally Bowles. Others objected to the lack of any real plot. In his defense, Van Druten admits that he had never been "good at either inventing or writing plots, and I have done my best work always without them." In his view, plots in the theater were becoming "less and less necessary."

What interested Van Druten was the inner life of the characters and the creation of a mood. In fact, the latter was the most important quality. And given the dictates of the stage, the playwright chose to confine the location of the plot to one room and set it in a boardinghouse of an anti-Semitic landlady.

Despite Isherwood's initial reservations about its content, the play moved forward. The casting of Julie Harris made a difference. Isherwood had met Harris during the rehearsal phase. Ironically, she had a reputation of being a serious actress, far from the image of the frivolous Sally.

Harris was well known at the time but not for ingénue roles (in 1950, she had won acclaim for her portrayal of Frankie Adams in the stage adaptation of Carson McCullers's *The Member of the Wedding*). She had appeared in dramatic roles on television before originating the role of Sally Bowles on stage. It helped that Isherwood himself thought Van Druten had made the right call. "Sally is not an obvious tart," he wrote in a letter to Van Druten. "She is a little girl who has listened to what the grown-ups said about tarts, and who was trying to copy those things." Van Druten needed to find an actress who could capture Sally's selfishness and yet still make her likable. Both the playwright and the author felt that Harris was the right match.

I Am a Camera is a three-act play that takes place in a room in Fräulein Schneider's flat in Berlin in 1930 before the rise of Hitler. The play begins with a knock on the door by Fräulein Schneider. Christopher tells her he is expecting one of his pupils to stop by ("She wanted to see where I lived."). In fact, she is the only student that he has at the moment since the others have gone away "for the summer." A friend, Fritz Wendel, drops in. He has

I Am a Camera lobby card.   *Photofest*

a reputation as a gigolo. It is Fritz who tells Christopher about Sally Bowles. "Hot stuff, believe me," he says. The character of Fritz Wendel is based on a young Jewish Hungarian businessman, Franz von Ullmann, who worked for a publishing company. According to Isherwood, he was fond of "tawny lads."

When Christopher casually mentions that he is expecting a visit from Natalia Landauer "of the big department store," Fritz is intrigued and decides to stay, hoping to make a pass at her even though he doesn't know what she looks like. Landauer was partly modeled on Gisa Soleweitschick, a cultured and earnest woman who did not suffer fools gladly. One of her favorite comments when Isherwood, or anyone else for that matter, failed to respond in the way she anticipated was, "Then I'm sorry. I cannot help you," a linguistic trait that Marisa Berenson continued in the film version. Natalia's physical appearance, though, is based on a friend of Gisa by the name of Annie Joël. Her father was a director of Wertheim's, an opulent department store on the Leipzigerstrasse.

Sally makes her grand entrance. She is described as wearing black silk "with a small cape over her shoulders and a page boy's cap stuck jauntily on one side of her head. Her finger-nails are painted emerald green." She turns down Christopher's offer of coffee, saying instead she prefers prairie oysters for breakfast. "Eggs with Worcester Sauce all sort of wooshed up together. I simply live on them."

The Hangover Cure

It is among the most famous hangover cures in theatrical and cinematic history (television too), the humble prairie oyster. Sally Bowles couldn't live without it. During the marriage proposal scene in the film version of *Cabaret*, Brian Roberts (Michael York) says to Sally Bowles (Liza Minnelli), "With this spiked Prairie Oyster, I thee wed."

But Sally isn't the only person who drank it on the big screen. Gary Cooper did too in *Mr. Deeds Goes to Town* (1936) and Fredric March in the 1937 version of *A Star Is Born*. It has also made an appearance in *The Nun's Story* (1959), *Back to the Future Part III* (1990), *Addams Family Values* (1993), and *The Man Who Wasn't There* (2001).

Although its origins are unknown, it apparently was popular in late-nineteenth-century New England. It has been said to have been invented by a cowboy on the American frontier for an ill comrade who thought only some sort of an oyster would shake his fever. True or not, it does help explain the appearance of the word "prairie." Typically, a proper prairie oyster consists of a raw egg, Worcestershire sauce, tomato juice, hot sauce, vinegar, salt and pepper. The egg is broken into a glass, the ingredients mixed up, and consumed in one big gulp. In the 2017 Roosevelt University production of *Cabaret*, the actress Maddie Dorsey was a trouper (who hid what looked like a carton of eggs in her coat)—downing the drink and seeming to enjoy it. But that's what you call acting.

Ingredients

 1 raw egg
 1 teaspoon Worcestershire sauce
 salt
 pepper
 2 dashes of hot sauce of your choice

The minimalist plot consists of a series of incidents, and mostly revolves around Sally's platonic and sometimes prickly friendship with Christopher

Maddie Dorsey as Sally Bowles in Roosevelt University's production of *Cabaret*, 2017.
Photo by Nic Mains. Courtesy Roosevelt University

Isherwood. Sally plays up her promiscuous past and does her best (unsuccessfully) to shock the young Isherwood. She has a lover, by the name of Klaus, her accompanist at the Lady Windermere cabaret who has abandoned her in order to return to England. Sally announces she is pregnant, which leads to Chris and Fräulein Schneider hastily arranging for Sally to have an abortion. Another plot point revolves around their friendship with Clive Mortimer, who, despite his very English-sounding name, is a "large," "blonde," "drunkish," and wealthy American in his late thirties who promises to sweep them off their feet and see the world (Christopher prefers India, Sally, Egypt). The character of Clive is based on John Blomshield. A closeted homosexual who was married, Blomshield decided that Isherwood, Jean Ross, and Stephen Spender deserved a taste of the "high life."

Another plot point includes Fritz's infatuation with and eventual marriage to Natalia Laudauer. Van Druten also introduces a new character, Mrs. Watson-Courtneidge, Sally's unbearable mother, but for some reason he turns the Isherwood character into a raging hypochondriac.

The play does have its serious moments. Clive tells Christopher that he heard shooting in front of one of the city's big department stores. "Seemed just like Chicago." Christopher surmises that "Nazi rioting" was going on. Fräulein Schneider worries that the National Bank will shut down. "There will be thousands ruined," she frets. "Such times we live in!" But she blames the Jews for Germany's turmoil. She insists "Germany must come first." Her outburst enrages Isherwood. "I've always been fond of you," he tells her. "Now I'm ashamed of you. And everything you say is horrible and dangerous and abominable." Unwilling to back down, she angrily shoots back, "You will see, Herr Issyvoo. You will see."

Other small, but important, details in the play appear in *Cabaret*. When Sally asks Clive to get a gift for Fräulein Schneider, Christopher suggests a pineapple. "It's her idea of real luxury." In the introduction to the play, Van Druten recommends that German music be "played as though by a bad night-club band of those years" between the acts and scenes.

Toward the conclusion, Christopher encourages Sally to go back home to England with him. "I'll see that you're all right," he tells her. But Sally turns down his offer, improbably opting instead to run off with a Yugoslavian film producer and a vague promise of making a movie somewhere in South America. Sally, the bohemian figure, retains her bohemian integrity. At one point early on in the play, Sally tells Christopher that she must have a "free soul." And then admits that she really thinks she is "a strange and extraordinary person," a tagline familiar to anyone who has seen the movie version.

Sally promises to write ("Postcards and everything."). She asks that Christopher dedicate one of his books to her. "The very first one," he replies. He looks out the window. The last time he sees her she turns a corner. And then she's gone. "Don't forget those postcards, Sally," he says to himself.

A Broadway Success Story

I Am a Camera had its premiere at the Empire Theatre on Broadway on November 28, 1951, under Van Druten's own direction. It was an immediate success. It ran for 214 performances. The set and lighting were by Boris

Aronson, who would later do the set design for the original Broadway musical of *Cabaret*, and costumes by Ellen Goldsborough. The play starred William Prince as Christopher; Olga Fabian as Fräulein Schneider; Martin Brooks as Fritz Wendel; Marian Winters as Natalia Landauer; Edward Andrews as Clive Mortimer; Catherine Willard as Sally's mother, Mrs. Watson-Courtneidge; and Julie Harris in the lead role of Sally Bowles.

Isherwood himself received 2½ percent of the royalties, "plenty to live on, but not enough to prevent him from having to earn a living again once the play ended its tour in 1953," according to biographer Brian Finney. It was also a smash hit in London.

Not everyone was impressed with the episodic nature of the play, however. Several critics commented negatively on the lack of a plot and its overall purposelessness. "It never accomplishes much," wrote the *New York Times*. *Time* complained that it had "no center." But the most memorably negative review—and presumably one of the shortest—was by Walter Kerr of the *New York Herald Tribune*, who wrote a three-word dismissal (and admittedly clever pun), "Me no Leica."

Despite their misgivings about the play, most critics were quick to praise Harris, from "amazing" (*Time*) to "brilliant" (*New Yorker*) to "a virtuosity" (*New York Times*). It also won its share of awards, including the New York Drama Critics Circle Award in 1952. Harris received her first Tony Award for her portrayal.

A few years later, in 1956, Harris reprised her role as Sally Bowles in the film adaptation opposite Laurence Harvey as Christopher and directed by Henry Cornelius. Cornelius (1913–1958), a native of South Africa, had worked for Max Reinhardt in Berlin but fled Germany after the Nazi takeover to make movies in England.

Isherwood had been asked to write the screenplay for *I Am a Camera*, but had to to turn it down because of other commitments. Cornelius then asked Van Druten to have his hand at it, but he also turned him down. Instead, both men recommended John Collier (1901–1980), a screenwriter and author best known for his *New Yorker* short stories (he also wrote the screenplay for the Charlton Heston flick *The War Lord* and helped with the script of the Bogart-Hepburn classic *The African Queen*). Once again, Julie Harris reprised her role of Sally Bowles. But when Isherwood actually saw the movie, he was angered at the introduction of a romance between Christopher and Sally.

Sally on the Big Screen

The movie opens up the action of the play, moving it outside its boarding-house setting to include scenes in the cabaret where Sally is the star attraction. Fritz takes Christopher to the nightclub, the Lady Windermere, where Sally performs. Sally wears a black-sequined skirt and a matching tuxedo jacket and bow tie, an English take on Marlene Dietrich's outfit in *The Blue Angel* but quite a departure from the first time we see Liza Minnelli's American Sally in the film version of *Cabaret*—black halter top and cocky black derby with a purple strip. Harris's Sally sings "I Only Saw Him in a Café in Berlin." The café, she notes in the song, is the "kind of place" where "love affairs begin." In the song, Sally, as the observer, admits she doesn't know this fleeting figure that she just observed from a distance nor does she ever see him again. He is a cipher—someone who comes in and out of her life in an instant. He stops to pick up his hat from a chair. Moments later, he pays the waiter, and then, like a Berlin phantom, is gone. And yet, she cannot forget him, and adds an enigmatic "I never met him." But she did meet him—once—in a café in Berlin.

The melody of the song runs throughout the film. It serves as Sally's theme. The song itself is based on Marlene Dietrich's "I Have Another Suitcase in Berlin" ("Ich Hab Noch Einen Koffer in Berlin") but with new lyrics. The song, it is said, is to Berlin what Tony Bennett's "I Left My Heart in San Francisco" is to Americans, a sentimental song about the love of a particular place and all the subsequent memories attached to it. All the joy that the singer remembers is held in a small suitcase. And whenever she is homesick, she returns to her native Berlin.

Because of its iconic status in Berlin—and its associations with Dietrich—Ronald Reagan referenced "I Have Another Suitcase in Berlin" during his "Tear Down This Wall" speech.

Ahead of Its Time

The film version of *I Am a Camera* was ahead of its time in certain respects: namely, its treatment of abortion—even though Sally, in the movie (unlike the play), never actually becomes pregnant. Still, just broaching the subject as well as the "gross promiscuity" of the amoral protagonist was enough for the Production Code Administration (PCA) in the United States to deny the film a Certificate of Approval. *I Am a Camera* was also condemned by the Catholic Legion of Decency.

As with the play, the critics generally praised Harris's portrayal of Sally, but the film itself was dismissed as trivial and superficial or as the persnickety Bosley Crowther of the *New York Times* wrote, "just plain cheap." The movie version of *I Am a Camera*, he writes, "is no more than a series of snapshots of an amoral and eccentric dame." He goes on to say that Julie Harris exercises "much the same glibness and abandon" as she did on stage and makes "a brassy, brittle sensualist out of the lightheaded playgirl Sally Bowles."

Philip Hartung in *Commonweal* admired Harris's performance but complained that the rest of the cast "can hardly keep up with her" and dismissed the abortion subplot as "vulgar and embarrassing." He writes, "There is a limit to what can be done with depravity in the movies, and 'Camera' exceeds that limit."

From a modern perspective, the film does, to this writer anyway, come across as dated and shallow. The sequence where Sally and Clive try to help Chris with his hangover at a never-ending party seems especially egregious. Harris's Sally is mannered and annoying—and not especially likable. She lacks Minnelli's vulnerability. This Sally is someone who quickly overstays her welcome. What's more, the subplot that Van Druten invented between Fritz Wendel (Anton Diffring), a gigolo, and Natalia Landauer (Shelley Winters), the Jewish department store heiress, is more of a distraction than adding immeasurably to the overarching story, unlike in the film *Cabaret*. Like the original play, it is a drawing room comedy with farcical elements. The storm clouds of Nazism are downplayed to the point of omission. As in the play, Fritz conceals his Jewish identity until later when, prompted by an anti-Semitic incident, he confesses to Natalia. Fortunately, though, Sally's mother, Mrs. Watson-Courtneidge, does not appear in the film.

John Van Druten: Beyond *Cabaret*

John Van Druten (1901–1957) first brought the character of Sally Bowles to the stage, and then the screen, and created a structure, if not a conventional plot, to Christopher Isherwood's diffuse source material. He is best known, of course, as being the author of the play *I Am a Camera*, which became the basis for *Cabaret*. But in recent years his work has been revived in London, New York, and elsewhere. In 2016, the critically acclaimed Den Theatre in Chicago in a Griffin Theatre production presented Van Druten's little-known drama *London Wall* (1931). *London Wall* is

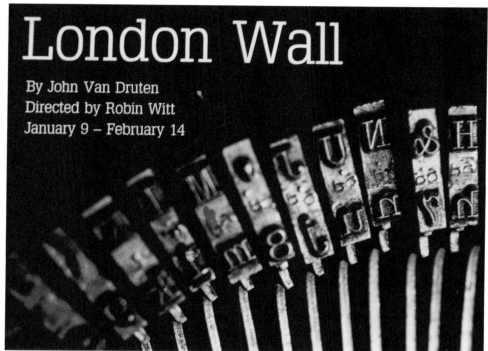

London Wall, considered one of the "lost" works of John Van Druten, is about the lives and love affairs of women employed as shorthand typists in a solicitor's office in 1930s London. Directed by Robin Witt for the Griffin Theatre Company at the Den Theatre, Chicago, 2016. *Author collection. Photo by Theresa Albini*

somewhat of a lost play by a playwright whose own work is overshadowed by the success of *Cabaret*. Set in a legal firm in London, *London Wall* is mostly about women and the community they build among themselves in a sexist and hostile environment; specifically about the typists and secretaries who do the brunt of the office work without being given much credit. More specifically, it is a portrait of the early years of women in the workplace in the days prior to the onset of World War II.

I Am a Camera

Screenplay by John Collier, adapted from the John Van Druten play. Directed by Henry Cornelius for Remus Productions. A Distribution Corporation of America presentation.

Sally Bowles: Julie Harris

Chris: Laurence Harvey
Natalia: Shelley Winters
Clive: Ron Randell
Fräulein Schneider: Lea Seidl
Fritz: Anton Diffring
Pierre: Jean Gargoet
American Editor: Stanley Maxted
Café Proprietor: Alexis Bobinskoy
Electro Therapist: Tutti Lemkow
Masseur: Henry Purvis

An Early Version of Cabaret

In the early 1960s, Christopher Isherwood first thought of collaborating on a musical based on his Berlin material, with W. H. Auden and Auden's young lover the American poet and librettist Chester Kallman. Movie director Tony Richardson, and father of Natasha Richardson, had expressed interest in directing it at the Royal Court in London. But nothing ever came of it.

Meanwhile, Isherwood learned that writer and actor Victor Chapin wanted to turn the Berlin stories into a musical. Chapin had already written the script and even found a composer and lyricist. A producer, Frank Taylor, expressed interest too. Isherwood, who read the script, was not impressed. He wrote back, pulling no punches, "I'm afraid I don't think this succeeds at all. . . . You have just taken scenes from my novel and reproduced them exactly." Nor did he think the songs had enough "sting" to them. When Taylor asked in turn whether he might be interested in working on it himself, Isherwood considered popping the question to Auden and Kallman to see if they had any interest in writing the lyrics. Auden not only immediately agreed but was also actually excited by the possibility. He wanted to bring the character of Mr. Norris into the script and even persuade Lotte Lenya to play the role of the landlady. Auden insisted that the script had to be as "brutal" as John O'Hara's *Pal Joey*, which was about a manipulative small-time nightclub entertainer.

At the same time, Isherwood learned from the screenwriter Arthur Laurents, who also happened to be a friend, that Hal Prince was also interested. As it turns out, Auden was concerned—because of the considerable geographical distance between them—that he and Kallman would be able to write the script as quickly as the producers wanted. And yet Isherwood preferred the two men. A delighted Auden suggested that all three of them meet at his summer home in Austria. He also thought that it would be beneficial for him to reread the necessary period work, including Isherwood's own writings such as his autobiographical novel *Lions and Shadows* to consider as "suitable raw materials for conversion into a musical that is definitely American yet as unsentimental . . . as Brecht." Kallman suggested that the Isherwood character should be replaced by "a new hero," a combination of Isherwood, Auden, and Stephen Spender. He should be, he continued, a writer but also "if we can dare it . . . overtly queer."

Sally Bowles would also be part of the story, but there would be no relationship between the two. The entire point of the musical, in Auden's view anyway, would be to emphasize the "indestructibility of landladies and artists." Thus, the final number, Kallman suggested, would be a duet between the writer "alone upstairs" and the landlady alone downstairs in a flat, which is now a "bombed ruin." In this version, both characters are now older and wiser but also resilient, singing the main theme of the musical, which in Auden and Kallman's version, can be summed up in one word: survival.

Isherwood traveled to New York to discuss the project with Auden and then returned to California to write an outline. As it turned out, many of Auden's more fanciful ideas were rejected, and instead the script revolved more around Sally Bowles. Most of the action took place in Fräulein Schroeder's flat and at the Lady Windermere bar. The characters of Natalia Landauer and Sally's mother were dropped; Fritz Wendel was replaced by Ernst, a bartender at the Lady Windermere. Ernst is Jewish and yearns to immigrate to America. The head barman, Bobby, and the anti-Semitic Fräulein Mayr were brought back from the Berlin stories as Fräulein Schroeder's tenants. Bobby had a more prominent role than in *Goodbye to Berlin*. Chris is a would-be novelist who persuades Sally to become a cabaret singer. He is furious, though, when she runs away with a young pianist by the name of Klaus. In this version, Chris is described as basically a control freak who is always telling people what they should be doing. "He is such a tyrant," writes Isherwood biographer Peter Parker. Parker believes this latter character trait was "clearly" one of Auden's contributions to the script.

The character of Clive remains, but he leaves after the Reichstag is burned down and Fräulein Mayr organizes a Nazi raid on the Lady Windermere. During the raid, Ernst is beaten to death by Nazi storm troopers. Klaus returns and takes Sally with him back to England with a band of musicians. Chris too comes to the conclusion that he must say "goodbye to

Berlin." As always, Fräulein Schroeder remains behind. Her building suffers considerable bomb damage during the war, but still she stays. She is a survivor. The musical ends with her sitting alone. But then, in an anticlimactic scene, Chris returns and declares that since the war is over he has decided to live in her building once again.

Despite Auden and Kallman's suggestions, Isherwood had serious doubts whether the times could cope with one of the main characters being openly homosexual. In fact, he suggested that rather than being a romantic lead he should be "a character part for a young not unattractive comedian." Isherwood also began to have doubts about Auden's suitability as a lyricist. Eventually, the project was set aside.

8

Cabaret Goes to Broadway

Happy to See You

I t is not entirely clear whose idea it was to adapt Isherwood's Berlin stories into a Broadway musical. Keith Garebian suggests lyricist Sheldon Harnick first considered the possibility when someone—we don't know who—suggested that the Berlin stories would make a wonderful musical. After reading Isherwood's book, Harnick concluded it couldn't be done.

Years later, it was Harold Prince's turn.

Prince already knew that others had considered turning Van Druten's *I Am a Camera* into a musical, but according to Garebian, the drafts that he had read were meant to be star vehicles for the likes of Gwen Verdon and Tammy Grimes. In late 1963, for example, playwright Sandy Wilson, who had written *The Boyfriend* in a 1920s musical style, had completed about two-thirds of the score, but Prince, having seen it, was not impressed with the results. Producer David Black suggested further revisions and hired Hugh Wheeler, who would later work on the film version of *Cabaret* as a research consultant and script doctor, to make the changes. Another wrinkle was the problem of obtaining rights to the Van Druten play. Prince, though, was sure he could get them. He told Wilson that he had asked Joe Masteroff, who had written the libretto for *She Loves Me*, to write the book. According to James Leve, it was Masteroff who came up with the idea of changing the nature of Sally and Christopher's relationship from friends to lovers and created an entirely new subplot of jettisoning altogether the Wendel-Landauer relationship with a sweet romance between Fräulein Schneider and an elderly Jewish fruit shop vendor, Rudy Schultz. Masteroff also softened the character of Fräulein Schneider—who was overtly anti-Semitic in Van Druten's *I Am a Camera*. In addition, Masteroff changed Christopher to an American writer, Clifford Bradshaw from Pennsylvania (the surname of the narrator in Isherwood's *The Last of Mr. Norris* but also one of the middle names of Isherwood himself). And in the biggest departure from the source material and Van Druten's play and film, Cliff is indisputably heterosexual. But his sexuality was a slow process, evolving gradually over the years. "In the original production, Cliff was totally sexless," admits Masteroff. "You couldn't have a gay leading man in those days. In the movie, he was bisexual. In the 1987 revival, as we traveled around the country, he was sort of bisexual. When we got to New York, we said, what the hell, let's make him homosexual." But Masteroff did retain Sally's out-of-wedlock pregnancy and abortion—a risky move for a Broadway musical in the mid-1960s. Finally, he invented a new character, Ernst Ludwig, a Nazi who befriends Cliff as his train arrives in Berlin.

Joe Masteroff

Born in Philadelphia in 1919, Masteroff served in the Army Air Corps during World War II. Although he is known as a playwright and as the book writer of *Cabaret*, he got his start in the industry as an actor—he made his Broadway debut in a now obscure Howard Lindsay and Russel Crouse play, *The Prescott Proposals* in 1953.

After his discharge from the army, Masteroff decided to go to New York to become a playwright, something he always wanted to do since he was a child. Coincidentally, the American Theatre Wing had just started a school for army veterans. Masteroff signed up for a course on playwriting. "They had you write at least a one-act play every week and then we would discuss it."

His career was off.

Masteroff's first play, *The Warm Peninsula*, a comedy, opened on Broadway in 1959 with a first-rate cast: Julie Harris, June Havoc, Farley Granger, and Larry Hagman. That show led, a few years later in 1963, to the writing of a book for the Sheldon Harnick-Jerry Bock musical *She Loves Me*, for which he received a Tony nomination. The director and producer was Harold Prince. (In 2016, it was revived on Broadway.) Coincidentally, *She Loves Me* is an adaptation of the 1937 Hungarian play *Parfumerie*, and the basis for the Judy Garland-Van Johnson 1949 movie *In the Good Old Summertime*, which featured the cinematic debut of Liza Minnelli (in a walk-on as the Garland and Johnson characters' daughter) and, further, the inspiration behind the popular Tom Hanks-Meg Ryan film *You've Got Mail* (1998).

Three years later, Prince hired Masteroff to write the book for *Cabaret* with lyrics by Fred Ebb and music by John Kander. They worked closely together, writing on it "bit by bit." But they knew they were heading into uncharted territory. "We knew we were doing a show with terribly dangerous things" for a Broadway musical in the 1960s, Masteroff told Mervyn Rothstein. "Musicals about abortions and Nazis were not particularly popular in those days." He knew too that success was not guaranteed. "We hoped that it would get good reviews, but we never thought it would be a commercial success because it was too different." Masteroff attributes changes to *Cabaret* partly to input from the cast, especially Alan Cumming, who played the Emcee in the 1993, 1998, and 2014 revivals. "I've told him that a lot of what he writes is better than mine."

In 1971, he again teamed up with Kander and Ebb in *70, Girls, 70*, which closed after only thirty-five performances.

Masteroff also wrote the libretto for the operatic adaptation of Eugene O'Neill's *Desire Under the Elms* and the book and lyrics for the musicals *Six Wives* and *Paramour*.

The problem, Prince thought, was the music. He didn't think Wilson's 1920s score was right for the material. Instead, Prince maintained that the music should evoke the Berlin of Kurt Weill and Lotte Lenya. Either way, Wilson was out of the picture once Prince secured the rights.

Nor did Prince have any interest in doing an old-fashioned Broadway musical. He was looking for material that could be turned into something new and innovative—something that would match the zeitgeist of the 1960s. By this time in his career, he had already worked with the legendary director George Abbott and directed and collaborated with Stephen Sondheim and Jerome Robbins.

Harold Prince

Producer and director Harold Prince (born 1928) has been a major figure on Broadway for decades. In addition to directing *Cabaret*, his other credits—a very long list—include *The Pajama Game* (1954; coproduer), *Damn Yankees* (1955; coproducer), *Fiorello!* (1959; coproducer), *A Funny Thing Happened on the Way to the Forum* (1962; producer), *She Loves Me* (1963; producer/director), *Fiddler on the Roof* (1964; producer), *Flora, the Red Menace* (1965; producer), *Zorba* (1968; producer/director), *Company* (1970; producer/director), *Follies* (1971; producer/director), *A Little Night Music* (1973; producer/director), *The Visit* (1973; director), *Candide* (1974; producer/director), *Pacific Overtures* (1976; producer/director), *Side by Side by Sondheim* (1977; producer), *Sweeney Todd* (1979; director), *Evita* (1979; director), *Merrily We Roll Along* (1981; director), *A Doll's Life* (1982;

producer/director), *The Phantom of the Opera* (1986; director), *Kiss of the Spider Woman* (1993; director), *Hollywood Arms* (2002; producer/director), and *Bounce* (2003; director).

In February 2016, Prince, along with Louis Armstrong, Placido Domingo, Yo-Yo Ma, Audra McDonald, and Leontyne Price, was selected for entry into the Performing Arts Hall of Fame at Lincoln Center. The honorees were inducted June 20, 2016, at Lincoln Center's Alice Tully Hall.

In early 2017, the eighty-eight-year-old Prince directed a new version of Leonard Bernstein's *Candide* for New York City Opera at the Rose Theater at Jazz at Lincoln Center. And in August 2017, *Prince of Broadway*, a celebration of Prince's sixty-year career, with original songs by Jason Robert Brown and directed by Prince himself, made its Broadway debut at the Samuel J. Friedman Theatre.

A visionary in his own right, Prince admired the productions of Joan Littlewood and subscribed to the aesthetics of the German theater director Erwin Piscator even if he didn't entirely agree with Bertolt Brecht's epic theatre. But he did believe in Piscator's promotion of unsentimental acting and appreciated the expressionistic theatrical techniques of German theatrical traditions.

Contemporary musical theater artists continue to appreciate Prince's visionary achievements. No less than Tommy Kail, the director of Lin-Manuel Miranda's *Hamilton*, has said that Prince is one of his heroes.

Cabaret evolved further under Prince's vision. *Cabaret* was a conceptual musical, one of the first—the songs commented on the action. Prince introduced the character of the Emcee to John Kander and Fred Ebb. The character developed over time, from a cardboard cutout to a more complicated figure that embodied the essence of Weimar Berlin. It was Prince's idea also to add the Emcee as a unifying symbol, a metaphor of the era. Kander and Ebb's score evokes the music, the sound of Kurt Weill, while Boris Aronson's paintings recall the work of George Grosz and Otto Dix, among other German artists.

Sets and Costumes

Boris Aronson's set design for *Cabaret* has been praised for its innovation. Steeped in European and American design traditions, Aronson (1898–1980) had worked with George Abbott, Max Reinhardt, George Balanchine, Lee Strasberg, Elia Kazan, Clifford Odets, Harold Clurman, and Jerome Robbins, among many others.

Roosevelt University's production of *Cabaret*, 2017. Costume drawing by Emily McConnell.　　*Photo by author*

Set design of *Cabaret* at Roosevelt University, 2017, by Michael Lasswell.　　*Photo by author*

The son of a rabbi, Aronson studied art in Kiev before moving to Moscow and then briefly living in Berlin, where he studied and painted and published several books. He immigrated to New York in 1923 and began work in the city's flourishing Yiddish theater. By 1935, he was associated with the Group Theatre, which led ultimately to Broadway. He did the set design work for Kurt Weill's *Love Life* (1948), Tennessee Williams's *The Rose Tattoo* (1951), John Van Druten's *I Am a Camera* (1951), Henrik Ibsen's *The Master Builder* (1955), William Inge's *Bus Stop* (1955), an adaptation of *The Diary of Anne Frank* (1955), *Fiddler on the Roof* (1964), *Zorba* (1968), *Follies* (1972), *A Little Night Music* (1973), and *Pacific Overtures* (1976).

For *Cabaret,* Aronson employed black velours to surround the rear and sides of the stage and an iron staircase that allowed observers (who served as surrogates of the German population) onstage. He used expressionistically lit storefronts for the street scenes. A flashing neon sign spelled out the word "Cabaret." But "the real coup," says Keith Garebian, was a nightclub with its own stage and "a large trapezoidal mirror . . . that hung center stage," reflecting the audience as they entered the theater—a major feature of the play and movie. Said Aronson, "Tilted one way, [the mirror] would reflect the audience. . . . It was a mirror of life—of a society." Indeed, the mirror has received the greatest praise of Aronson's design. Remarks Garebian, the mirror "forced members of the audience to be aware of themselves not only as voyeurs but also as participants in the cabaret, and thus it urged them to see a parallel between themselves" and the Germans "who tacitly observed Nazi horrors."

The look of *Cabaret* was created by costume designer Patricia Zipprodt (1925–1999). She had previously designed the costumes for an off-Broadway production of Jean Genet's *The Blacks*, Arthur Kopit's *Oh Dad, Poor Dad, Mamma's Hung You in the Closet and I'm Feeling So Sad*, and *Fiddler on the Roof.* As research, Zipprodt (and Aronson) watched the films of G. W. Pabst and Josef von Sternberg—especially his films with Marlene Dietrich—and studied the drawings of George Grosz. She was particularly taken with Grosz's *Lovesick* (1916), a strikingly bizarre image of a bald man in a dark suit seated at a round table in a cabaret while holding a cane and set in a nightmarish Van Gogh-like twilight. He has sickly white skin and thin bright red lips with a small tattoo over his reddish-hued ear. (Bob Fosse was also influenced by this work). The clothing of the cast used a mixture of German Expressionism and what Garebian calls "trashy glitz."

Among her other productions were *She Loves Me* (1963), *Zorba* (1968), *1776* (1969), *Pippin* (1972), *Chicago* (1975), and *Sweet Charity* (1986).

Michael Lasswell, set designer at Roosevelt University, had a particular look in mind that was different than the famous Aronson set. His influences are significant, which include Glasgow's Citizens Theatre and the theater's singular approach to design ("the sets look like the way the characters see the world," says Lasswell) as well as the craggy angles of F. W. Murnau's classic film *Nosferatu*. He tried to create the look of a subterranean, down-market club. At the chilling climax, a wall (which previously had appeared as the doors of Fräulein Schneider's boardinghouse) collapses in a loud boom to reveal a gas chamber. "We wanted the last moment to be violent," said Lasswell. According to Lasswell, the inspiration behind the "collapse" occurred the day after the 2016 American presidential election. Lasswell was targeted in a downtown Chicago parking lot by some "frat boys in a convertible" because his car displayed Clinton and Obama bumper stickers. Amid cries of "You lost!" he told me he felt "harassed and bullied." But there was more. "The realization that the bullies now felt empowered hit me like a ton of bricks. It was like being slapped in the face." As it turns out, it also came as an artistic epiphany. "We wanted the audience to be hit with the same force."

In the opening moments of Aronson's *Cabaret*, the large "Cabaret" sign is illuminated—letter by letter. Then it disappears. In Lasswell's *Cabaret*, the large Kit Kat Klub sign noticeably disintegrates as the show progresses like a musical theater equivalent of Oscar Wilde's *The Picture of Dorian Gray*.

Casting Sally and Cliff

Numerous actresses were considered for the iconic role of Sally Bowles in the original Broadway production. One of them was Sarah Miles, best known today for her performances in *Blowup* (1966), *Ryan's Daughter* (1970), *Lady Caroline Lamb* (1972), *The Sailor Who Fell from Grace with the Sea* (1976), and *Hope and Glory* (1987).

Harold Prince flew John Kander to London to see Miles. At the time she was living with the playwright Robert Bolt, whom she later married. They took him out to dinner, but what Kander really wanted was to hear her sing. Both Miles and Bolt insisted she could sing "just fine." When Kander finally heard her sing in a small church, he was horrified to learn that he couldn't hear her voice. She didn't project. She was standing at the front of the church, he at the back. Even as he got closer, he still couldn't hear her.

Miles didn't get the part, but Prince continued to insist that the role be given to an English actress.

Prince knew he wanted Joel Grey as the Emcee from the start, but finding the right Cliff Bradshaw and especially the right Sally Bowles was problematic. According to Garebian, more than two hundred actresses/singers auditioned for Sally, including Liza Minnelli. From the start, John Kander and Fred Ebb thought Minnelli would make a good choice, but Joe Masteroff and Prince were not so sure. In fact, they thought she was entirely wrong for the role because (1) she was too American and (2) she was just too talented to play a third-rate singer in a shabby Berlin club.

Still preferring an English actress, they chose instead someone with little musical theater experience. Prior to snaring the role of Sally Bowles, Jill Haworth had a small part as one of the doomed children in *Village of the Damned* (1960) and other roles before getting her one break when the famously temperamental director Otto Preminger hired her for *Exodus* (1960). She had other parts in *The Cardinal* (1963), *In Harm's Way* (1965), and *The Greatest Story Ever Told* (1965), but her career was going nowhere fast.

Until Hal Prince came along.

When Haworth auditioned for him and he asked her to sing, she flatly refused. Upon further prompting, she sang "Happy Birthday" more than a dozen times and the first line of "Someone to Watch over Me." With that he told her to return to London and take singing lessons. Still not quite catching his drift, he explained why. He wanted to cast her in the role of mediocre but ambitious Sally Bowles.

She burst into tears and thanked everyone.

Why did Prince insist on casting a musical neophyte for such a crucial role? As Keith Garebian notes, Prince was a gambler at heart. He was impressed with her loud, brassy, and untrained voice. She had just the kind of voice that the version of Sally that he had in his head would have had.

"I never understood the criticism that Jill received," Fred Ebb told Greg Lawrence. Said Prince, "When Jill . . . auditioned, she nailed it. That's what we wanted, and that's what she delivered." Joel Grey has described her as someone who liked to have a good time. "I understood why [Prince] chose her. She was so Sally Bowles." Walter Kerr's criticism in the *New York Times* was typical. "She is a damaging presence," he wrote, "worth no more to the show than her weight in mascara."

Valerie Jill Haworth was born in Sussex, England, on August 15, 1945, the daughter of a textiles magnet father and a mother who trained as a ballet dancer.

Getting the coveted role of Sally Bowles was the high point of her career. After she left the show, she appeared in several horror movies and made appearances on American television series, including *Mission: Impossible*, *Bonanza*, and *Baretta*. But she would never regain the fame that *Cabaret* brought her. She was succeeded in the role by Anita Gillette, Melissa Hart, and Tandy Cronyn.

Haworth died in Manhattan in January 2011 of natural causes at the age of sixty-five.

On the other hand, the actor who was chosen to play Cliff, Bert Convy (1933–1991), had much more experience as both an actor and a singer. Among other roles, he had performed in *The Fantasticks* off-Broadway, appeared on television commercials, did game shows, and had small parts in numerous television shows, but the role that led him to *Cabaret* was Perchik in the 1964 Broadway production of *Fiddler on the Roof.*

Lotte Lenya and Jack Gilford

John Kander and Fred Ebb had Lotte Lenya, the Austrian-born singer and actress and widow of the German composer Kurt Weill, in mind when they were composing Fräulein Schneider's songs. Lenya (1898–1981) originated the role of Jenny in Brecht-Weill's *The Threepenny Opera* in 1928; she won her first Tony for the same role in Marc Blitzstein's English-language version of *Threepenny* in 1956. She also appeared in other Weill-Brecht works, including *Happy End* and *Rise and Fall of the City of Mahagonny* as well as Max Reinhardt's *The Eternal Road*, Maxwell Anderson's *Candle in the Wind*, and the Weill-Gershwin collaboration *Fireband of Florence*. In 1933, she sang the lead in Brecht-Weill's *The Seven Deadly Sins* and sang in the revue *Brecht on Brecht*.

With her untrained, pure soprano voice, Lenya was considered "the living symbol" of Weimar Germany at the time she was cast in *Cabaret*. Her best-known films were *The Roman Spring of Mrs. Stone* (1961), for which she was nominated for an Academy Award, and as the sadistic Russian spy Rosa Klebbe in the James Bond film *From Russia with Love* (1963).

Jack Gilford (1907–1990), a vaudeville and Borscht Belt veteran, was nominated for an Academy Award for best supporting actor for his role opposite Jack Lemmon in *Save the Tiger* (1973). Born Jacob Gellman in New York, Gilford appeared in numerous Broadway productions, including *The Diary of Anne Frank* (1955), *A Funny Thing Happened on the Way to the Forum* (1963), a revival of *No, No, Nanette* (1971), and *The Sunshine Boys* (1973).

The Plot

Cabaret begins as Cliff arrives at the train station in Berlin on New Year's Eve. He has come to Berlin from England to write his second novel. On the train he meets Ernst Ludwig, who encourages him to attend the Kit Kat Klub, the "hottest spot in Berlin. Telephones on every table. Girls call you. You call them."

Cliff thanks him for his kindness but admits he doesn't have a place to stay yet. Herr Ludwig recommends "the finest residence in all of Berlin," the boardinghouse of Fräulein Schneider. Cliff laments that he can't afford the "finest." Unfazed, Ludwig maintains that the Fräulein has all kinds of rooms to fit every budget. In the next scene, Fräulein Schneider offers the room for "only" one hundred marks, a price that the money-strapped Bradshaw still cannot afford. "Fifty marks," he says, trying to bring the price down.

"But for a professor. . . ," she maintains.

An author, he corrects her. And a starving one at that. "What do you have for a starving author?"

She accepts the fifty-mark reduction. "Is fifty more than I had yesterday, ja?" she sings in response.

Within no time, he meets another resident, Fräulein Kost ("a large and happy woman who works diligently at her profession"), who lives across the hall, and Fräulein Schneider's friend and future suitor Herr Schultz, a proprietor of the "finest" fruit market on the Nollendorfplatz.

Cliff then meets Sally Bowles, a singer at the Kit Kat Klub. They flirt. He asks her questions, which she refuses to answer ("If I want to tell you anything, I will."). In the next scene, we learn she had just been fired by her former boyfriend, the owner of the club. The subject of a mutual acquaintance, Ernst Ludwig, comes up. She offhandedly mentions that he smuggles money from Paris to support "some political party." After sharing a prairie oyster, she notices a book, written in German, lying on Cliff's writing table. She looks at the cover. *Mein Kampf.* Cliff says it is not his work. "I thought I should know *something* about German politics," he innocently offers.

With nowhere to go, Sally depends on Cliff's American generosity—and naiveté—and convinces him to take her in as a roommate, insisting she would not be a distraction. Besides, she insists, she will only stay a day or two.

The developing romance between Fräulein Schneider and Herr Schultz sets up a crucial plot point. Herr Schultz brings her a gift from his fruit shop—a large pineapple. But, as it turns out, it is more the beginning of the end than the start of a long relationship.

Mein Kampf

In 2016, an annotated version of *Mein Kampf* became a best-seller in Germany, according to its German publisher, Der Spiegel. Banned in Germany for seventy years, the new version spent thirty-five weeks on the best-seller list. The two-thousand-page edition (which includes a massive thirty-five hundred critical and historical annotations) allowed scholars to explain the origins of Hitler's worldview, and to understand his totalitarian ideology's effect on the German public at a time when populist parties and ideas were gaining popularity around the world.

In the next scene, a group of well-scrubbed German waiters sing what at first seems to be an innocent, pastoral ballad about the joys of the German countryside, until the lyrics suddenly turn ominous with references to the Fatherland that the children of Germany have waited to see. With the rise of Nazism and especially in the powerful figure of Adolf Hitler, the song seems to indicate that Germany is about to turn the corner; that the days of humiliation are over and that Germany will once again be the powerhouse that it was in its so-called glory days.

Meanwhile, the relationship between Sally and Cliff has turned intimate. Sally becomes pregnant. In need of money, he accepts an offer from Ernst Ludwig to smuggle contraband from Paris to Berlin. "[I] promise you are giving help," he says, "to a very good cause." Cliff doesn't what to know any of the details—the less he knows the better. Cliff and Sally agree to marry, as do Fräulein Schneider and Herr Schultz. At the engagement party for the older couple, we clearly see that Ernst is wearing a swastika armband on his overcoat.

Cliff and Ernst get into a heated discussion over *Mein Kampf*. Cliff can't understand how anyone could be a follower of a man who is "out of his mind. It's right there on every page." Realizing that Herr Schultz is Jewish, Herr Ludwig strongly advises Fräulein Schneider to reconsider the marriage proposal. Herr Schultz is not a German, he declares. "But he was born here!" Fräulein Schneider counters. "He is not a German," he repeats. As he is about to leave the party, Fräulein Kost sings a song—"Tomorrow Belongs to Me," the same song that the German waiters sang—for Herr Ludwig. The guests join in. As their voices grow louder, the song, and its meaning, becomes clear, and frightening. Fräulein Schneider and Cliff listen with great concern while Sally and Herr Schultz laugh, unaware of the song's deadly implications.

The wedding between Fräulein Schneider and Herr Schultz is cancelled. Fräulein Schneider can no longer dismiss the Nazis. Meanwhile, Cliff refuses to make the "business" trips to Paris for Ernst and Sally considers going back to the Klub. They argue over politics. ("But what has *that* to do with us?" she asks.) Meanwhile, Fräulein Schneider returns Sally and Cliff's engagement present. Cliff insists that he and Sally must leave Berlin. ("Sally—wake up!," he tells her. "The party in Berlin is *over!*")

Cliff tries to convince Sally to leave the Kit Kat Klub behind, too. He gets into a fight with Ernst Ludwig and his Nazi henchmen. When Sally returns to the boardinghouse, she no longer has her fur coat, which she has used to pay for an abortion.

They both know it is over.

Major Characters in *Goodbye to Berlin*, *I Am a Camera*, and *Cabaret* (the Musical and the Film):

The Berlin Stories
   Sally Bowles (English) Based on Jean Ross (Anglo-Scots)
   Christopher Isherwood (English) Based on Christopher Isherwood (English)
   Fräulein Schroeder (German) Based on Fräulein Meta Thurau
   Fräulein Kost (German)
   Clive (American)
   Bobby (bartender at the Troika)
   Fritz Wendel (German) Based on Franz von Ullman
   Klaus Linke (Sally's accompanist and lover)
   Natalia Landauer (German Jew) Based on Gisa Soleweitschick
I Am a Camera (play, 1951)
   Sally Bowles (English) (Julie Harris)
   Christopher Isherwood (English) (William Prince)
   Fräulein Schneider (German) (Olga Fabian)
   Clive Mortimer (American) (Edward Andrews)
   Fritz Wendel (German Jew) (Martin Brooks)
   Mrs. Watson-Courtneidge (Sally's mother) (Catherine Willard)
   Natalia Landauer (German Jew) (Marian Winters)
I Am a Camera (film, 1955)
   Sally Bowles (Julie Harris)
   Christopher Isherwood (Laurence Harvey)
   Fräulein Schneider (Lea Seidl)
   Fritz Wendel (Anton Diffring)

Natalia Laudauer (Shelley Winters)
Clive (Ron Randell)
Cabaret (musical, 1966)
    Sally Bowles (English) (Jill Haworth)
    Clifford Bradshaw (American) (Bert Convy)
    Ernst Ludwig (Edward Winter)
    Fräulein Schneider (Lotte Lenya)
    Fräulein Kost (Peg Murray)
    Max (Kit Kat Klub owner) (John Herbert)
    Bobby (Jere Admire)
    Herr Schultz (Jack Gilford)
    Emcee (Joel Grey)
Cabaret (film, 1972)
    Sally Bowles (American) (Liza Minnelli)
    Brian Roberts (English) (Michael York)
    Ernst Ludwig (Ralf Wolter)
    Fräulein Schneider (Elisabeth Neumann-Viertel)
    Fräulein Kost (Helen Vita)
    Maximilian von Heune (Helmut Griem)
    Fritz Wendel (German Jew) (Fritz Wepper)
    Natalia Landauer (Marisa Berenson)
    Emcee (Joel Grey)
Cabaret (musical, 1998 revival)
    Sally Bowles (Natasha Richardson)
    Emcee (Alan Cumming)
    Clifford Bradshaw (John Benjamin Hickey)
    Fräulein Schneider (Mary Louise Wilson)
    Ernst Ludwig (Denis O'Hare)
    Fräulein Kost (Michele Pawk)
    Bobby (Michael O'Donnell)

Kander and Ebb

Born in New York, Fred Ebb (1928–2004) graduated from New York University in 1955 and earned a master's from Columbia University two years later. John Kander was born in Kansas City, Missouri, in 1927. He graduated from Oberlin College in 1951, and also received his master's at Columbia. Kander began his career in 1956 as a pianist for *The Amazing*

John Kander and Fred Ebb, the geniuses behind *Cabaret*.   *Photofest*

Adele and *An Evening with Beatrice Lillie*. In 1962, he cowrote *A Family Affair* with James and William Goldman, in which he made his Broadway debut as composer. That same year he met Ebb, who was writing material for various nightclub acts as well as contributing to revues. Ebb also wrote for the television show *That Was the Week That Was*.

John Kander, the mild-mannered Midwesterner, and Ebb, the witty New Yorker with an acerbic side, were about to begin the start of a productive professional relationship. Both grew up in Jewish families. Kander's family had been in Kansas City for several generations "so being a Jewish family meant practically nothing except that we knew we were Jewish," he told Greg Lawrence. He grew up in a family where art and music were an accepted part of daily life. Ebb, on the other hand, came from a family where culture was an alien commodity. "As a boy, I had very little exposure to the arts," he said.

Ebb met Kander in 1962. They wrote their first musical together, *Golden Gate*, but it was never produced. Harold Prince learned of their work, though, was suitably impressed, and hired them to write the score for *Flora, the Red Menace*, which starred a young Liza Minnelli. Although it was a commercial flop, it did earn Minnelli a Tony Award. Their second collaboration, *Cabaret*, changed everything. They teamed up with Minnelli again for the television concert *Liza with a Z*, the film *New York, New York*, and the musical *The Rink*. Additional collaborations included *The Happy Time*; *Zorba*; *70, Girls, 70*; *Chicago*; *Kiss of the Spider Woman*; and *The Visit*. The final collaboration between Kander and Ebb was *The Scottsboro Boys* in 2010, which was performed in the style of a minstrel show in which stock characters join the nine performers onstage, each playing one of the "boys." (The Scottsboro boys refers to the nine African American teenagers in Alabama who were accused of raping two white women on a train in 1931.)

Since Ebb's death, Kander, now working with Greg Pierce, composed *The Landing* (2013) and *Kid Victory* (2015), about a team of small-town Christian teens abducted by an older online friend who spend a year in captivity in a dark basement. In early 2017, *Kid Victory* opened at the Vineyard Theater in New York. Kander has also scored numerous motion pictures, including *Kramer vs. Kramer*, *Places in the Heart*, and *Billy Bathgate*.

Cabaret's Score

Before Prince commissioned Kander and Ebb to write the score of *Cabaret*, they had precious little experience on Broadway. As mentioned, they had a flop with *Flora*, but even so, Prince had liked what he had heard and thought they would be the perfect team to create the *Cabaret* score.

To create the sound of *Cabaret,* Kander initially listened to German jazz recordings from the 1920s, including the piano of Peter Kreuder (1905–1981) and the cabaret songs of Friedrich Hollaender. He was aware of the work of the great German cabaret singers, many of them women, such as Trude Hesterberg, Rosa Valetti, and Claire Waldoff, and, of course, Marlene Dietrich (although he would know her mostly through her film roles). According to Garebian, Kander refused to listen to Weill's best-known German works (such as *The Threepenny Opera* and *Rise and Fall of the City of Mahagonny*). Instead, he listened to the popular music and Berlin cabaret music of the time. Specifically, Kander tried to write songs that one might have heard in a nightclub in late 1920s, early 1930s Germany. But he especially kept in mind the tough but vulnerable voice of Lotte Lenya, the widow of Kurt Weill. "I had Lenya and the sound of her voice in my head the entire time I was composing," he told Donald Spoto. Lenya had already been cast as Fräulein Schneider when Kander began writing the music, and he wrote specifically with her in mind.

Although some critics would later criticize the music as being "watered-down Kurt Weill," Lenya, for one, thought the team had hit the mark and praised them for finding their own voice and the essence of Berlin. Otis Guernsey quotes her: "It is not Weill. It is not Kurt. When I walk out on stage and sing those songs it is *Berlin*." She later elaborated: "For me it's as if I just left the Kit Kat Klub in Berlin last night. It's so authentic, it's frightening. The way they caught the atmosphere, everything of that era—the telephones at the tables, the girls, the kick line, the monkey number. I was just like Fräulein Schneider in the play. I had a suitcase full of money. At 2 it was worth 3 million marks. At 2:30 it was worth nothing. The people in the show are too young to have lived through that, but they have caught it. Am I pleased? That is an understatement. I am very happy about it."

As far as the lyrics, Ebb used the records that Kander listened to as his chief source of information to approximate the mood of the time.

Parallel Scores

The cabaret songs comment on the book scenes. In addition, the songs set the mood for each selection. "Collectively, the cabaret songs reflect the moral decline in Germany: they start out as risqué diversions but gradually become racist political propaganda," notes James Leve.

As Leve showed, Kander and Ebb created two parallel scores, "one consisting of traditional book songs and one of novelty numbers." They initially began writing a group of songs that, they felt, captured the decadent atmosphere of the Berlin they were trying to recreate. They called them "Berlin Songs"—songs that were intended to be performed throughout the show by various characters. At one point, the Emcee was supposed to sing some of these songs in a single scene. The characters for these songs included a fat man, an operatic tenor, a streetwalker, two Chinese girls on the radio, and a group of college boys. The themes of the songs ranged from poverty to prostitution.

The Berlin Songs consisted of the following:

- "Angel of Love" (not used)
- "I Don't Care Much" (later to appear in the 1998 *Cabaret* revival)
- "I Never Loved a Man as Much as Herman" (not used)
- "If You Could See Her (The Gorilla Song)"
- "A Mark in Your Pocket" (not used)
- "Tomorrow Belongs to Me"
- "Two Ladies"
- "Willkommen"

While both men were well aware of Kurt Weill's influence, they wanted to create a sound that would evoke the Weillian-Brechtian sound and yet still stand on its own. Leve argues that only one song, "Willkommen," can really be considered Weill-like (the latter shares musical traits with "Mack the Knife"). Otherwise, what connects the songs with Weill is less the sound than their shared cynicism.

Originally, Kander and Ebb composed nearly fifty songs, but only fifteen were used. Several scholars have observed that they actually wrote a double score since the songs in the Kit Kat Klub comment on the book scenes, but more than this they reflect the moral malaise of Germany at the time. Even so, notes Garebian, songs from the cabaret score refer back to songs in the book score (the introductory music of "Don't Tell Mama" recalls the opening moments of "Willkommen," while the introduction of "Perfectly Marvelous" is an instrumental repeat of "Don't Tell Mama").

The original script called for three acts until Harold Prince and Joe Masteroff, taking the advice of George Abbott, reduced it to two acts, which led to the elimination of several songs: "Good Time Charlie" by Sally and Cliff; "Song of Love" by the Emcee; and "The End of the Party" which closed the first act. What's more, "Room Mates" was replaced by "Perfectly

Marvelous," a duet by Sally and Cliff. According to Garebian, an early draft of the three-act libretto had "I Don't Care Much" as a production number in which the Emcee was backed up by girls in men's suits. Prince cut that too, although the song, if not the girls in men's suits, was reinserted during the 1987 Broadway and subsequent revivals. (When Cumming sang it in Mendes's version, the Emcee was high on heroin.)

"Willkommen" begins with a few seconds of drumroll and clashing cymbals. Other elements enter: lyrics in several languages (German, French, and English), spoken word, an out-of-tune piano, a trumpet.

> Kander and Ebb wrote numerous songs that never made it into the final script: "Angel of Love," "Herman, My German," "A Mark in Your Pocket," "Yodelin'," "Liebchen," "Policeman," "Bücher," "Berlin, Berlin, Berlin," "A Little Geld" (also called "Good Neighbor, Cohen," which later Fosse used for the melody of the "Money Song" in the film), "Haven't They Ever," "Welcome to Berlin," and "This Is Life."

Originally, Kander and Ebb had in mind a dramatic play with songs in the prologue that described the decadent atmosphere in Berlin. Gradually, they began to change the structure so it would conform to that of a traditional Broadway musical. They replaced some songs with tunes that better reflected the plot. They also changed Isherwood's characters from the novel. The Isherwood character became an American writer who teaches English to students to get by; the formerly anti-Semitic landlady became more sympathetic and with a Jewish suitor to boot; two new characters were added: the prostitute Fräulein Kost who lives in the same boardinghouse as Bowles and the Isherwood character and the Nazi Ernst Ludwig. This new version told two stories simultaneously: the scenes at the club and the story outside the club.

There are six non-cabaret songs: a solo for Fräulein Schneider, a duet for Sally and Cliff, two duets for Fräulein Schneider and Herr Schultz, and a solo each for Sally and Cliff.

The Emcee introduces Sally as "the toast of Mayfair." Her first song, "Don't Tell Mama," is a racy, vibrant romp featuring Sally doing her best version of a 1920s flapper performing a Charleston-like dance who tries to keep her secret life hidden from her staid mother back in England, a leftover plot point perhaps from Van Druten's stuffy mother figure in *I Am a Camera*.

The next two selections, "Telephone Song" and "Two Ladies," are light-hearted novelty songs in sharp contrast to what is to come. The latter, sung gleefully by the bawdy Emcee, is a ménage à trois between the Emcee and his two lady friends, both outrageous and hilarious. Similarly lewd is "Money Song." Garebian notes that it evolved from "A Mark in Your Pocket" and "Sitting Pretty." Here the chorus girls parade the various national currencies in a vulgar display of wealth, or at least the pursuit of it (and for many the lack of it in inflationary Weimar Germany). "Why Should I Wake Up?," a solo outing for Cliff, is a lush ballad in which Cliff admits to having fallen under Sally's decadent spell.

Next, Fräulein Schneider sing-talks "So What?," which essentially functions as her philosophical statement about life, about Berlin, and about her marginal status in an increasingly precarious city and country. And to that she offers a shrug. So what! On the other hand, the Schneider/Schultz soft-shoe duet "It Couldn't Please Me More" is sentimental and romantic with some mild scatological humor about passing gas as Herr Schultz attempts to court her not with wine or chocolates or flowers but with the much more practical . . . pineapple (which always elicits guffaws from the audience).

"Married" is a lovely duet between Fräulein Schneider and Herr Schultz as Schneider considers Schultz's marriage proposal. On the other hand, "Meeskite," sung by Herr Schultz in his fruit shop, is the most Jewish-sounding song of the score. "Meeskite" is a Yiddish word that means "ugly" or "unattractive." It is also the song in which Schultz reveals his Jewishness. After learning this at the party meant to celebrate their future union, Ernst Ludwig informs Fräulein Schneider that the wedding is "not advisable."

The mood changes further with the final song before the end of the first act, the chilling (but also very beautiful) Nazi anthem "Tomorrow Belongs to Me." Sung by the cabaret waiters, it sounds (intentionally) like the type of song performed at a German beer garden. A lovely boy tenor with the purest of voices is heard before the chorus joins in. At first the images are bucolic, harmless, with references to the sun shining on a meadow under a summer sky as the stag runs free in the forest.

But then the mood darkens and the images turn nationalistic and ominous, as the lyrics turn increasingly jingoistic.

The song seemed so authentic that some audience members were certain that they had heard it as children in Germany. Either way, Ebb was criticized by some for writing a pro-Nazi anthem. The song, the Emcee, and the Kit Kat Klub reflect the real world outside as the nation teeters on the edge of fascism. The troubles that the audience was told to leave behind have now entered the cramped, claustrophobic quarters of the club.

In "If You Could See Her (The Gorilla Song)" in Act II, the Emcee performs a soft-shoe with a gorilla dressed like a woman. According to Ebb, the striking image came to him in a dream.

A comment on anti-Semitism and specifically on the now doomed romance of Fräulein Schneider and Herr Schultz, the last couplet in the song caused the cast much consternation: if we in the audience—and more importantly, the members of German society—could see her, she wouldn't look "Jewish at all."

During the Boston tryout preview, a rabbi asked Kander and Ebb if they would consider removing the offending line since it still remained a sensitive topic to thousands of Jews, many of whom would be attending the show. The controversy continued even when it opened in New York. Indeed, the pressure was so unrelenting that Ebb felt compelled to change "Jewish" to the Yiddish "meeskite." By the 1987 Broadway revival, though, it was put back in.

In the poignant "What Would You Do?"—the most Weill-like song of the score—Fräulein Schneider addresses her dilemma of marrying a Jew in Nazi Germany.

The title song, "Cabaret," is Sally's anthem to self-indulgence but also her defiant renouncing of stable family life. James Leve maintains the song actually has two functions: not only as an obvious anthem to hedonism but also, specifically during the Elsie segment, as a moment of self-reflection. When Sally sings "I think of Elsie to this very day," she drifts into what Leve calls a "limbo" space, as she struggles to regain composure. The actual stage directions of the original production clearly state:

> SALLY *has walked off the Kit Kat Klub stage. She heads directly downstage as the Kit Kat Klub disappears.* SALLY *stands alone.*

In the Mendes revival, Sally begins to break down after she recalls a friend, Elsie, that she knew back home in the London neighborhood of Chelsea. Elsie was a prostitute that she shared "four sordid rooms" with. She recalls the day she died—by consuming too much "pills and liquor." Her observation that Elsie looked like a queen reposing in her coffin is reminiscent of the classic line coined by Chicago writer Willard Motley, "live fast, die young, and leave a good-looking corpse" in his 1947 novel *Knock on Any Door.* "Goodtime Charlie" was cut during the pre-opening rewrites.

Songs Not Used in *Cabaret*

"Anywhere You Are" (Cliff and Sally)

"Come the End of November" (Cliff and Sally)

"Down, Down, Down" (Sally, Cliff, Herr Schultz)

"The End of the Party" (Sally, Cliff, Herr Schultz)

"Goodtime Charlie" (Sally, Cliff, Fräulein Schneider)

"I Wish I Never Met Her/Him" (Cliff and Sally)

"I'll Be There" (Sally and Cliff)

"It'll All Blow Over" (Cliff, Sally, and Herr Schultz)

"Mama Loves Papa" (Cliff and Sally)

"Man in the Mirror" (Cliff and Sally) (two versions)

"Maybe Down That Street" (Cliff)

"My Room-mate" (Sally and Cliff) (also known as "Room Mates")

"Never in Paris" (Cliff)

"Perfectly Marvelous" (Sally and Cliff) (different from final version)

"Practical People" (Cliff and Sally)

"Soliloquies" (Cliff and Sally)

"We Can't Stand Still" (Cliff and Sally)

Other songs were replaced altogether: "It'll All Blow Over" was deemed redundant and was replaced by "Tomorrow Belongs to Me," while "Room Mates" was replaced by "Perfectly Marvelous."

Types of Musical Theater Songs in Cabaret

In *The Musical from the Inside Out*, Stephen Citron describes the various styles of songs in the musical theater tradition. *Cabaret* follows the format, with some variations.

According to Citron, the popular song format is typically AABA, generally a thirty-two-bar chorus with each segment divided into eight-bar segments. The letters signify:

A = A strong statement

A = repetition

B = a new statement acting as contrast

A = return to the original statement

ABAC (show tune format) follows the typical show tune. Songwriters consider this format more sophisticated than the AABA form since it can offer more intense emotions as its final section can become climactic.

Another popular form is Verse Chorus. Especially popular in comedy, it conveys a story that is often interrupted with a short chorus or refrain. The verse is usually eight lines long, and the chorus is often an exact repetition—though sometimes it can have a different punch line each time—but should not be more than four lines.

Cabaret, says Citron, follows the following song forms:

- "Willkommen" = ABA
- "So What?" = Verse Chorus
- "Don't Tell Mama" = Lead in Verse; Chorus AABA
- "Telephone Song" = Verse Chorus
- "Perfectly Marvelous" = ABAC
- "Two Ladies" = Verse Chorus
- "Pineapple Song" = AABA
- "Tomorrow Belongs to Me" = 4 Line Hymn Stanza
- "Married" = AABA
- "Meeskite" = Verse Chorus
- "If You Could See Her (The Gorilla Song)" = ABAC
- "What Would You Do?" = Verse Chorus
- "Cabaret" = AABA; Interlude and Extension

How Does That Song Go Again?

"Cabaret," the song, almost never appeared in *Cabaret*. It turns out when Kander and Ebb first played it for Hal Prince, he wasn't too thrilled with it. Prince figured he already had a title song with "Willkommen" and didn't want another one. But when choreographer Ron Field heard it, he thought it wonderful. He met with Prince and vouched for the song. Kander and Ebb played it for Prince again, and he agreed. "Cabaret" would be the title song.

The Eleven O'Clock Number in *Cabaret*

In traditional music theater, the first act rarely ended before 10:00 p.m. With the intermission, second act curtain usually rose at 10:25 p.m., which meant that the climax of the second act usually occurred near 11:00 p.m. Today many critics consider it an old-fashioned device. Now if the number occurs at all, it more than likely occurs around 10:15 p.m., but still the phrase remains. The eleven o'clock number must do two things, says Citron. It must serve as the climax of the play while stating the concept or theme of the play. And it must be a showstopper. The "Cabaret" musical motif can be heard at various times throughout the play, so by the time Sally Bowles sings the title song, the audience has become familiar with it. The song states Sally's philosophy on life. To Citron, it is "the ultimate eleven o'clock number."

Joel Grey

He was the hottest thing in town. At least that was what Joel Grey was told. And so, he had to see him.

Grey was trying to make it in the unpredictable world of show business. It should have been easy for him. Well, easier. After all, his father, Mickey Katz, was a popular entertainer in his own right.

It was the early 1950s. Grey was on his night off during his nightclub tour in St. Louis. He wanted to see the competition; that's who this unnamed entertainer that he had come to see this night represented. But when he came to the stage, Grey couldn't believe his eyes: This guy was his competition? Clearly, he had seen better days. What's more, he told stale joke after stale joke. And yet he was killing it. The audience loved him. He did anything for a laugh, and it worked. The crowd ate it up.

This crowd-pleaser, Grey writes in his memoir, "was the epitome of everything that I had been trying to escape" ever since he was a green teenager in his hometown of Cleveland, Ohio, in his father's variety show, known as the "Borscht Capades."

But what Grey saw that night stayed with him. Years later, this has-been entertainer became the foundation for his portrayal of the Emcee in *Cabaret*.

Never Good Enough

Grey's father, Meir Myron Katz, better known as Mickey Katz, was a minor celebrity in his hometown of Cleveland. He was a clarinet and alto saxophone player in the city's biggest music halls and nightclubs. A dapper man and spiffy dresser, he wore a small pencil mustache and parted his hair to the side.

Joel Katz was named after his mother's favorite movie star, Joel McCrea. The moment he stepped inside the Cleveland Play House as a nine-year-old—his first time he had been to the theater—he knew instinctively where he belonged. He began acting in children's plays, and slowly earned a reputation. When his father was hired to play with the American band leader Spike Jones, who was known for his satirical arrangements of popular songs, the Katz family had moved west to Los Angeles, where they were "seduced" by the California sun and the glamour of the one-industry town.

Soon Mickey Katz became known for his parodies: Yiddish-inflected versions of standard American songs, from the "Barber of Schlemiel" to "She'll Be Coming 'Round the Katzkills." Despite his success, the Katz family was keenly aware of the anti-Semitism reverberating under the surface. "We were here but not entirely welcome," notes Grey.

And yet one thing led to another. As a teenager Grey (still going by his birth name, Katz) played famous clubs like the Mocambo in Hollywood and the El Rancho in Las Vegas. He worked in summer stock, regional theater, and off Broadway. When his father went on the road with the Borscht Capades, young Joel traveled with him throughout North America, from Boston and Chicago to Toronto and Montreal: anywhere there was a sizable Jewish population. In Miami Beach, they played the thousand-seat Roosevelt Theatre to sell-out crowds. The younger Katz was already making a name for himself. In the audience that night was Eddie Cantor, who came specifically to see Joel. This led to Joel's appearance on *The Colgate Comedy Hour* on national television, which led in turn to being signed to the prestigious William Morris Agency.

Other engagements followed. Joel auditioned at the famous Copacabana nightclub. He got a gig: at midnight. The only problem was he had no idea what he was doing. Despite his showbiz experience, he felt he was over his head here. He donned a tuxedo, as the fishnet-stocking Copa Girls went by him. "How old are you, anyway?" one of them asked the youthful Joel. Onstage, the audience paid little attention to him, and yet his agent told him later that night that they loved him.

By the time he earned a four-week engagement at the Chez Parée in Chicago, a favorite hangout for gangsters, he had become Joel Grey.

Grey's fledgling Hollywood career began with a cameo in *About Face*, a musical-comedy remake of *Brother Rat*. Small parts in numerous television shows followed, including the "plum part" of Jack in NBC's 1956 telecast of a musical version of *Jack and the Beanstalk* as well as roles in such popular television westerns as *Bronco, Lawman,* and *Maverick,* where he played the part of Billy the Kid, which he called "creative casting." He got small parts in movies too, such as *Come September* starring Rock Hudson and Gina Lollobrigida.

These roles helped pay the bills, but what he really wanted was to be in the theater, the legitimate theater.

His career changed with one telephone call. In the winter of 1961, he was asked to come to New York to audition for the replacement for one of the leads in Neil Simon's *Come Blow Your Horn.* (In an example of six degrees of separation, Grey's understudy at the time was the young Ron Rifkin, who would later play Herr Schultz in the 1998 Broadway revival of *Cabaret.*)

Soon after he got another important role, that of the circus clown Littlechap in the 1963 national touring production of *Stop the World—I Want to Get Off,* the role later made famous by Anthony Newley. Littlechap was a tragic figure, and Grey identified with him completely. At the end of the show, he sits alone at the edge of the stage and sings the play's showstopper, "What Kind of Fool Am I?," which became a hit for Newley.

The success of *Stop the World* led Grey to believe that his career was now on the upturn. There would be no more struggles, no more worrying about the next gig. But, as he recalls in his memoir, just the opposite happened. Nothing. "I didn't receive *any* offers at all." He began to wonder if he was in the right industry, if he would ever get his lucky break. By this time, he had a wife and small children to take care of. His future seemed uncertain, his career on shaky ground.

But then fate intervened. He received a phone call from Hal Prince. When the *Stop the World* production stopped in Westport, Connecticut, Prince happened to be in the audience and liked what he saw.

Prince told Grey that he was working on a new musical with a score by Kander and Ebb. Joe Masteroff, who received a Tony nomination for the musical comedy *She Loves Me,* wrote the book. Ron Field had already been hired as choreographer.

Before the show opened in Boston, Prince invited his friend Jerome Robbins to watch the run-through. Although Robbins thought the show "wonderful," he suggested to Prince that any musical numbers that did not take place at the Kit Kat Klub be cut. But Prince thought otherwise.

"And there's a role we think you'd be swell for!" he told Grey, leaving him to ponder what he had in mind.

"We're calling it *Cabaret.*"

A few days later, Grey showed up at John Kander's Upper West Side townhouse to hear the score. Ebb and Prince were there along with others who were to be part of the show. Prince offered a few words of welcome, and then Kander began to play the piano as Ebb sang the now familiar lyrics, "Willkommen! Bienvenue, welcome! Fremder, etranger, stranger. . . ."

Cabaret was the first time Grey didn't have to audition for a role. But when he read the script, he was disappointed. His character had no name. He was simply known as the Emcee. Worse, he didn't make an appearance until Scene 3 in Act 2, and he had no interaction with the other characters Sally Bowles, Clifford Bradshaw, Fräulein Schneider, or Herr Schultz, other than the Kit Kat Klub dancers and band members. "No words, no lines. . . . My heart sank. I was nothing more than a song-and-dance man—a German song-and-dance man."

Despite his misgivings about the script, Grey knew it was an opportunity he couldn't turn down. But the feelings of uncertainty continued, especially when he learned that the dancers and the actors were to rehearse separately and in separate locations, "as if there were two shows." Once again he felt that he didn't belong. But what really bothered him, what unnerved him, was that he had no idea what he was doing. He hadn't yet found the essence of the character. He wore too much makeup, yet was larger than life. To Grey, he was just a metaphor—the epitome of the corruption of the Weimar Republic—but how do you build and develop a character from a mere metaphor? That was his challenge, and his frustration.

The musical numbers commented on the book scenes. It took him a while to understand that. But a few weeks before the show's tryout in Boston, Grey had a moment of revelation in the unlikely reappearance of the vulgar St. Louis comedian he had met many years before, that same entertainer mentioned earlier. He came to realize that the comedian and the Emcee were one and the same person. "It had taken me so long to 'find' the Emcee because all my life he was who I never wanted to be," he admitted. Having achieved a proper breakthrough, he very quickly came up with a backstory: where the character lived in Berlin, what his flat looked like, how he behaved backstage (in a word, reprehensible). Was he Jewish? It was a question he never quite came to terms with.

He also knew how the Emcee should look. He soon learned that using women's makeup—base, rouge, lipstick, and eyelashes—wouldn't work ("My character was androgynous, not trying to pass as a woman."). He wanted to make him iconic but also an individual: or, as he puts it, as a flesh and blood second-rate talent in a tacky Berlin cabaret. He was nothing less than a "low vaudevillian," someone Grey was very familiar with.

Sitting in front of his wife's vanity mirror, Grey experimented with different kinds of makeup. First, he used a pink "stick," matted down with Johnson's baby powder. He drew thick, dark, and slightly arched eyebrows

Joel Grey as the Emcee in the national touring production of *Cabaret*, 1987, at the Chicago Theatre.

Photofest

and "dark orange underbrows" with blue eye shadow on his lids. Next, he applied a pair of his wife's old and thick-with-mascara eyelashes. The finishing touches were an application of raspberry rouge to his cheeks and an "old German" shading stick. He then parted his hair in the center, flattening it with a dash of Dippity-do.

Rehearsals for *Cabaret* were held in a "big, cold" dance studio ten blocks away from the George Abbott Theatre, where Prince also held the main rehearsals with the actors.

Grey realized it would take effort, reflection, and self-knowledge to create the inner life of what would become an iconic character. It would mean embracing "everything that was in poor taste." It would mean becoming someone he did not want to be: the cheap tricks, the vulgar jokes, the dark underside of show business. But who in their right mind would want to pay money to watch a creep? he wondered.

Ruth Gordon met with Fosse about appearing as the Emcee in the film version of *Cabaret*.

They came. Grey won a Tony and an Academy Award for his portrayal of the figure he called a "creep." But life did not end after *Cabaret*. Since his star turn as the Emcee, he has starred as George M. Cohan in the musical *George M!* opposite Bernadette Peters. He replaced Brad Davis in Larry Kramer's *The Normal Heart*. And he played the role of the cuckolded husband, Amos Hart, in the revival of *Chicago*, a role that he had initially turned down. (In the original Fosse production, the role had been played by a physically more robust actor—Grey didn't think he was physically right for the role until he reconsidered and accepted the juicy part.)

He toured with Liza Minnelli in a nightclub act, although he had reservations about doing it since he "loathed" working in nightclubs. But Minnelli convinced him otherwise. Their first show together was at the Riviera in Las Vegas, where he sang a medley from *George M!* He opened the show, Minnelli did her act, and then they did several encores together.

Other movie roles came: the thriller *Man on a Swing* (1974); Robert Altman's revisionist western *Buffalo Bill and the Indians* (1976), where he played Nate Salisbury, Buffalo Bill's press agent; the Sherlock Holmes movie *The Seven Percent Solution* (1976); and Lars von Trier's *Dancer in the Dark* (2001). Back on Broadway, he originated the role of the Wizard in *Wicked* (2003) and appeared in the 2011 revival of Cole Porter's *Anything Goes*.

In December 1998, Grey performed "Wilkommen" with Alan Cumming in a tribute at the Kennedy Center honoring Kander and Ebb. In December 2016, he received the 25th annual Oscar Hammerstein Award for lifetime achievement in musical theater.

Opening Night

Cabaret was scheduled to open, in previews, at the Shubert Theater in Boston on October 10, 1966, when it was still consisted of three acts, but Prince thought it was too long and that the main characters were still undeveloped. George Abbott suggested he reduce the action to two acts. Prince agreed.

The Boston reviews were mostly positive. Critics praised the set design and the performances, especially Lotte Lenya's. The sticking point for some, though, was Sally herself, and Haworth's portrayal of her. But not all agreed. Others found Haworth to be a worthy Sally.

Another potential problem involved audience expectations, especially given the somber content of the material. Masteroff in particular was worried that the lighthearted title might bring people in who were expecting more *Moulin Rouge* and not the harsh glare of life as depicted in Nazi Germany. Masteroff was sure it would be a flop with audiences even as he took some consolation in its possible critical appeal.

After twenty-one previews, the original Broadway production opened on November 20, 1966, at the Broadhurst Theatre. It then transferred to the Imperial Theatre and finally the Broadway Theatre before completing its 1,165-performance run.

The Original Broadway Cast and Crew (1966)

Cabaret was first presented on November 20, 1966, by Harold Prince in association with Ruth Mitchell at the Broadhurst Theatre in New York, with the following cast (in order of appearance):

Master of Ceremonies (Emcee): Joel Grey
Clifford Bradshaw: Bert Convy
Ernst Ludwig: Edward Winter
Customs Officer: Howard Kahl
Fräulein Schneider: Lotte Lenya
Fräulein Kost: Peg Murray
Herr Schultz: Jack Gilford

Girl: Tresha Kelly
Sally Bowles: Jill Haworth
Girl Orchestra: Maryann Burns, Janice Mink, Nancy Powers, Viola Smith
Two Ladies: Mary Ehara, Rita O'Connor
Maitre D': Frank Bouley
Max: John Herbert
Bartender: Ray Baron
German Sailors: Bruce Becker, Steven Boockvor, Roger Briant, Edward
    Nolfi
Frau Wendel: Mara Landi
Herr Wendel: Eugene Morgan
Frau Kruger: Miriam Lehmann-Haupt
Herr Erdmann: Sol Frieder
Kit Kat Girls:
    Maria: Pat Gosling
    Lulu: Lynn Winn
    Rosie: Bonnie Walker
    Fritzie: Marianne Selbert
    Texas: Kathie Dalton
    Frenchie: Barbara Alston
Bobby: Jere Admire
Victor: Bert Michaels
Greta: Jayme Mylroie
Felix: Robert Sharp

Replacements later in the run were as follows:

Anita Gillette and Melissa Hart as Sally Bowles
Ken Kercheval and Larry Kert as Cliff Bradshaw
Martin Ross as the Emcee

Directed by Harold Prince. Dances and cabaret numbers by Ronald
Field. Scenery by Boris Aronson. Costumes by Patricia Zipprodt. Lighting
by Jean Rosenthal. Musical direction by Harold Hastings. Orchestrations
by Don Walker. Dance arrangements by David Baker

Cabaret: Original Broadway Cast Recording (1996)

Side 1
- "Willkommen" (5:10): Joel Grey and Company
- "So What?" (3:21): Lotte Lenya
- "Don't Tell Mama." (4:00): Jill Haworth, Joel Grey, and Girls

- "Telephone Song" (2:30): Bert Convy and Company
- "Perfectly Marvelous" (3:27): Bert Convy and Jill Haworth
- "Two Ladies" (2:22): Joel Grey, Rita O'Connor, and Mary Ehara
- "It Couldn't Please Me More (A Pineapple)" (3:17): Lotte Lenya and Jack Gilford
- "Tomorrow Belongs to Me" (2:12): Robert Sharp, Joel Grey, and Waiters

Side 2
- "Entr'acte" (2:22): Kit Kat Band
- "Why Should I Wake Up?" (2:28): Bert Convy
- "Money Song" (1:50): Joel Grey and Cabaret Girls
- "Married" (2:40): Lotte Lenya and Jack Gilford
- "Meeskite" (3:43): Jack Gilford
- "If You Could See Her (The Gorilla Song)" (2:51): Joel Grey
- "What Would You Do?" (3:24): Lotte Lenya
- "Cabaret" (4:27): Jill Haworth
- "Finale" (3:37): Bert Convy, Jill Haworth, Lotte Lenya, Jack Gilford, Joel Grey, and Company

Cabaret: Original Broadway Cast Recording (Reissue, 1998)

Act I

- "Willkommen" (5:10): Joel Grey and Company
- "So What?" (3:21): Lotte Lenya
- "Don't Tell Mama" (4:01): Joel Grey, Jill Haworth, and Girls
- "Telephone Song" (2:30): Company
- "Perfectly Marvelous" (3:28): Jill Haworth and Bert Convy
- "Two Ladies" (2:24): Joel Grey, Mary Ehara, and Rita O'Connor
- "It Couldn't Please Me More (A Pineapple)" (3:17): Lotte Lenya and Jack Gilford
- "Tomorrow Belongs to Me" (2:12): Robert Sharp, Joel Grey, and Waiters
- "Why Should I Wake Up?" (2:28): Bert Convy
- "Money Song (Sitting Pretty)" (1:51): Joel Grey and Girls
- "Married" (2:40): Lotte Lenya and Jack Gilford
- "Meeskite" (3:45): Jack Gilford

Act II
- "Entr'acte" (3:45): Kit Kat Band
- "If You Could See Her (The Gorilla Song)" (2:52): Joel Grey
- "What Would You Do?" (3:24): Lotte Lenya

- "Cabaret" (4:29): Jill Haworth
- "Finale" (3:43): Company
- Bonus Tracks
- "Berlin Songs Intro" (0:28): John Kander and Fred Ebb
- "I Don't Care Much" (1:32): John Kander and Fred Ebb
- "Room Mates Intro" (0:09): John Kander and Fred Ebb
- "Room Mates" (5:55): John Kander and Fred Ebb
- "Good Time Charlie Intro" (0:20): John Kander and Fred Ebb
- "Good Time Charlie" (3:19): John Kander and Fred Ebb
- "It'll All Blow Over Intro" (0:32): John Kander and Fred Ebb
- "It'll All Blow Over" (4:04): John Kander and Fred Ebb

Songs Deleted from the Original Production

"I Don't Care Much" was deleted from the original production only to be restored in the 1987 production as well as the subsequent 1998, 2012, and 2014 revivals.

"Room Mates" was replaced by "Perfectly Marvelous"

'It'll All Blow Over" was originally planned for the end of Act I; Sally tells Cliff and Fräulein Schneider that everything will be all right.

Other Deviations from the Original Production

"Mein Herr" was written for the film but replaced "Telephone Song" in the 1998, 2012, and 2014 revivals.

"Maybe This Time," which first appeared in the movie version, was actually written for Kander and Ebb's unproduced musical *Golden Gate*. It first appeared in the 1998 revival and in the 2012 and 2014 revivals.

In the 1987 revival, a new song, "Don't Go," was written for Cliff, and replaced "Why Should I Wake Up?" Prince reinstated "I Don't Care Much" in this revival. But in Mendes's 1998 revival, the Emcee sings the song while on heroin.

9

Cabaret

What the Critics Said

T he critical response to the original Broadway production of *Cabaret* was mostly positive with one notable exception. Even those critics that admired the show felt that the weakest link was the casting of Jill Haworth as Sally Bowles.

In the November 21, 1966, *New York Times*, for example, Walter Kerr called *Cabaret* "stunning" but with "one wild wrong note." But first he discusses what is right with the show. He compares "Wilkommen" approvingly to the songs in the Dietrich movie *The Blue Angel*. He calls Joel Grey "cheerful" and "charming" but also "soulless" and "wicked." Lotte Lenya, he proclaims, "has never been better."

And then comes the "wrong note." The mistake, in his estimation, is Haworth. She is more of a "profile" than a full-fledged human being and "worth no more to the show than her weight in mascara." He considers the casting a lapse in judgment on Harold Prince's part.

Meanwhile, Richard Gilman in the December 5, 1966, issue of *Newsweek* finds *Cabaret* both serious and fun as well as salty in a "grown-up way."

He acknowledges the four-piece female band, which plays "gay-somber Kurt Weillish tunes," and praises the choreography by Ronald Field and David Baker as "good as anything in recent years."

And then the wrong note surfaces again. Jack Gilford is "fine"; Grey, "splendid," but Haworth is a "wide-eyed sawdust doll."

On the other hand, he concludes that the Nazi anthem "Tomorrow Belongs to Me" in a moment of "beauty and anguish" is musical theater "at its highest."

The outlier here is Harold Clurman. In the December 12, 1966, issue of *The Nation*, Clurman complains that *Cabaret* is "stunning in its ugliness." He acknowledges the decadent period that *Cabaret* portrays on stage and mentions by name some of the most notable figures associated with the era, including Erwin Piscator, Ernst Toller, Bertolt Brecht, George Grosz, Hanns Eisler, Kurt Weill, Ernst Lubitsch, Emil Jannings, and Marlene Dietrich.

He compares the tone of *Cabaret* with *Sweet Charity*, and finds it lacking. *Sweet Charity*, he maintains, had "real style of Broadway jingle-jangle," whereas *Cabaret* is not even a parody. "In *Cabaret* very little is successful beyond the box office."

Even the Kander and Ebb score comes under attack. With the exception of "Willkommen," which he refers to as "Welcome," he finds the lyrics flat. The only time that he considers the score worthwhile is when it echoes "old German tunes." The choreography too he calls "ineffective" except for its occasional "grotesquerie" and with the assistance of Joel Grey (referred to as "Joe" Grey in the review).

As far as the fabled Lotte Lenya is concerned, Clurman wishes she had more opportunity to display "her own tart contemptuousness." He also dismisses Jack Gilford as Herr Schultz, while Bert Convy as Cliff Bradshaw sings "acceptably." Nor does Jill Haworth escape his wrath. He admires her brassiness but finds her best feature is not her voice but her beautiful back: "credit where credit is due." Ouch.

But he does greatly admire the set design by Boris Aronson and the lighting of Jean Rosenthal.

10

Tours and Revivals

Beyond the Great White Way

Broadway National Tour (1968)

After its successful Broadway run, *Cabaret* enjoyed equally successful productions on the road. The Broadway Company national tour of 1968 featured

Melissa Hart as Sally Bowles
Signe Hasso as Fräulein Schneider
Leo Fuchs as Herr Schultz

The tour included stops at the Los Angeles Civic Light Opera, the Ahmanson Theatre, also in Los Angeles; the Curran Theatre in San Francisco; with additional stops in Atlanta and Dallas.

Original London Production (1968)

For the London production, Hal Prince considered several leading actresses of stage and screen for the role of Sally Bowles, including Vanessa Redgrave (Redgrave, of course, is the mother of Natasha Richardson, who would play Sally most memorably in Sam Mendes's 1998 revival). But, much like the casting of Jill Haworth, he made an unconventional choice: Judi Dench.

Dench had made her first professional stage appearance with the Old Vic Company at the Royal Court Theatre in Liverpool as Ophelia in *Hamlet*, and remained a member of the esteemed company for four seasons. In late 1961, she joined the Royal Shakespeare Company. A few years later she made her film debut in the British drama *The Third Secret*. She was widely acclaimed as a terrific actress, but she was no one's idea of a singer. Thus, when her agent first told her that Prince wanted to offer her the role of Sally Bowles, she blurted out, "You have to be joking."

But Prince was deadly serious. He recommended that she read the original source material to see if she could see herself as Sally, who was after all just a middle-class girl from England. But Dench had doubts not about her acting ability but about her vocal skills. When Prince suggested that she act as if she was someone who knew she would never achieve great artistic heights but sought the limelight anyway, she was able to reach a creative breakthrough.

Dench, as was her wont, worked hard throughout the rehearsal phase. She watched her diet and took singing lessons. But when she opened on February 28, 1968, all the preparation and hard work wasn't enough. To say that the critics were not enthralled is an understatement. They found fault with the modest set design and with some of the cast, especially Kevin Colson's Cliff but also Dench herself. Some complained she was physically miscast. And some found the libretto weak.

The show ran for nine months.

The original West End production opened on February 28, 1968, at the Palace Theatre with the following cast:

Sally Bowles: Judi Dench
Cliff Bradshaw: Kevin Colson
The Emcee: Barry Dennen
Fräulein Schneider: Lila Kedrova
Herr Schultz: Peter Sallis

The production ran for 336 performances. It closed on January 1, 1970.

London Revival (1986)

The 1986 revival in London was presented at the Strand Theatre. The cast included Kelly Hunter as Sally Bowles, Peter Land as Cliff Bradshaw, and Wayne Sleep as the Emcee. It was directed and choreographed by Gillian Lynne. It opened on July 17, 1986, and closed on June 4, 1987.

Broadway Revival (1987)

The first Broadway revival of *Cabaret* opened on October 22, 1987, at the Imperial Theatre, before transferring to the Minskoff Theatre. For the first time in the play's history, Joel Grey received top billing. It had a 261-performance run. It was directed and choreographed by Harold Prince and Ron Field.

Prince had agreed to direct the revival but with one caveat—and it was a big one. He asked the original book writer Joe Masteroff to rewrite the book in order to reinterpret the major characters. Among the changes was the dropping of the song "Meeskite," the song that Jack Gilford sang in the original 1966 production. Prince thought that Gilford's portrayal of Herr Schultz was more Jewish than German—the point being that German Jews, he maintained, had already assimilated into Germany society, which was what made the Holocaust so surprising, and, of course, shocking. With this change in mind, the German actor Werner Klemperer was cast as the new Herr Schultz.

Cliff Bradshaw was also given more complex shades of character. Times had changed. And in 1980s America, homosexuality no longer had to be swept aside. It had, culturally speaking, come out of the metaphorical closet. He was now bisexual. Sally would be his last chance at a heterosexual relationship. Given this change, his song, the passive "Why Should I Wake Up?," was replaced by the more aggressive "Don't Go." Also different was the role of the Emcee. He would become a more menacing figure, less Borscht Belt vaudeville and more Weimar-era ruffian. Sally too was tougher: no longer the amoral naïf stranded in a strange land.

If the original Broadway production was intended to serve as a mirror to countercultural America, this late 1980s version was Prince's attempt to convince people that all was not well in Reagan's America. This *Cabaret* was a warning: to not become complacent, to not look away from the despair on the streets. Prince asked Americans not to do what Good Germans did: to not look the other way.

The revival received mixed reviews: it was not quite a reinvention but rather something in between. And yet the revival ran until June 1988 before resuming its national tour.

This time around, though, it was intended as a star vehicle for Joel Grey, which some critics found to be problematic, and unfair. "To have a 'Cabaret' reliant on its emcee is almost like reviving 'Oklahoma!' as a star vehicle for the actor playing Jud," wrote the *New York Times*' Frank Rich. "While Mr. Grey does his job as expertly as ever, he needs help during the long stretches when he's not at center stage."

Nor did Rich appreciate David Chapman's sets, which were based on Boris Aronson's original design. Rich described them as "tacky, stripped-down cannibalizations of the influential originals. . . . Even the original costume designer, Patricia Zipprodt, is at less than her brilliant best: How could chorus girls wear transparent plastic aprons in 1929?" Worse, Rich and other critics found Masteroff's script "tame" in light of some of the "franker Prince musicals ('Evita,' 'Sweeney Todd') that came later."

Rich was especially withering in his estimation of Gregg Edelman's Cliff: "Mr. Edelman's writer . . . is so mild that one is constantly taken aback to discover he is the toast of two sexes in at least that many nations. With his corduroy suit and hayseed accent, he seems less likely to write a novel than a homeowner's insurance policy."

Alan Cumming performing in his cabaret show, *Alan Cumming Sings Sappy Songs*, at the Oriental Theatre, Chicago.
                                                                    Photo by Theresa Albini

Broadway 1987 Revival

Directed by Harold Prince. Book by Joe Masteroff, based on the John Van Druten play and stories by Christopher Isherwood; music by John Kander; lyrics by Fred Ebb; directed by Harold Prince; dances and cabaret numbers by Ron Field; scenic design, David Chapman, based on original set designs by Boris Aronson; costume design, Patricia Zipprodt; lighting design, Marc B. Weiss; sound design, Otts Munderloh; assistant director, Ruth Mitchell; additional orchestrations, Michael Gibson; orchestrator, Don Walker; musical supervisor, Don Pippin; musical director, Donald Chan; production stage manager, Scott Faris.

   Presented by Barry and Fran Weissler. At the Imperial Theatre, 249 West 45th Street.

The Emcee: Joel Grey

Sally Bowles: Alyson Reed

Clifford Bradshaw: Gregg Edelman

Fräulein Schneider: Regina Resnik

Herr Schultz: Werner Klemperer

Ernst Ludwig: David Staller

Fräulein Kost: Nora Mae Lynn

   With Stan Chandler, Laurie Crochet, Bill Derifield, Mark Dovey, Noreen Evans, Karen Fraction, Laurie Franks, Ruth Gottschall, Caitlin Larsen, Sharon Lawrence, Mary Munger, Panchali Null, Steve Potfora, Lars Rosager, Mary Rotella, Gregory Schanuel, Michelan Sisti, Jon Vandertholen, David Vosburgh, Jim Wolfe.

London Revival (1993)

The *Cabaret* reinvention of the late twentieth century began not in New York, not on Broadway, but rather at the Donmar Warehouse in London's West End in 1993. And the director, the instigator, was an Englishman, Sam Mendes. He returned to the numerous sources: the original Broadway musical and the Fosse movie—and before them, the original source material, Christopher Isherwood's *Berlin Stories* and John Van Druten's 1952 play, *I Am a Camera.*

   Mendes was considered the wunderkind of British theater. He had his own very specific ideas on how to stage *Cabaret*. *Cabaret*, Mendes told Matt Wolf, belonged on the same pedestal as "*The Crucible* or *The Homecoming* or any other play of the twentieth century that deserves to be reinvented and rediscovered generation to generation." What would set this revival apart was turning the interior of the Donmar into the Kit Kat Klub itself. But more than just transforming a theater space into a Weimar-era cabaret was involved. Mendes had to rediscover the spark that caused the original *Cabaret* to ignite. What made it fresh to begin with and how to transfer that into something new for a different generation?

The paintings of George Grosz and Otto Dix were pinned to the rehearsal room walls as a reminder of what the denizens of a Weimar-era cabaret might look like. Mendes also encouraged the Kit Kat Klub chorus members to write their characters' own backstories; that is, to internalize Ebb's lyrics—to make them an organic part of their characterizations—before actually singing the words.

Stephen Spender, a contemporary of Isherwood as well as his friend and colleague, met with the staff and helped them understand the ambiance of the era and, in particular, about life in the Berlin bars and cafés of the period.

Mendes also came up with unique ideas to open up the production: to make it more Brechtian, to remove the fourth wall between audience and performers. It was at the Donmar, for example, at the end of the Entr'acte that the Emcee picks a random person from the audience as a dance partner. It has since become a signature part of any musical production of *Cabaret*.

Starting Over Again

This 1993 revival was a bit of a misnomer. It was more of a full-throttle reinvention, a complete rethinking of the material. The secret to the revival was the mode of presentation. Mendes turned the Donmar into the Kit Kat Klub to give the audience a you-are-there feel. When the audience walked into the theater, they were seated at tables and served food and drinks by a wait staff that bore bruises and tattoos and then walked onto the stage, dragging their instruments and doubling as the Kit Kat Klub's orchestra. In another intentional and well-thought-out detail, Mendes did not distribute playbills until after the show ended in an effort not to break the precious mood. Mendes's *Cabaret* was actually performed in an actual cabaret, albeit a late twentieth-century version as envisioned by an English director in London.

Changes that Mendes made:

- the Emcee became edgy, slightly dangerous, and hypersexual

- the satiric "Sitting Pretty" was combined with "Money"
- instead of "Tomorrow Belongs to Me" performed by a male choir, the Emcee played a recording by a boy soprano
- In the final scene, the Emcee removes his outer clothing to reveal a striped uniform typically worn by concentration camp victims. Two badges are pinned to it: a yellow badge, identifying him as being Jewish, and a pink triangle, indicating he is a homosexual.

The Mendes production also made it clear that Cliff was bisexual and even included a brief scene showing him kissing one of the Kit Kat boys. "I Don't Care Much," which was removed from the original production, was reinserted; and the rousing "Mein Herr" was added from the movie version.

The revival productions dropped scenes, added scenes, and conflated scenes; songs were dropped, songs were added; dialogue was inserted from the movie. In Act I, Scene 3, Fräulein Schneider emphasizes to Chris the view from his window, and its central location, in an effort to persuade him to take the room in her boardinghouse.

> And look—your window! You can see the whole of the Nollen-dorfplatz! And there—that little house—the U-bahn station. What you call the Metro. Ja? In ten minutes, you are anywhere in Berlin!

A few pages along in this scene, Herr Schultz, proprietor of the "finest fruit market on the Nollendorplatz" refers to Italian oranges. It was Seville oranges in the original production. A few lines down, when Herr Schultz wishes Cliff "mazel" in the New Year, a befuddled Cliff asks, "Mazel?" In the 1966 production, Herr Schultz explains it's "Jewish" for good luck. In the Mendes production, "Jewish" was changed to the more specific, and accurate, "Yiddish."

In Act I, Scene 5 (previously Act I, Scene 4), Sally, who longs to hear English spoken, asks Cliff to say anything in English. In the original production, he recites a few lines from Matthew Arnold's quintessential 1867 English poem "Dover Beach" ("The sea is calm tonight."), but Mendes replaces it with the very American baseball poem "Casey at the Bat" (1888) by Ernest Thayer ("Somewhere in this favored land the sun is shining bright."). In the same scene, Cliff bumps into Bobby at the Kit Kat Klub, who reminds him that they met at the Nightingale Bar in London.

In Act I, Scene 6, Ernst Ludwig complains about the grammatical inconsistencies of English, much like the character of Fritz Wendel does in the movie:

Ernst: You know what is the trouble with English? It is not an exact language. Either one must memorize fifty thousand words either one cannot speak it correctly.

Cliff: Either one must memorize—or one cannot speak. . . .

Ernst: Aha! Either-or.

In Act I, Scene 10 (Scene 9 in the original production), Cliff receives a check from his mother. To Cliff, it is enough to pay the rent. To Sally, it possibly means dinner (and a bottle of champagne) at the upscale Adlon restaurant, a historic Berlin venue, which is also mentioned in Van Druten's *I Am a Camera*. Cliff admits how much he loves being in "tawdry" Berlin ("tacky" in the original script). Also in this scene Sally tells Cliff she is pregnant—and actually uses that word, something that skittish 1960s Broadway would not allow.

Another big change was the portrayal of the Emcee. Alan Cumming was as singular as Joel Grey's original, only younger, more sexual, definitely more dangerous. He wore a white tuxedo but no shirt, a black bowtie, black trousers, and spats under his black jacket. Once he removed the jacket, he revealed bruises on his arms—the Emcee–this Emcee–was a drug addict. Whether rubbing against Cliff on the train or grabbing his crotch when dancing the soft-shoe with the gorilla in "If You Could See Her," the androgynous Emcee was part cheeky boy, part satanic overseer. Cumming as the Emcee did more too. He introduced a scene, he served as a dramatic chorus, he even was given his own torch song, "I Don't Care Much," which he sang while wearing a sequined dress. While playing a gramophone recording of "Tomorrow Belongs to Me," he squatted down, then abruptly stopped the song to say the title lines, foreshadowing the dark days to come.

The cast of the 1993 London West End revival featured

Jane Horrocks as Sally Bowles
Adam Godley as Cliff Bradshaw
Alan Cumming as the Emcee
Sara Kestelman as Fräulein Schneider

Cumming received an Olivier Award nomination for his performance; Kestelman won the Olivier for best supporting performance in a musical.

Broadway Revival (1998)

The second Broadway revival of *Cabaret* was based on Sam Mendes's 1993 production in London. For the Broadway rendition, though, director/choreograph Rob Marshall was brought along as codirector and choreographer.

The production opened after thirty-seven previews on March 19, 1998, at the Kit Kat Klub, which was housed in the former Henry Miller's Theatre (now the Stephen Sondheim Theatre). Later that year, it was moved to Studio 54, where it remained for the rest of its long run.

Like the arrangement at the Donmar in London, the theater in New York was turned into a cabaret. Rows of orchestra seats were removed to make room for small round black tables with red Tiffany lamps and straight-backed chairs. Henry Miller's Theatre was even renamed the Kit Kat Klub for the run. The rear of the theater had banquettes. Patrons who sat at the tables could order drinks from a wait staff dressed like the band members onstage. The Emcee also invited patrons to be part of the festivities, just like the London production. At the beginning of Act II, the Emcee would choose someone from the audience to dance with him onstage. Audience participation was definitely part of the show.

The Kit Kat dancers, just as bruised and battered as the Emcee, would saunter onstage before the show began and did stretching exercises, the splits, and somersaults—encouraging interaction with the audience.

The stage consisted of two black doors, black metal staircases, and a tilted picture frame that suggested Boris Aronson's original mirror. Overlooking the stage sat the Kit Kat band, male and female musicians dressed like punk rockers out for a night on the town: black caps, sleeveless t-shirts, black boots.

Alan Cumming's Emcee looked a bit different from his Donmar days. He still wore a long black leather jacket and black boots, but his eyes now had blue eye shadow and some red touches. His nipples were rouged. Needle marks ran up one forearm. There was a tattoo on his upper left arm. He wore a bowtie that was attached to some kind of harness that wrapped around his crotch. It looked painful, like an S&M exercise gone wrong.

He was a voyeur, a sexual exhibitionist, a charming host, an outcast, and a cynic all rolled into one. Similar to the London production, the Emcee served many roles. He was omniscient. But his behavior was unpredictable. At one point he posed as a uniformed German guard. Another time he danced in drag in the club. And, most brazenly, he mooned the audience, a swastika on his bare buttocks at the end of the first act. By the show's finale, though, the mood had darkened even more. The doors of the club were shut, lending the theater a claustrophobic feel. The ending was just as shocking as it was inevitable. The walls of the club appear whitewashed as the sound of a single gunshot rings out and the lights black out. Smoke fills the stage. The characters appear as if prisoners in a concentration camp. As if there was any doubt, the Emcee reveals that he too dons the uniform of a concentration camp decorated with the yellow star of Judaism and the pink triangle indicating homosexuality. Two strikes against him.

And then there was Sally Bowles herself—here embodied by Natasha Richardson. This Sally was a far cry from Jill Haworth's Sally. She still enjoyed her prairie oysters, but she drank harder, smoked, and snorted cocaine. This Sally was broken and bruised, knocked about by life and her own inadequacies and flaws. When, after singing the last words of "Cabaret," she knocked over the microphone stand and stumbled off the stage, the city and the world that she knew were also about to come to an end. Richardson reinvented the role for a new generation of theatergoers.

Richardson plays an older, if not necessarily wiser, Sally Bowles. But she is defiant and stubborn, especially when she sings the title song. And then there is the Emcee. As Richard Zoglin noted in *Time*, Alan Cumming, with his blue and red eye shadow and "sequined nipples and suspenders wrapped around his crotch," looks more like Alex from Stanley Kubrick's film adaptation of *A Clockwork Orange* while "filtered through Madonna's Sex book." Even the usually bland Cliff Bradshaw character (John Benjamin Hickey) had been sexed up. No longer coy or unambiguous, here he is overtly bisexual.

By the time director Sam Mendes, then a thirty-two-year-old wunderkind, took the Cabaret revival to Broadway he already was the artistic director of the Donmar Warehouse in London. Past productions included everything from Chekhov to Shakespeare to Sondheim, and Mendes had spent five years with the Royal Shakespeare Company.

Mendes spent more than two years looking for the proper space in New York that was comparable to the Donmar in London. He found the venue on the former site of Xenon, a once popular disco. An admirer of movie musicals, he turned to *Cabaret* after he read the original Broadway script and realized how much different it was from Fosse's movie—and how much had been changed, and left out, including the subplot between the landlady and her Jewish suitor, which he reinserted. "[Herr] Schultz is a beautiful character. He very much loves this woman. But he's one of those Germans who didn't really believe he would ever not be a German, one of those Jews who just didn't see it happening," said Ron Rifkin, who played the role in the 1998 Broadway revival.

Mendes made further revisions in the book with original writer Joe Masteroff. What's more, he intentionally cast actors with little or no musical experience. "I didn't want a produced sound," he told Zoglin. "The singing voices come out of their speaking voices."

The Reviews

The reviews were ecstatic. The critics loved it.

In the April 26, 1998, *New York Times*, Michiko Kakutani found the Broadway revival so "inventive, so galvanic" that it was as if theatergoers were experiencing "something entirely new." She goes on: "It is a production . . . that conclusively demonstrates that Broadway musicals can be treated like Shakespeare and other classic texts, that in the hands of a gifted direc- tor they can be repeatedly reimagined and made to yield new truths."

Also in the *New York Times*, Vincent Canby praised Natasha Richardson for a "radiant performance that lights up the year" as well as the overall "wonderful and inventive score." Fellow *Times* theater critic Ben Brantley also commented on the rawness of Richardson's performance. Richardson as Bowles not only looks raw but also "brutalized and helplessly exposed." Referring to the title cut, he notes that "now she's going to sing us a song, an anthem to hedonism" but she "might as well be inviting you to hell."

Meanwhile, Nancy Franklin in the *New Yorker* found everything about the production "raw and immediate, including the audience's proximity to the actors." The intimate nightclub setting allowed audiences to be brought into the experience, making the theatergoers feel that they were more than mere spectators, more than just members of a passing parade. And it is a parade, she writes, that you can't look away from. "[T]he figures onstage are garish, ghoulish, and aggressively arresting, beginning with Alan Cumming."

The 1998 Cabaret Revival in a Nutshell

- At Kit Kat Klub: March 19, 1998 to November 8, 1998
- At Studio 54: November 12, 1998 to January 4, 2004
- First Preview: February 13, 1998
- Total Previews: 37
- Opening Date: March 19, 1998

- Closing Date: January 4, 2004
- Total Performances: 2,377 performances

Cabaret began previews in February 1998 at Henry Miller's Theatre on West 43rd Street (later renamed the Kit Kat Klub) and opened on March 19, 1998. It moved to the Studio 54 space on West 54th Street in November 1998.

Cabaret won four Tony Awards in 1998, for best musical revival, best actor (Alan Cumming) and best actress (Natasha Richardson) in a musical, and best featured actor in a musical (Ron Rifkin). It also won three Drama Desk Awards and three Outer Critics Circle Awards.

Other details:

- Alan Cumming made his Broadway debut with *Cabaret*. The choreography of Rob Marshall tried to reflect the lines and angles of a George Grosz or Otto Dix painting.
- Nineteen casting sessions were conducted before Marshall and Mendes chose the final six Kit Kat Klub girls. Many dancers were too good. In addition to singing, dancing, and acting, they had to be able to play an instrument as well.
- Sally Bowles's signature corset was constructed of whalebone and had three different kinds of lace; underneath their corsets, bras, panties, and garter belts, the women wore two pairs of underwear; their bras had microphones sewn into the seams.
- Cumming's equally singular harness was constructed by pinning together four pairs of suspenders.

Broadway Revival 1998 Cast and Crew

Roundabout Theatre Company at Henry Miller's Theatre

Todd Haimes, Artistic Director; Ellen Richard, Managing Director; and Julia C. Levy, Executive Director, External Affairs

Emcee: Alan Cumming
Sally Bowles: Natasha Richardson
Clifford Bradshaw: John Benjamin Hickey
Ernst Ludwig: Denis O'Hare
Customs Official: Fred Rose
Fräulein Schneider: Mary Louise Wilson
Fräulein Kost: Michele Pawk
Rudy: Bill Szobody
Herr Schultz: Ron Rifkin

Max: Fred Rose
Gorilla: Joyce Chittick
Boy Soprano (recording): Alex Bowen
The Kit Kat Girls
    Rosie: Christina Pawl
    Lulu: Erin Hill
 Frenchie: Leenya Rideout
    Texas: Michele Pawk
Helga: Kristin Olness
The Kit Kat Boys
    Bobby: Michael O'Donnell
    Victor: Brian Duguay
    Hans: Bill Szobody
    Herman: Fred Rose
Swings: Linda Romoff, Vance Avery

Sound Design by Brian Ronan. Orchestration by Michael Gibson. Dance and Incidental Music Arranged by David Krane. Original Dance Music Arranged by David Baker. Musical Coordinator John Monaco. Production Stage Manager Peter Hanson. Dialect Coach Tim Monich. Associate Choreographer Cynthia Onrubia. Make-Up and Hair Design by Randy Houston Mercer. Casting Jim Carnahan and Pat McCorkle, C.S.A.

Associate Director Jennifer Uphoff Gray. General Manager Sydney Davolos. Founding Director Gene Feist. Press Representative Boneau/Bryan-Brown. Director of Marketing David B. Steffen. Musical Director Patrick Vaccariello. Codirected and Choreographed by Rob Marshall. Directed by Sam Mendes.

Other cast members included Joyce Chittick, Leenya Rideout, Erin Hill, Christina Pawl, Kristen Olness, Michael O'Donnell, Bill Szobody, and Fred Rose. The Broadway revival was nominated for ten Tony Awards, winning three actor awards for Richardson, Cumming, and Rifkin and the Tony for Best Revival of a Musical.

Notable replacements included:

As Sally Bowles: Jennifer Jason Leigh, Susan Egan, Joely Fisher, Gina Gershon, Deborah Gibson, Teri Hatcher, Melina Kanakaredes, Jane Leeves, Molly Ringwald, Brooke Shields, Lea Thompson, Mary McCormack, Kate Shindle
As the Emcee: Michael C. Hall, Raúl Esparza, Neil Patrick Harris, Adam Pascal, Jon Secada, Norbert Leo Butz, John Stamos
As Cliff Bradshaw: Boyd Gaines, Michael Hayden

As Herr Schultz: Tom Bosley, Dick Latessa, Hal Linden, Laurence Luckinbill, Tony Roberts

As Fräulein Schneider: Blair Brown, Polly Bergen, Mariette Hartley, Carole Shelley

Songs from the 1998 Broadway Revival

Act I

- "Willkommen": Emcee and the Kit Kat Band
- "So What?": Fräulein Schneider
- "Don't Tell Mama": Sally Bowles and the Kit Kat Girls
- "Mein Herr": Sally Bowles and the Kit Kat Girls
- "Perfectly Marvelous": Sally Bowles and Cliff Bradshaw
- "Two Ladies": Emcee, Lulu, and Bobby
- "It Couldn't Please Me More": Fräulein Schneider and Herr Schultz
- "Maybe This Time": Sally Bowles
- "Money": Emcee and the Kit Kat Girls
- "Married": Herr Schultz, Fräulein Schneider, Fritzie
- "Tomorrow Belongs to Me" (Reprise): Fräulein Kost, Ernst Ludwig, and the Company

Act II

"Entr'Acte": The Kit Kat Band

"Kick Line": The Kit Kat Band

"Married" (Reprise): Herr Schultz

"If You Could See Her (The Gorilla Song)": Emcee and Gorilla

"What Would You Do?": Fräulein Schneider

"I Don't Care Much": Emcee

"Cabaret": Sally Bowles

"Finale": The Company

Alan Cumming

For many fans of *Cabaret*, he is the only Emcee they know. Others only recognize him from his seven seasons on *The Good Wife*, for which he received many Golden Globe, Emmy, and SAG nominations. But Alan Cumming is one of the more eclectic performers working today. He has appeared on Broadway, in movies, on television. He has performed his "sappy songs" at

Carnegie Hall and at New York's premier cabarets, the Café Carlyle and Feinstein's. He has written a memoir, performed in concert, done voice-over commercials (including for "Scotland, a Spirit of Its Own"), hosted award shows.

Cumming was born in the town of Aberfeldy in Perthshire, Scotland, but after brief stays in the Highland towns of Dunkeld and just outside Fort William, he mostly grew up on a country estate near Carnoustie, on the east coast of Scotland, as the son of the head forester of Panmure Estate. As he makes clear in his searing memoir *Not My Father's Son*, it was a brutal existence ("feudal and a bit *Downton Abbey*, minus the abbey and fifty years later" is how he describes it). His father abused him both physically and verbally. At one point, his father even denied that Cumming was his own son. Cumming and his brother, Tom, took a DNA test to uncover the truth. Ultimately, he learned that he was indeed his father's son, but by then his self-identity had gone through several transformations.

"One of the ways I survived was just being able to switch away from something, and I think that's how acting should be," he told the *New York*

Cabaret 1998 Revival Intermission Incidents

Alan Cumming as the Emcee chooses a pair of audience members on stage to dance with him. But sometimes things didn't go as planned.

Famous people who have been lucky, or unlucky, enough have included Mikhail Baryshnikov ("I always go for the butchest men," Cumming joked) and Walter Cronkite, by accident. Cumming reportedly didn't recognize him even at the time, though he knew who he was.

In 2014, actor Shia LaBeouf was arrested for drunken behavior. During the first act, he stood up from his seat and began yelling at the actors onstage. During intermission, he was handcuffed and escorted outside. He was charged with two counts of disorderly conduct and one count of criminal trespassing.

Cumming told comedian Conan O'Brien, "As I walked past him, he was at the table in the end of the row and he . . . whacked me. He did say the reason he did it is I was the sexiest man he had ever seen."

Times. And then added, "I choose to be in the light, but I have access to the darkness."

He trained at the Royal Scottish Academy of Music and Drama in Glasgow and has has a long track record in British television. He made his British television debut in the popular and long-running Scottish show *Take the High Road* (a very enjoyable little soap opera) and the highly regarded Glasgow crime show *Taggart.* Other British shows include the BBC comedy *Bernard and the Genie,* with Rowan Atkinson; and the BBC sitcom *The High Life,* cowritten by Cumming and his costar Forbes Masson. In 2011, he starred as a transvestite named Desrae on the Sky series *The Runaway.*

He made his film debut in Gillies MacKinnon's *Passing Glory* in 1986, when he was still in school, and his feature film debut in Ian Seller's *Prague,* which premiered at the Cannes Film Festival in 1992. But he first came to public attention with his creepy turn as Sean Walsh in the Irish film *Circle of Friends* (1995) starring Minnie Driver and a very young Chris O'Donnell. Other major film roles include the James Bond film *GoldenEye* (1995), *Romy and Michele's High School Reunion* (1997), Stanley Kubrick's *Eyes Wide Shut* (1999), Julie Taymor's *Titus* (1999), *Emma* (1996), *Get Carter* (2000), the *Spy*

Alan Cumming's cabaret show in 2016 at the Oriental Theatre in Chicago.

Theresa Albini

Kids Trilogy, and *X2: X-Men United* (2002). With Jennifer Jason Leigh, he wrote, produced, directed, and acted in *The Anniversary Party* (2001).

Cumming remains a supporter of indie films. One of his more obscure, but significant, roles was in the 2006 indie film *Sweet Land*, which he also produced and which was based on Will Weaver's story of the same name. *Sweet Land* won a Spirit Award for best first feature. More recently, in 2012, he appeared in Travis Fine's *Any Day Now*, in which he played a 1970s drag queen. In 2016, he made *Battle of the Sexes*, costarring Emma Stone and Steve Carell, as well as starring in *After Louie*.

Cumming has popped up on any number of television programs. Before capturing the plum role of Eli Gold on CBS's *The Good Wife* (he of the dancing eyebrows), he has made numerous appearances on many shows: the HBO comedy *Sex and the City*, a cameo role in the popular sitcom Frasier (he played Niles' yoga instructor), a guest spot on *3rd Rock from the Sun*. On season 3 of Showtime's *The L Word* he played the role of Bill Blaikie, a gay drag queen promoter and nightclub manager. In 2007, he appeared in the *Wizard of Oz*-inspired *Tin Man* and guest-starred in Lisa Kudrow's improvised web series *Web Therapy*. In addition, he hosted the Oxygen cable television show *Eavesdropping with Alan Cumming* and *Midnight Snack*. He's also been the voice of a Smurf and is the host of PBS's *Masterpiece Mystery*.

Cumming has also made several documentaries, including *My Brilliant Britain*, a journey throughout Scotland exploring Scottish humor, and *The Real Cabaret* (2009), for which he traveled to Berlin to follow in the footsteps of Christopher Isherwood. He appeared on the BBC's genealogical program *Who Do You Think You Are?*, where he discovered that his maternal grandfather, Tommy Darling, was a war hero during World War II who died in Malaysia while playing a game of Russian roulette.

Cumming began his theater career in his native Scotland. He performed with the Royal Lyceum in Edinburgh, Dundee Rep, the Tron in Glasgow, and toured with Borderline, Theatre Workshop, and Glasgow Citizens' TAG. During his final year at drama school in Glasgow, he made his professional theater debut as Malcolm in the Tron Theatre's production of *Macbeth*. He played the role of Slupianek in Edinburgh's Traverse Theatre's 1988 production of *Conquest of the South Pole*, which later transferred to the Royal Court in London and for which he received an Olivier Award nomination as most promising newcomer. He also performed at Bristol's Old Vic and the Royal Shakespeare Company, as well as the Lyric. In 1991, he played the Madman in the Royal National Theatre production of Dario Fo's *Accidental Death of an Anarchist*, for which he won the Olivier Award for best comedy performance. A few years later, in 1993, he received great acclaim for the title role in the English Touring Theatre's *Hamlet*, playing opposite his then-wife Hilary Lyon as Ophelia.

It was while still performing *Hamlet* that Cumming began rehearsals to play the Emcee. *Cabaret* was to tour England before culminating at the Donmar Warehouse. It was an exhausting, yet exhilarating, time for him. "Here I was, the bright new London theatre star, playing Hamlet alongside his wife's Ophelia, about to start a family. I had everything going for me, and I felt I had no control over anything." In fact, he was going through what is commonly called a nervous breakdown (or a "Nervy B," as he once called it). He couldn't eat and his relationship with his wife was rapidly falling

Club Cumming

Alan Cumming appreciates a good party. He was, after all, "your host" as the Master of Ceremonies in *Cabaret,* the most famous Emcee this side of Joel Grey. And after the lights went out on the Broadway stage, he welcomed guests to his *Cabaret* dressing room at Studio 54, the ultimate after-party. The festivities typically raged until 1:00 or 2:00 in the morning. Wednesdays were known as "soup nights" since he made a different vegan soup every week. The "club" also featured music played on Cumming's laptop. The set list leaned toward the upbeat, from the Black Eyed Peas to Beyoncé.

The guest list was eclectic, including cast members, friends, and assorted others (big names have included James Franco, Cate Blanchett, Woody Harrelson, and even Monica Lewinsky). He called it "Club Cumming." The name has lived on in the charming dining sets that the equally charming—and goofy—store, Fishs Eddy, sells in New York's Union Square neighborhood. The items include a Club Cumming shot glass, a bar tray, and a gift box set of four.

The shop with the odd moniker opened in 1986. It takes its name from a tiny hamlet in upstate New York, northeast of Hancock village in Delaware County, off State Route 17.

A portion of the proceeds go to Broadway Cares/Equity Fights AIDS. In August 2017, Cumming announced that he plans to open a nightclub, also called Club Cumming, in the East Village in September 2017. The club will be open to all ages and all genders.

apart. By the time *Cabaret* ended in the spring of 1994, he said he was "a zombie. I went to work, but I spent most days in bed if I had no appointments. I was in a deep depression." So when he was offered a chance to shoot a film in Ireland, *Circle of Friends*, he jumped at the chance. It was an escape, "a happy respite," from his misery.

He played the role of the Master of Ceremonies in Sam Mendes's 1993 revival of *Cabaret* in London's West End opposite Jane Horrocks's Sally Bowles despite having initial misgivings. He had told the director that he didn't do musicals.

He received an Olivier Award nomination for best actor in a musical. He reprised the role in 1998 for Mendes and Rob Marshall in the Broadway revival, opposite Natasha Richardson as Sally Bowles. He won the Tony Award, Drama Desk Award, and Outer Critics Circle Award, Theater World.

Other roles on Broadway include the part of Otto in the 2001 production of Noël Coward's *Design for Living* and Mack the Knife in the Brecht-Weill musical *The Threepenny Opera* opposite Cyndi Lauper. He has done work Off-Broadway too, including his adaptation of Jean Genet's *Elle*.

He costarred with Dianne Wiest in the Classic Stage Company's production of Chekhov's *The Seagull*. In 2006, he played the lead role in *Bent* in London's West End. The following year he starred in the National Theatre of Scotland's production of *The Bacchae*, directed by John Tiffany (the director of the critically acclaimed *Black Watch* and *Once*), which premiered at the Edinburgh International Festival before moving on to the Lyric Theatre in London and then to Lincoln Center in New York. He collaborated with Tiffany again in the National Theatre of Scotland's radical interpretation of *Macbeth*, which premiered at the Tramway in Glasgow and in which he played virtually all of the roles. (Actually, his character is a patient in a psychiatric unit who acts out the entire play). It moved to Lincoln Center in 2012 and then to Broadway at the Ethel Barrymore Theatre in 2013, where, wrote Charles Isherwood in the *New York Times*, his "rich, rolling accent brings a whiff of the green highlands with it." Unfortunately, Isherwood was not entirely taken with Cumming's nearly one-man *Macbeth* ("while Mr. Cumming had persuasively differentiated all the key roles, he had not fully inhabited any one of them."). In 2015, he appeared in a video role in David Bowie's *Lazarus* at the New York Theatre Workshop.

In 2014, he returned to Broadway in his iconic role of the Emcee in Sam Mendes's Roundabout Theatre Company revival of *Cabaret*, starring opposite Michelle Williams and then Emma Stone and Sienna Miller. *Cabaret* opened on April 24, 2014, and ran until March 29, 2015.

Club Cumming refers to the name given to Alan Cumming's legendary *Cabaret* dressing room after-party held at Studio 54, where the Scotsman played genial host to an eclectic guest list. A portion of sales of Club Cumming bar sets go to Broadway Cares/Equity Fights AIDS.   *Author collection. Photo by Theresa Albini*

He has performed in concert with Liza Minnelli, most recently at New York's historic Town Hall. He published a novel, *Tommy's Tale*, in 2002, and has contributed articles to the *New York Times, Harper's Bazaar, Out*, the *Globe and Mail, Marie Claire, Newsweek, Out*, and the *Wall Street Journal*. He has also written introductions and prefaces to the works of Nancy Mitford, Andy Warhol, and Christopher Isherwood.

As evidence of his eclecticism, he had his own line of fragrances called, of course, "Cumming" and "Second (Alan) Cumming," and a line of scented bath lotions and body washes. In 2012, he held his first photography exhibition, *Alan Cumming Snaps*.

Natasha Richardson

The daughter of actress Vanessa Redgrave and film director Tony Richardson, Richardson (1963–2009) received stellar reviews for her portrayal of Sally Bowles in *Cabaret* and won a Tony Award. She made her West End debut in Chekhov's *The Seagull* in 1985 and her Broadway debut in the 1993 revival of *Anna Christie*, opposite her future husband Liam Neeson. Other Broadway appearances include *Closer* (1999). She portrayed Blanche DuBois in the Roundabout Theatre revival of Tennessee Williams's *A Streetcar Named Desire* in 2005.

In January 2009, two months before her death in Quebec from a skiing accident, she appeared with her mother in a concert production of Stephen Sondheim's *A Little Night Music*.

Her more notable films include *Patty Hearst* (1988), *The Handmaid's Tale* (1990), *Nell* (1994), *The Parent Trap* (1998), *Maid in Manhattan* (2002), *Asylum* (2005), *The White Countess* (2005), and *Evening* (2007).

Other Cast Members

Mary Louise Wilson (b. 1931) is a veteran of stage, film, and television. Her major Broadway productions include *Flora, the Red Menace* (1965); *Promises, Promises* (1968); *Grey Gardens* (2006), for which she won a Tony; and *On the Twentieth Century* (2015). Among her many movie appearances are *Klute* (1971), *Up the Sandbox* (1972), *The Best Little Whorehouse in Texas* (1982), *Zelig* (1983), and *Nebraska* (2013).

Ron Rifkin (b. 1939) has made many movie and television appearances. He was a regular on *Alias* and the family drama *Brothers & Sisters*. For his role as Herr Schultz in *Cabaret*, he won a Tony Award for best supporting actor.

Denis O'Hare (b. 1962) has appeared on Broadway in *Take Me Out* and *Sweet Charity* and in the films *21 Grams*, *Michael Clayton*, *Charlie Wilson's War*, *Milk*, *Changeling*, and *Dallas Buyers Club*, among others. He has appeared on various seasons of the television anthology *American Horror Show*, on *True Blood*, and *The Good Wife*.

O'Hare won a Tony for best performance by a featured actor in a play for *Take Me Out* and the Drama Desk Award for outstanding featured actor in a musical in *Sweet Charity* (2005). Other Broadway appearances include Stephen Sondheim's *Assassins* (2004)

John Benjamin Hickey (b. 1963) originated the role of Arthur in Terrence McNally's *Love! Valour! Compassion!* (1995) and appeared in the 2002 revival of *The Crucible*. He won the Tony in 2011 for best performance by a featured actor in *The Normal Heart*. He also appeared in numerous films, including *The Ice Storm*, *Flags of Our Fathers*, *Infamous*, and *Pitch Perfect*.

2014 Broadway Revival

In 2014, the Roundabout Theatre Company presented a second revival of *Cabaret*. Alan Cumming reprised his role as the Emcee with Michelle Williams as Sally Bowles, Linda Emond as Fräulein Schneider, Danny Burstein as Herr Schultz, and Bill Heck as Cliff Bradshaw.

The reviews were mostly excellent, although critics either loved or hated Michelle Williams' interpretation of Sally Bowles. Hilton Als opined that she "wears her loneliness like a cloak over her fur coat." She speaks in a "metallic voice, like the clatter of a typewriter; the voice is a defense, a remnant of the Jazz Age, out of sync with this corroding world." He felt she gave an "authentic performance in a synthetic medium, the American musical." He goes on: "[S]he digs and digs for those moments, in herself and in the script, that will lift the production to a level that can't be explained. Her performance may baffle those who know only the Minnelli version and don't realize that Williams is playing Sally as Isherwood envisioned her: talentless, more verbal about sex than sexual . . . adrift—and intent on being fascinating." Cumming plays the Emcee, says Als, as a snob; his role, as always, is flashier because, he insists, it has to be. His function, after all, is "to draw us into his world and then trap us there."

As for the supporting cast, Als called Linda Emond's Fräulein Schneider "outstanding," while Danny Burstein is "a new Karl Malden, subtle and down to earth."

"The Emcee's hedonism, Fräulein Schneider's anti-Semitism, and Herr Schultz's willingness to turn a blind eye to it are all nails in the coffin of European civilization," notes Hilton Als. As he looks toward the audience, the Emcee removes his overcoat "to reveal a pink triangle and a Star of David." Sally appears "impassive, as if she'd been swallowed whole by the horror of the world."

For this third Broadway revival, Sam Mendes and Rob Marshall returned as director and codirector/choreographer, respectively. The production began a twenty-four-week limited engagement with previews beginning on March 21, 2014. Opening night was April 24, 2014. It was later extended to a thirty-six-week run; it concluded its run on March 29, 2015.

Replacements for Michelle Williams included Emma Stone and Sienna Miller as Sally Bowles.

The *Cabaret* 2014 touring cast consisted of the following:

Andrea Goss as Sally Bowles

Randy Harrison as the Emcee

Shannon Cochran as Fräulein Schneider

Mark Nelson as Herr Schultz

The Emcee's Dance Partners

One of the many highlights of *Cabaret* productions is the dance sequence at the end of the entr'acte where the Emcee selects an audience member to dance. It started when Alan Cumming tried it out at the first preview at the Donmar in London's West End and it has followed him from London to Broadway to touring productions to even high school productions.

Michelle Williams

Like Jill Haworth before her, Michelle Williams had virtually no singing or dancing experience when she got the coveted role of Sally Bowles after Emma Stone dropped out of the running (ironically, it was Stone who would later replace Williams after Williams left the show). Williams made her Broadway debut in the role. Prior to *Cabaret*, she snared another significant song and dance role: that of Marilyn Monroe in the indie film *My Week with Marilyn*, in which she costarred with Eddie Redmayne.

To get up to speed for the role of the "Queen of Mayfair," and to bring her singing up to what she called an "acceptable, nonembarrassing level," Williams rehearsed privately with *Cabaret* music director Patrick Vaccariello and associate choreographer Cynthia Onrubia. What was especially nerve-wracking was that Williams followed in the footsteps of so many other Sallys: from Harris to Dench to Richardson on the stage, to Minnelli on the big screen.

"Sally is a part that bears repeating," she told Charles McGrath of the *New York Times*. "That's why people keep coming back to it, because it really holds up."

In order to make the part her own, Williams made Sally into someone who was fragile and yet confident: she found the vulnerability within the grand gestures.

Critics were torn about Williams's performance. "Miss Bowles is supposed to be an emotional mess . . . and that is precisely what Williams delivers," wrote Chris Jones in the *Chicago Tribune*. But he thought her rendition of the musical's many famous songs lacked the proper "force of a great Broadway singer." On the other hand, he applauded her effort, which "feels deep and truthful and earned."

Williams is best known, of course, for her roles on the big screen. In addition to *My Week with Marilyn*, for which she received a Golden Globe Award and an Academy Award nomination, she has also appeared in Kenneth Lonergan's *Manchester by the Sea*; Derek Cianfrance's *Blue Valentine*; Ang Lee's *Brokeback Mountain*; Kelly Reichardt's *Meek's Cut-off, Wendy and Lucy*, and *Certain Women*; Martin Scorsese's *Shutter Island*; Charlie Kauffman's *Synecdoche, New York*; Todd Haynes's *I'm Not There*; Ethan Hawke's *The Hottest State*; and Thomas McCarthy's *The Station Agent*. She received Academy Award nominations for *Blue Valentine*, *Brokeback Mountain*, and *Manchester by the Sea*.

Other Cast Members

Linda Emond received a Tony nomination for her role as Fräulein Schneider in *Cabaret*. She also appeared in *Death of a Salesman* and *Life (x) 3* on Broadway, receiving Tony nominations for both. Her many films include *Pollock, The Dying Gaul, North Country, Stop-Loss, Across the Universe*, and *Julie & Julia*.

Danny Burstein was nominated for a Tony for his performance as Herr Schultz in *Cabaret*. His many Broadway appearances include *Company, Follies, Women on the Verge of a Nervous Breakdown, South Pacific, The Drowsy Chaperone*, and *Fiddler on the Roof*. His films include *Transamerica, Deception, Blackhat*, and *Indignation*.

Bill Heck, who played Clifford Bradshaw, appeared in numerous plays, including *Angels in America, Orphans' Home Cycle, Brooklyn Boy*, and *Chopin's Preludes*.

Other cast members included Aaron Krohn as Ernst Ludwig; Gayle Rankin as Fräulein Kost; Will Carlyon as Swing; Kaleign Cronin as Lulu and one of the "Two Ladies" dancers; Caleb Damschroder as Swing; Benjamin Eakeley as Herman, the Customs Officer, and Max; Andrea Goss as Frenchie (and that's her in the Gorilla suit in "If You Could See Her"); Leeds Hill as Bobby and one of the "Two Ladies" dancers; Kristin Olnes as Helga; Kelly

Paredes as Swing; Jessica Pariseau as Texas; Dylan Paul as Victor; Jane Pfitsch as Rosie; Evan D. Siegel as Hans and Rudy.

2014 Revival Musical Numbers and the Kit Kat Band

Act I
- "Willkommen": Emcee and the Kit Kat Band
- "So What?": Fräulein Schneider
- "Don't Tell Mama": Sally and the Kit Kat Girls
- "Mein Herr": Sally and the Kit Kat Girls
- "Perfectly Marvelous" Sally and Cliff
- "Two Ladies": Emcee, Lulu, and Bobby
- "It Couldn't Please Me More": Fräulein Schneider and Herr Schultz
- "Tomorrow Belongs to Me": Emcee
- "Maybe This Time": Sally
- "Money": Emcee and the Kit Kat Girls
- "Married": Herr Schultz, Fräulein Schneider, Fritzie
- "Tomorrow Belongs to Me" (Reprise): Fräulein Kost, Ernst Ludwig, and the Company

Act II
- "Entr'Acte": The Kit Kat Band
- "Kick Line": The Kit Kat Band
- "Married" (Reprise): Herr Schultz
- "If You Could See Her (The Gorilla Song)": Emcee and the Gorilla
- "What Would You Do?": Fräulein Schneider
- "I Don't Care Much": Emcee
- "Cabaret": Sally
- "Finale": The Company

The Kit Kat Band

Musical Director and Piano: Patrick Vaccariello

Associate Conductor: Maggie Torre

Drums: Eric Poland

Bass: Billy Sloat

Trumpet: Jeremy Miloszewicz

Trumpet/Euphonium: Stacey Sipowicz

Trombone: Dylan Paul

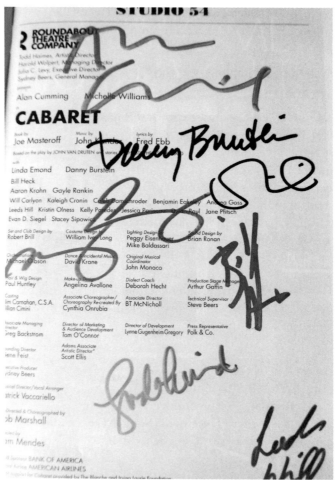

Broadway cast autographs of the 2014 *Cabaret* revival at the
Roundabout Theatre Company, New York.

Author collection. Photo by Theresa Albini

Clarinet/Soprano Sax/Alto Sax: Benjamin Eakeley

Clarinet/Tenor Sax: Jessica Pariseau

Clarinet/Tenor Sax: Kristin Olness

Alto & Tenor Sax: Evan D. Siegel

Alto Sax: Kaleign Cronin

Cello: Will Carylon

Violin/Piano: Andrea Goss

Violin/Clarinet: Leeds Hill

Violin/French Horn/Trumpet: Jane Pfitsch
Violin/Viola: Kelly Paredes
Accordion: Gayle Rankin
Banjo/Bassoon: Caleb Damschroder
Banjo: Aaron Krohn
Understudies: Kaleigh Cronin and Andrea Goss (Sally Bowles), Caleb Damschroder (Emcee), Benjamin Eakeley (Clifford Bradshaw, Ernst Ludwig), Leeds Hill (Emcee), Dylan Paul (Ernst Ludwig, Clifford Bradshaw), Stacey Sipowicz (Fräulein Kost)
Standbys: Kristie Dale Sanders (Fräulein Schneider), Philip Hoffman (Herr Schultz)

Other Crew

Book: Joe Masteroff
Music and Lyrics: John Kander and Fred Ebb
Director: Sam Mendes
Codirector, Choreographer: Rob Marshall
Set and Club Design: Robert Brill
Costume Design: William Ivey Long
Lighting Design: Peggy Eisenhauer and Mike Baldassari
Sound Design: Brian Ronin
Orchestrations: Michael Gibson
Dance and Incidental Music: David Krane
Associate Choreographer/Choreography Re-created By: Cynthia Onrubia
Hair and Wig Design: Paul Huntley
Make-up Design: Angelina Avallone
Dialect Coach: Deborah Hecht
Associate Director: BT McNicholl
Casting: Jim Carnahan
Production Stage Manager: Arthur Gaffin
Stage Manager: Lee Micklin
Assistant Stage Manager: Jeff Siebert
Founding Director, Roundabout Theatre Company: Gene Feist
Artistic Director, Roundabout Theatre Company: Todd Haimes

Changes Between the 1993 and 1998 Revivals

"Two Ladies" was performed with the Emcee, a Kit Kat girl, and a Kit Kat boy in drag and featured a shadow play (similar to a scene in the movie) simulating various sexual positions.

The score was reconsidered, with synthesizer effects; more significantly, the instruments of the Kit Kat Klub Orchestra were now played by the cabaret girls and boys, meaning that the musicians were also actors.

"Sitting Pretty" was removed.

"Money" was performed as a stand-alone song.

"Mein Herr" and "Maybe This Time," both from the movie, were added.

The Kit Kat Klub menu at Studio 54, 2014

Small Plates

Farmstead Cheeses 17
   Assorted Cheeses, Candied Walnuts,
   Fig Jam, Strawberries, Grapes, Crackers
Charcuterie 17
   Salami, Black Forrest Ham, Peppadews,
   Olives, Brown Mustard, Crackers
Pretzel Ham Sandwich 12
   Black Forrest Ham, Brie, Green Apple and Fig Jam on a Pretzel Roll with Pickle
Sweets Platter 17
   German Chocolate Brownie Bites, Pecan Drops, Mini Linzer Tarts, Pretzel
Rods
Bavarian Pretzel 5

Kit Kat Klub Cocktails 19

The Toast of Mayfair
   Gin, Kirschwasser, Kupferburg Gold Sparkling Wine, Fresh Lime, Raspberry-
   Bay Laurel Syrup, Bittermens Burlesque Bitters

Don't Tell Mama
> Vodka, Apple Schnapps, Fresh Lemon, Gooseberry Preserves, Honey-Caraway Syrup, Seltzer

Mein Herr
> Paulaner Beer, Barenjager Honey Liqueur, Black Cherry-Cacao Syrup

Other Revivals

1999–2001 North American Tour

The opening date of the North American tour was February 23, 1999; the closing date, May 20, 2001. Teri Hatcher might have been the name star, but Norbert Leo Butz, a veteran of *Rent*, as the Emcee received most of the acclaim. Just as the Roundabout Theatre production on Broadway transformed the theater space to recreate as much as possible a Weimar-era cabaret, so too did the national tour productions. At the Schubert Theatre in Chicago, for example (now the Private Bank Theatre), the management removed the first nine rows of orchestra seats (268 in total, according to writer Sid Smith) and replaced them with tables and chairs, which could accommodate up to one hundred people.

The cast consisted of the following:

Emcee: Norbert Leo Butz
Sally Bowles: Teri Hatcher
Fräulein Schneider: Barbara Andres
Clifford Bradshaw: Rick Holmes
Herr Schultz: Dick Latessa
Ernst Ludwig: Andy Taylor
Herman, Max, Customs Official: Corey Brill
Victor: Thomas Cannizzaro
Bobby: Michael Curry
Lulu: Alison Ewing
Frenchie: Lisa Ferguson
Hans: Paul Lincoln
Texas: Shana Mahoney
Fräulein Kost: Jeanine Morick
Rosie: Jessica Perrizo
Helga: Susan Taylor
Boy Soprano (recording only): Alex Bowen

Fräulein Kost and the Orchestra

The 1999 national touring production of *Cabaret* consisted of a twenty-piece orchestra. What makes the Kit Kat Klub band distinctive then—and now—is that members of the band are also cast members. Casting director Jim Carnahan told writer Anne Taubeneck that it was a challenge to find performers who could not only sing but also dance and act—and look sexy onstage to boot. Another challenge was the casting of Fräulein Kost ("the single hardest role to cast," he said). Fräulein Kost, played by Jeanine Morick during the 1999–2001 tour and perhaps most famously by Michelle Pawk during the Broadway revivals, had to learn German, a language she did not know, in order to sing "Married" in German, while Fräulein Schneider and Herr Schultz sing it in English. Making it even more complicated, she had to sing it with a Berlin accent. She also had to know how to dance and how to play the accordion. During rehearsal, she practiced for three hours every night because the fingering, she told Taubeneck, "has to be ingrained in your body."

London Revival (2006)

In September 2006, a new production of *Cabaret* opened at the Lyric Theatre with the following cast:

Sally Bowles: Anna Maxwell Martin
Emcee: James Dreyfus
Fräulein Kost: Harriet Thorpe
Fräulein Schneider: Sheila Hancock

Hancock won the Olivier Award for best supporting performance in a musical.

Replacements in the run included

Sally Bowles: Kim Medcalf and Amy Nuttall
Fräulein Schneider: Honor Blackman and Angela Richards
Emcee: Julian Clary and Alistair McGowan

Directed by Rufus Norris, it closed its run in June 2008 and then toured nationally for two years. The touring cast included Wayne Sleep as the Emcee and Samantha Barks and Siobhan Dillon as Sally Bowles. For additional commentary, see the Lyric Theatre entry on page 174.

London Revival (2012)

The 2012 revival opened in the West End at the Savoy Theatre on October 3, 2012, prior to a four-week tour of Britain. The cast included

Sally Bowles: Michelle Ryan
Emcee: Will Young

Other cast members included Siân Phillips, Harriet Thorpe, and Matt Rawle. In 2013, the production went on tour again, with Young reprising his role as the Emcee, Dillon as Bowles, and Lyn Paul as Fräulein Schneider.

Other Notable Productions

BBC Radio 2 broadcast, 1996, at the Golders Green Hippodrome. The cast included Claire Burt as Sally Bowles, Steven Berkoff as the Emcee, Alex Hanson as Cliff Bradshaw, Keith Michell as Herr Schultz, Rosemary Leach as Fräulein Schneider.

In 2008, the Stratford Shakespeare Festival performed a critically acclaimed production at the Avon Theatre. The cast included Bruce Dow as the Emcee, Trish Lindström as Sally Bowles, Sean Arbuckle as Cliff Bradshaw, Nora McClellan as Fräulein Schneider, and Frank Moore as Herr Schultz. Directed by Amanda Dehnert.

In 2014, *Cabaret* was performed at the Shaw Festival at Niagara-on-the-Lake in Ontario, from April 10 to October 26, at the Festival Theatre. The cast included Juan Chiroan as the Emcee, Deborah Hay as Sally Bowles, Gray Powell as Cliff Bradshaw, Benedict Campbell as Herr Schultz, Corrine Koslo as Fräulein Schneider, Jay Turvey as Ernst Ludwig. With choreography by Denise Clarke. Directed by Peter Hinton.

U.S. tours: 1967, 1969, 1987, 1989

U.K. tours: 2008, 2012, 2013

North American tours: 1999, 2016

International productions have been staged as well, including in Argentina (1988, 2007), France (2006, 2011), Latvia (2014), Mexico (1980, 2004), The Netherlands (2005), and Spain (1992, 2003, 2015). Other productions took place in Australia, Brazil, Colombia, Greece, Israel, Malaysia, Peru, Serbia, South Africa, and Venezuela.

Additional Significant Stage Productions

Countless productions of *Cabaret*—professional, community theater, and high school—have been presented throughout the country, and indeed the world, for decades. Several in particular have stood out because of their innovative staging and daringly different conception.

Among the highlights are the following:

Stratford Shakespeare Festival of Canada (1987)

Sheila McCarthy as Sally Bowles, Scott Wentworth as Cliff Bradshaw, and Brent Carver as the Master of Ceremonies, Denise Fergusson as Fräulein Schneider, Richard Curnock as Herr Schultz. Directed by Brian Macdonald. Although McCarthy's Sally received her share of critics (she lacked "sexiness" to some and her voice was "too slight" to others), this Stratford production was much praised for Carver's reinterpretation as the leering emcee. He was recognized, too, for his "spectacular" dancing; James Leve describes him as "magnificently androgynous, roguish, and sinister." Fun fact: Eric McCormack of *Will and Grace* fame played a transvestite waiter in the Kit Kat Klub.

Lyric Theatre, London (2006)

Anna Maxwell Martin as Sally Bowles, Michael Hayden as Cliff Bradshaw, Sheila Hancock as Fräulein Schneider, James Dreyfus as the Emcee. Directed by Rufus Norris.

In Norris's vision, the lurid atmosphere of the Kit Kat Klub reflected the self-absorbed and self-indulgent Weimar society. By referring back to German Expressionism, the grotesque paintings of George Grosz and Otto Dix, anti-Semitic imagery, and German propaganda films (think Leni Riefenstahl), Norris emphasized the depravity of the era. Whether onstage or outside, the point was that both worlds were threatening places.

This production toured the United Kingdom in 2008–2009 with a regional company.

Arena Stage, Washington, D.C. (2006)

Brad Oscar as the Emcee. Directed by Molly Smith.

Smith's Cabaret was criticized by some for its "sledgehammer approach" and lack of subtlety (Nazis giving one of the main characters a terrific beating and then posing Abu Ghraib style)

Stratford Shakespeare Festival of Canada (2008)

Trish Lindstrom as Sally Bowles, Sean Arbuckle as Cliff Bradshaw, Bruce Dow as the Emcee. Directed by Amanda Dehnert.

Amanda Dehnert presented a major reimagining of *Cabaret*. But first, according to Leve, she did some serious research on the social milieu of Weimar Germany, consulting books, watching contemporary films (such as Walter Ruttmann's silent film documentary *Berlin: Symphony of a Great City*, 1927), and uncovering original materials (underground tabloids, playbills, postcards, verboten travelogs, hotel brochures, and "naughty" guides). Through this research she was able to get a better sense of the decadence of the period. Berlin between the wars, notes Leve, had more than six hundred sex establishments, from sex clubs to private torture dungeons. "The city's cabarets, too," he notes, "were remarkable for their perversities." The most "notorious," he contends, was the Cabaret of the Nameless. Promoter Erwin Lowinsky used mentally ill and talent-challenged performers—the more untalented the better.

Dehnert tapped into all these sources to reinterpret her vision of *Cabaret*. Unlike other productions, Dehnert felt Cliff formed the center of the story. Cliff not only as embodying the essence of Isherwood himself but also as someone who observed the world with a jaundiced eye. Dehnert used multimedia, movable platforms, expressionistic lighting, and various Brechtian techniques. Her biggest concept was to adapt a play-within-a-play framing device. The internal world of the Kit Kat Klub and the external world of Weimar Berlin were intertwined.

Dehnert's treatment of the Emcee (a portly Bruce Dow) was also novel. Wearing white makeup, his outfit consisted of a white shirt, black trousers, and a Mohawk parted down the middle. He was truly omniscient—and the only one on the stage who was aware of the past and unable to stop the future. Although portrayed, in Leve's words, as "a warm-hearted, empathetic Everyman," he was keenly cognizant of the moral decay that surrounded him and that he, in return, was part of. All of Berlin contributed to Germany's failure as a society; all of Berlin was part of a collective illusion that created Nazism. No one was off the hook, not even the "paternal" Emcee.

Cabaret National Tour (2016–2017)

As part of their fiftieth anniversary season, the Roundabout Theatre Company presented a national touring company of *Cabaret* in 2016 and 2017.

The 2016 cast consisted of

Emcee: Randy Harrison
Sally Bowles: Andrea Goss
Fräulein Schneider: Shannon Cochran
Fräulein Kost/Fritzie: Alison Ewing
Herr Schultz: Mark Nelson
Ernst Ludwig: Ned Noyes
Clifford Bradshaw: Lee Aaron Rosen
Swing: Kelsey Beckert
Helga: Sarah Bishop
Texas: Margaret Dudasik
Rosie: Hillary Ekwall
Swing: Lori Eure
Frenchie/Gorilla: Aisling Halpin
Bobby: Leeds Hill
Victor: Andrew Hubacher
Swing: Joey Khoury

Andrea Goss as Sally Bowles in the 2016 national touring company production of *Cabaret*.
Courtesy Margie Korshak, Inc.

Herman/Customs Official/Max: Tommy McDowell
Hans/Rudy: Evan D. Siegel
Lulu: Dani Speller
Swing: Steven Wenslawski
Standby for Herr Schultz: John Little
Standby for Fräulein Schneider: Lucy Sorlucco

The 2017 cast consisted of

Emcee: Randy Harrison
Sally Bowles: Andrea Goss
Cliff: Benjamin Eakeley
Fräulein Kost/Fritzie: Alison Ewing
Fräulein Schneider: Mary Gordon Murray
Herr Schultz: Scott Robertson
Ernst Ludwig: Patrick Vaill
Swing: Kelsey Beckert
Helga: Sarah Bishop
Lulu: Chelsey Clark
Hans/Rudy: Ryan DeNardo
Swing: Lori Eure
Texas: Kendal Hartse
Victor: Andrew Hubacher
Bobby: Joey Khoury
Swing: Chris Kotera
Herman/Customs Official/Max: Tommy McDowell
Rosie: Samantha Shafer
Frenchie/Gorilla: Laura Sheehy
Swing: Steven Wenslawski
Standby for Herr Schultz: Bob Amaral
Standby for Fräulein Schneider: Lucy Sorlucco

Other *Cabaret* Productions

2002: Australian tour of the Mendes production.
2003: Spanish production at the Teatro Nuevo Alcala in Madrid. Directed by B. T. McNicholl.
2005–2006: Mexican production. Directed by Felipe Fernández del Paso.
2006: French-language version at the Folies Bergère.

2008: Cuban version, featuring a new libretto by Nicholas Dorr with contributions from Cuban dramaturges and directors Héctor Quintero and Jose Milian. Directed by Tony Diaz. This version also added new choreography and even gave it a new name, *Musical Cabaret*.

2009: Peruvian production at the Teatro Segura in Lima. Directed by Mateo Chiarella.

High School and College Productions of *Cabaret*

At first blush, some may find it surprising that high schools throughout the United States perform *Cabaret*.

But they do.

And quite often. A quick search on the web proves this handily. Yes, occasional controversy erupts. One letter writer—a parent and teacher from Syracuse, New York—objected to a performance of it in 2015, because of its "vulgar, adult content." "High school is not Broadway," she wrote. A few years earlier in 2013, there was a Stop *Cabaret* petition to prevent this "vulgar and immoral play" being performed at St. Genevieve Catholic High School in Panorama City, California.

I attended the sold-out opening night production of *Cabaret* at Jones College Prep in April 2016, one of Chicago's best high schools, which is located in the city's downtown—the first of three performances. The rehearsal process was a very lengthy eight weeks.

The role of the Emcee was portrayed by the charismatic Jack Siebert, a junior at the time. His hair parted in the middle, he wore a red bowtie, a cutaway black tuxedo, white shirt, and black and red vest. With his slightly red cheeks and youthful features, he looked Bowies-esque in bone structure, in build, in facial features.

But what made this production so distinctive was its diverse casting: Sally Bowles was played by a young African American; Bobby, one of the Kit Kat Boys, a Korean American. (In the Mendes revival, when Sally admits she doesn't know who the father of her baby is, she says the father might be "an Oriental. I seem to recall a rather taciturn Malaysian.")

"I think it's important that Sally was black because then we got to focus on another part of that time period, which was the objectification of black people in cabaret clubs for 'entertainment,' as well as the lack of black performers in this time period," Siebert told me, smeared eyeliner still on his face.

According to Peter Jelavich, "German stages had hosted African American song-and-dance numbers since the turn of the century. They received considerably more attention during the Weimar era, as jazz . . . became a prominent style of popular music."

The script departed from the Roundabout Theatre script in several ways:

* Fräulein Heidi performed "Don't Tell Mama," not Sally Bowles, and was introduced by the Emcee as "The Toast of Berlin," rather than Sally's "Toast of Mayfair."

Cabaret program at Jones College Prep High School, Chicago, 2016.

Author collection

- Sally pretended to be English when she first met Cliff, but soon revealed herself to be an American (Cliff says, "Let's talk about Sally Bowles. You're English.").
- It quoted several lines from the movie (such as when Sally announces in Act I, Scene 10, "I'm going to have a baby.").
- When Cliff says he has only been with women three times, Sally counters, "Only with girls three times? Even I have a better track record than that." When Sally receives a letter from her ambassador father explaining why he had to cancel his dinner engagement with her, Sally reads the note she received from him:

> "Dear Sally. Sorry. Hope nose doesn't fall off.' Ten words. . . ."

The audience reacted vociferously several times. When Sally announced to Cliff that she was going to have a baby, there was an audible gasp. And when Cliff questioned who the father was, Sally admitted it could even be Bobby. "Perhaps a Korean. I do remember a drunken night with Bobby."

Audible oohs and ahs erupted too when Sally and Cliff kissed for the first time; and a Democratic socialist comment, clearly referencing Bernie Sanders, who was then running again Hillary Rodham Clinton during the Democratic presidential primaries, elicited a few chuckles. When Cliff says to Sally, after learning about her pregnancy, "You have a new career as a mother," there was noticeable disapproval from a displeased audience.

Posters around the school promoting the production featured swastikas, which troubled some. "People started ripping them down and complaining, which I understand given little context about the show," Siebert told me, "but I think it's important to include swastikas. Censoring history is pretending it didn't happen."

Siebert says he saw the movie first, which he didn't particularly like. "Too 'Hollywoodized'" is how he described it. But he also saw the touring production of *Cabaret* when it played in Chicago in February 2016, which he considered "awesome." Prior to being cast as the Emcee, he didn't know a lot about the Weimar era, but after doing his research, he acknowledged "so much relevance" to what's going on today. *Cabaret* "directly mirrors what's going on in politics today," he said. High school students, certainly the ones at Jones, says Siebert, "do get it."

Siebert adds, "I thought of the Emcee as an enigma. . . . The Emcee also represents the journey the show takes from a dream ("Wilkommen" and the Kit Kat Club) into a nightmare (Finale), or transition from Impressionism to Expressionism, also depicted in my costume and makeup."

In early 2017, Roosevelt University, also in Chicago, mounted a terrific production of *Cabaret*. The director and choreographer, Jane Lanier, had worked with Bob Fosse as a young dancer: in the revival of *Sweet Charity* in 1986–1987 and in the musical revue *Fosse* from 1999 to 2001. In the production, she included small details that added tremendously to the ambiance and verisimilitude, such as inserting announcements in German (by Sid McConnell) at the beginning of the show and asking the audience to turn off their cell phones. During the dramatic climax, Lanier included an authentic recording of Adolf Hitler.

The cast, which featured a mesmerizing Maddie Dorsey as Sally Bowles, rehearsed for six weeks, "five days a week, three and a half hours a night," says Lanier. The cast did their research and were totally committed to the play. Dorsey, in particular, "owned Sally," said Lanier. "She was so disciplined . . . a complete pro."

Cabaret, the Film

On the Big Screen

In 1968, the distribution company Cinerama Releasing Corporation bought the rights to *Cabaret* for $2.1 million but seven months later dropped out. The following year, Allied Artists moved in, purchasing the rights at the lower price of $1.5 million. Finally, in early 1970, Allied lined up with ABC Pictures: ABC would produce the film and Allied would distribute for a relatively low budget of $5 million.

Marty Baum, the president of ABC Pictures, hired Broadway veteran Cy Feuer as the producer. Feuer had a background in the movie industry. He had produced *Guys and Dolls* (1950), *Can-Can* (1953), and *How to Succeed in Business Without Really Trying* (1967), but he had also directed a few musicals, too, including *The Boy Friend, Silk Stockings*, and *Little Me*. Feuer in turn hired Jay Presson Allen to write the screenplay. Allen had previously written the screenplay for Alfred Hitchcock's *Marnie* (1964) and adapted Muriel Spark's novel *The Prime of Miss Jean Brodie* (1969) into an acclaimed motion picture, for which Maggie Smith won an Academy Award as best actress.

Allen drew on three sources: Isherwood's original Berlin stories; Van Druten's play, *I Am a Camera*; and Joe Masteroff's book of the 1966 original Broadway production.

Both producer and screenwriter also agreed on three crucial changes to the Broadway musical. The relationship between the middle-aged Fräulein Scheider-Herr Schultz plot would be replaced with a love story about two considerably younger characters, Natalia Landauer, the Jewish department store heiress, and Fritz Wendel, the German gigolo who masks his Jewishness. In fact, the character of Herr Schultz was removed altogether, while Fräulein Schneider's role was drastically reduced to minimal screen time.

The second major change involved the nationalities of the major characters (and the sexuality of one of them). The nationality of the Isherwood character—renamed Brian Roberts—remained English, but now his sexuality was fluid: he would be bisexual. And as for Sally Bowles herself, the toast of London's Mayfair—she was now a brash American living in Berlin.

The third change, though, was perhaps the most controversial, certainly the most innovative. Feuer, as producer, decided to flex his producing muscles by jettisoning all of the book songs from the stage production that were performed outside the Kit Kat Klub, with the exception of the Nazi anthem, "Tomorrow Belongs to Me," which was now set in an outdoor German beer garden.

Allen, along with Feuer and later director Bob Fosse, also altered the basic plot. The story now revolved around the evolving relationship between Sally (Liza Minnelli) and Brian (Michael York).

The movie begins in complete silence. At the thirty-three-second mark, we hear some muffled background noise. Voices. Laughter. Then distorted black-and-white images fill the screen before gradually turning into color before we realize that what we have been watching is the twisted reflection of a mirror. Then the grotesque, vaguely shocking image—the white face, the bright red lips, the lascivious grin—of the Emcee abruptly appears.

Brian Roberts arrives in Berlin. He is working toward his doctorate of philosophy degree at King's College, Cambridge University, but has decided to come to the German capital for a break. From his wide-eyed look, it is clear he is happy to be here—and makes his way toward Fräulein Schneider's boardinghouse, where he meets up with Sally Bowles, his neighbor.

Brian: *How long have you been here?*

Sally: *Forever.*

Brian: *How long is that?*

Sally: *Almost three months.*

Sally, as portrayed by the indomitable Liza Minnelli, is a whirlwind, and someone you feel instantly comfortable with, as if she has been a lifelong friend. She introduces some of the residents of the boardinghouse to Brian, including Fräulein Kost, who she describes as "a terribly sweet streetwalker."

She tells him that she is constantly "dashing" off here and there and that she performs at the Kit Kat Klub. That night he attends a show, watching Sally at the Klub ("You know you are very good," he says to her), and they begin a tentative relationship.

But it starts off on the wrong foot. In fact, it's a disaster. She makes a pass at him, which he ever-so politely fends off.

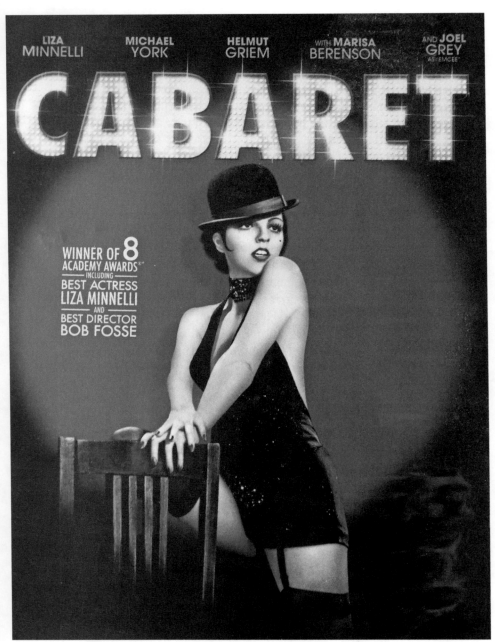

Cabaret motion picture soundtrack with Liza Minnelli as Sally Bowles.

Author collection. Photo by Theresa Albini

Sally: *Maybe you just don't sleep with girls.*

Brian: *I've gone through the motions of sleeping with girls exactly three times.
All of them disastrous.*

They agree to be just friends.

Brian teaches English to pay the rent. One of his new students is the very proper Natalia Landauer (Marisa Berenson), a Jewish heiress. The charming gigolo Fritz Wendel (Fritz Wepper), a mutual friend, expresses interest in Natalia, sight unseen, solely because of her vast wealth. But then he slowly starts to fall in love with her.

Meanwhile, Sally returns to the boardinghouse, devastated that her ambassador father once again did not show up for a dinner engagement. She reads a letter from him explaining his absence, but it is written in the form of a terse telegram. "'Dear Sally. Sorry. Schedule revised at last minute. Writing. Love.' Ten words exactly. After ten, it's extra," she says. When she breaks down ("Maybe I'm just nothing—nothing."), Brian reassures her that she is "a perfectly marvelous girl," echoing the title of one of the songs from the stage musical that does not appear in the film. The friendship now turns into a full-fledged romance.

Strange and Extraordinary

Sally Bowles often refers to herself as a "most strange and extraordinary person." The first time Liza Minnelli utters the famous phrase is early on in the film as she and Brian Roberts (Michael York) are walking down a Berlin street at night, getting to know each other better. After she learns that she is pregnant, she says to Brian that the unborn child will be "a most strange and extraordinary baby."

It is during these early scenes too that we learn that Sally's cinematic heroine is a now obscure Lya De Putti (1897–1931), a Hungarian silent film actress (she later changes her mind, insisting she makes "too many faces"). In fact, Sally references numerous historical theatrical and cinematic figures. Cavorting on filthy rich Maximilian's boat with Brian one sunny day, she imitates what she calls a Clara Bow pose. Clara Bow (1905–1965) was an American actress who transitioned from silent films to the talkies. During an angry moment, she blurts out, "One of these days Max Reinhardt is going to drift into the club."

Sally is movie mad ("It's crazy. Me, wanting to be an actress."). Other names she mentions include Emil Jannings (1884–1950), the German actor and costar opposite Marlene Dietrich in *The Blue Angel*; director, actor, producer Erich von Stroheim (1885–1957); the American stage and film actress Kay Francis

(1905–1968); and even the casting director at UFA, the great German movie studio that produced, among other movies, *The Blue Angel*, *Dr. Mabuse*, *Metropolis*, and Leni Riefenstahl's Nazi propaganda film *Triumph of the Will* (1935). UFA was also the studio of such great German directors as Fritz Lang and Josef von Sternberg and veterans of German cabaret Kurt Gerron and Friedrich Hollaender.

But things get complicated when Sally inadvertently meets the handsome and very rich Maximilian van Heune (Helmut Griem)—in Van Druten's *I Am a Camera* he was a wealthy American—who promises to wine and dine them to their heart's delight. "I think it's my duty to corrupt you," he tells both Sally and a glum Brian over dinner. "Agreed?" Sally gleefully agrees; Brian is not so sure. He promises to whisk them away to Africa. Either way, both end up sleeping with him. And then, just as quickly as he arrived, he vanishes from the scene altogether, leaving for Argentina. Making matters more complicated, though, Sally learns she is pregnant (she is uncertain who the father is). Brian proposes to her and offers to take her back to England with him. Free spirit Sally cannot accept the notion of a traditional marriage as a wife and mother in small-town Cambridge. Without telling Brian, she has an abortion. When he asks why, she shrugs and weakly offers, "One of my whims?" The relationship is over: Brian says goodbye to Berlin while Sally remains behind, still searching for some kind of stardom on the eve of Hitler's Germany.

The collapse of Sally and Brian's relationship parallels the downfall of Germany. With conditions at their nadir, Fräulein Schneider back at the boardinghouse sighs, "I wish the Kaiser was back. In those days, we had order."

In the closing moments, the Emcee reappears, his face now representing more of a Nazi death mask than that of a gleeful entertainer, and then a drum roll. He says goodbye (perhaps for the last time?) and disappears. Echoing Boris Aronson's inventive tilted mirror in the original Broadway production, Bob Fosse also uses a mirror, for his final statement. The images of the Kit Kat Klub that fill the screen are disturbing ones, as we see the distorted faces of Weimar Berlin but now there are plenty of Nazi uniforms.

Just as it began, the movie ends in (chilling) silence.

The *Cabaret* Film Score

Numerous changes in the score were made from the transition to the big screen. Two of the Kit Kat Klub numbers were dropped. Sally's very

English-sounding "Don't Tell Mama" didn't make much sense since Sally was now an American, so it was replaced by the Dietrich-esque "Mein Herr." The Emcee's "Money Song (Sitting Pretty)" was replaced with "Money, Money," now a duet between Sally and the Emcee.

Money, Money

"Fosse insisted we wear costumes when rehearsing "Money," Joel Grey told Liz McNeil. Liza Minnelli chose a gown, Grey chose a tailcoat and top hat. "[M]y body was running so hot, doing the song over and over," he said, which made Minnelli break out in laughter. "It was like we were Judy [Garland] and Mickey [Rooney] putting on a show in a barn!"

Other additions were an instrumental version of "Money Song" on the soundtrack and a lovely German rendition of the old Fräulein Schneider-Herr Schultz song "Married" by the Austrian singer-actress Greta Keller (heard on a creaky gramophone as Sally and Brian toast to their soon-to-be-parents status). In fact, the "Married" melody is heard several times throughout the film: when Fräulein Schneider dances with another resident, Fräulein Mayr, at the boardinghouse as Bobby plays the piano; when Brian and Sally are picnicking in the woods; and when Brian, about to leave Berlin altogether, walks Sally to the train station.

Greta Keller: 1903–1977

Born Margaretha Keller in Vienna, Keller was a contemporary of Marlene Dietrich and, like Dietrich, had a singular personality. She was also known for her double entendres. She appeared onstage with Dietrich, in the musical *Broadway*. She portrayed cabaret singers in several German films and performed regularly at the Waldorf Astoria and the Stanhope hotels in New York. She also made many recordings, including the songs of Kurt Weill.

She was considered a "singer's singer."

There's also a new song, "Maybe This Time," a torch song for Sally to sing as she celebrates her relationship with Brian. Ironically, she sings it to a mostly empty club. Those who are in the audience look bored. A dour German businessman smokes a cigar. There is a shot of a member of the Kit Kat Kat band, wearing a blank expression. At one point there is even a brief shot of the Emcee.

"Maybe This Time" has an interesting backstory of its own. Kander and Ebb wrote "Maybe This Time" for an earlier, and unsuccessful, musical of theirs, *Golden Gate*. In a coincidental twist, Minnelli recorded it on her first album, *Liza! Liza!*, in 1964 (on that album, she performed another Kander and Ebb song, "If I Were in Your Shoes"). According to Stephen Tropiano, she convinced Bob Fosse, who had his doubts about it, to include it in the movie. Frank Rich has referred to "Maybe This Time" (as well as "Cabaret" and Kander and Ebb's "New York, New York") as "hyperbolic anthems of survival." Kander himself called them "screamers." They are songs written for a diva—in the best and most generous sense of the word—and so, perfect for a full-throated singer like Minnelli.

Other changes in the script included the addition of a new character, Sally's diplomatic father, who works for the American embassy in Romania. But various people, including Cy Feuer, screenwriter Robert Alan Aurthur and playwright Neil Simon (friends of Fosse), and Fosse's wife, Gwen Verdon, objected to the character, and he was eventually dropped. Instead, in the final draft and in the film, his presence is always felt but he is never seen.

12

The Making of Cabaret

Gathering the Team

Cy Feuer knew the business. Show business. It was in his blood.

He grew up in New York. His father, Herman, was the general manager of a Yiddish theater on Second Avenue on the Lower East Side, who died of cancer when Cy was only thirteen. He had to grow up fast. After his father's death, Cy became the head of the family, but he also had music in his blood. He began playing the trumpet in various New York clubs. He turned professional before he was even fifteen and graduated from Juilliard in 1932.

When he moved west, he quickly found work in the Hollywood studios, scoring "a truckload of pictures" between 1938 and 1948, he says in his autobiography. He felt at home in Los Angeles—but there were limits. "All those transplanted palm trees and transplanted East Coast Jews were right at home on the western fringe of America," he wrote. "We joined clubs, we socialized, and we acted as if we really belonged." He was head of the Music Department at Republic Pictures. "I played sandlot polo with a group of Jews (Jews on horseback, what a scene!)"

Cy Feuer knew all about movies. He knew all about musicals too. He knew people in the industry. He also knew what it meant to be an outsider in the place where you lived. So when Marty Baum, head of ABC Pictures who was offered the film rights to *Cabaret*, asked Feuer if he would "take it on" as a producer, Feuer had his doubts. He didn't have a high opinion of the Broadway musical. So he held off until he was convinced it could work as a film.

When he saw a road company production of *Cabaret* in Seattle, it reinforced his initial reaction. "The entire secondary story—that soupy, sentimental, idiotic business with the little old Jewish man courting Sally's landlady by bringing her a pineapple every day—had to be thrown out," he said. But he loved the goings-on at the Kit Kat Klub, and the "diabolical M.C. was terrific."

Somewhere along the line he picked up a limited-edition copy of George Grosz's 1923 *Ecce Homo*, a collection of his drawings and watercolors that depicted human nature at its most depraved: images of lust, greed, and cruelty. The phrase is Latin and refers to the words used by Pontius Pilate (roughly, "Behold the man!") when he presented a scourged Jesus Christ, crowned with thorns, to a hostile crowd before his Crucifixion. Grosz, who had volunteered for military service and was well aware of the horrors of warfare, was a virulent opponent of World War I and had a history of satirizing the German army and German establishment. In fact, in 1921, he was sentenced for insulting the German army with his *God with Us* collection of drawings; and in 1928, he was accused of blasphemy for drawing *Christ with Gas Mask*, and fined 300 marks. He was later acquitted.

Either way, Feuer was impressed with the Grosz collection and saw in its depravity "the cruel decadence of Berlin between the wars." With these images as a bleak inspiration, he thought he could do something "important." He told Baum, "If you throw out the pineapples and put in a secondary love story—something that could appeal to young people—I'll do it." He also wanted the sexual orientation of the Isherwood character clarified and insisted that no "unjustified singing" take place. It had to be realistic; the musical numbers had to be organic.

He told screenwriter Jay Presson Allen to return to the original sources—the Berlin stories and Van Druten's *I Am a Camera* for plot details. "I also thought we should have the secondary love story take place between a young Jewish heiress who cannot marry out of her faith and a gentile." The gentile, Fritz Wendel, portrayed by Fritz Wepper in the film, was a Jew who was passing as a gentile.

When Bob Fosse got word that Feuer was looking for a director (see the next chapter for a discussion of Fosse and his work), Feuer said Fosse was "kinda desperate." His film adaptation of the musical *Sweet Charity* had flopped, and Fosse was looking for a project where he could redeem himself, and rescue his floundering career.

"We met for lunch. I had pasta, he had a pack of cigarettes," Feuer recalled.

But Manny Wolf, head of Allied Artists, and Baum of ABC, wanted a big-name director, a big-name star, such as Joe Mankiewicz or Billy Wilder. Even Gene Kelly's name was floated around. But Feuer knew Fosse's work and had always wanted him. His mind was made up before he even asked the other directors.

So, Fosse it would be.

Verisimilitude

Cabaret was shot at the Bavaria Studios, located eight miles south of Munich, for a modest $3.4 million. But money was always a concern. "We were working with a very tight collar," Feuer admits.

From the start, too, there was a conflict over the choice of cinematographer. Fosse had worked with Robert Surtees on *Sweet Charity* and wanted to bring him him aboard for *Cabaret*. After much turmoil and mounting tension—including accusations of lying and broken promises—Surtees was out and the English cinematographer Geoffrey Unsworth was in.

Rehearsals for the film began on February 22, 1971, in Munich. Shooting began nearly six months later, on July 9, 1971. The interior scenes, including those at the Kit Kat Klub, were shot at Bavaria Studios. The exterior scenes were shot on various locations around Germany, including West Berlin and the Eutin area in northern Germany. The baronial home of the Duke of Oldenberg, outside Hamburg, was used as Maximilian's country estate. It boasted an enormous ballroom ("sixty feet across, high ceilings, and great big fireplaces at both ends," said Feuer), which was used to great advantage in the drunken, swirling seduction scene between Sally, Brian, and Max.

Fosse worked closely with his technical crew to create the look that he wanted for the Kit Kat Klub. He was particularly inspired by the artwork of George Grosz (1893–1959) and Otto Dix (1891–1969). Among Dix's most famous paintings—and which Fosse particularly admired—was *Portrait of the Journalist Sylvia von Harden* (1926). It depicts what was then called the New Woman, a short-haired female German journalist and poet sitting at a table in a café with a cigarette in her right hand and wearing a monocle on her right eye. She has bright red lips, her teeth exposed. A cocktail drink with a straw, a matchbox, and a cigarette holder lies on the table.

Sylvia von Harden (1894–1963) wrote a literary column for the monthly *Das junge Deutschland* (the young Germany) from 1919 to 1923. Dix's painting embodied the New Objectivity movement.

Divine decadence. Green nail polish. Paraphernalia from the 2014 Broadway revival of *Cabaret*.

Author collection

Fosse re-created the painting as a still shot in the opening moments of *Cabaret* when the Emcee sings "Willkommen."

Control Freak

One of the most fascinating back-stories is the shooting of the beer garden scene, where a handsome German youth—the epitome of Aryan Germany—sings the Nazi anthem, "Tomorrow Belongs to Me." The young boy was twelve at the time. But there was a problem. He had long hair "down to his ass," said Feuer, as did most of the German youth at the time. So, as an incentive, the producers offered "hair payments." This didn't work for the young boy. But Feuer noticed he took a keen interest in an old army jeep. How would he like to learn how to drive it? And then drive it around the set?

Another problem was the boy's voice. He had the look, but not the right sound. Feuer auditioned members of the Vienna Boys Choir, but when that didn't work Feuer heard a "perfect" boy back in Hollywood who was in a rock band. "[I]t was his voice we dubbed into the picture." Nor were the other Germans in the beer garden actually singing. They were just moving their lips to the words. Their voices were also dubbed in later. "But the lips had to move to the right words and none of them spoke English, so we put up huge blackboards around the tables. . . . The lyrics were written in phonetic German."

Fosse was a control freak. Every scene was shot according to the script. There would be no variation—with one exception: the two women mud wrestling on the Kit Kat Klub stage. That scene involved so many takes that shooting stretched past midnight. Finally, Fosse said there would be one more take before wrapping for the night. Everyone was exhausted. At the end of the last take, Joel Grey, as the Emcee masquerading as the wrestling referee, bent down and placed some mud on his right forefinger and smeared it across his upper lip, imitating Hitler and then giving a "Heil Hitler" salute. The only problem was it wasn't in the script: it was a moment of sheer inspiration. He felt it was something the Emcee would have done.

Joel Grey worked with a dialogue coach, Osman Ragheb, to make sure he had a Berlin accent, not just a generic German accent.

But Fosse was furious. "Cut!" he screamed and walked off in a rage. Assistant director Wolfgang Glattes shouted, "That's a wrap!" Ultimately, though, Fosse (after he had calmed down) thought it was a good creative move on Grey's part.

13

Cabaret Cast and Crew

Hello Stranger

Bob Fosse: Dancin' Man

He always wanted to be in show business. Even as a boy, he was a natural performer.

Bob Fosse got his start in show business in his native Chicago by being a part of a dancing duo, with friend Charles Grass, called the Riff Brothers. Fosse and Grass made their professional debut at an amateur show at the Oak Theatre in Chicago in February 1939. Once a grand vaudeville palace, by the time the duo made their debut it was little more than a fading glory.

The movie that was being shown that winter night at the Oak was *Swing Time* starring Fred Astaire and Ginger Rogers. During those waning days of vaudeville, theaters such as the Oak were called "presentation houses," where various acts were "presented" between movies. On Friday nights, some theaters offered amateur shows as extra attractions where just-getting-started young ones could get some early exposure.

Fosse thought Astaire to be the perfect dancer. Fosse and Grass mimicked Astaire; they stared up at the screen "sidewise" and copied his moves. When the music from the orchestra pit started, the Riff Brothers would take the stage themselves, performing a light dance routine before Fosse took a solo turn to "Stars and Stripes Forever," pantomiming gunfire while donning a soldier's cap. For their grand finale, the "brothers" did their best to dazzle the audience with their fanciest moves. The whole act lasted eleven minutes. Bob Fosse was all of thirteen years old.

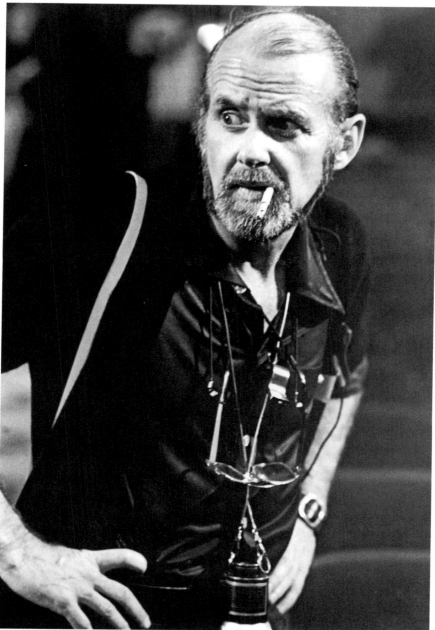

Classic Bob Fosse on the set of *All That Jazz*: a camera dangling from his neck and the
ubiquitous cigarette hanging from his lip.   *Photofest*

Learning the Trade

Fosse learned his dancing trade at the Chicago Academy of Theatre Arts, originally located in a couple of rooms in a converted apartment above a drugstore at the corner of Montrose and Ashland, which was a short walk from his house (the school later moved to 1961 West Lawrence Avenue). Frederic Weaver, its dapper manager, preferred pinstripe suits, red bow ties, vests, and spats. "With the added accents of a monocle and a small, waxed mustache, he looked like a threadbare Adolphe Menjou," writes Fosse biographer Martin Gottfried. Perhaps in an effort to add an element of class to his neighborhood academy, he spoke with a "vaguely" English accent.

Report card for five-year-old Robert Fosse at Ravenswood Elementary School in Chicago. Offense: "Did not get out of bed."

Everyone seemed to love the avuncular Weaver. Fosse in particular looked up to him and saw him as a mentor, a father figure. Best of all, he was Fosse's entrée to show business, the Chicago variety at least. His father, Cy, was a salesman who tried his hand at show business but failed. He played the spoons; his brother—Fosse's uncle—played the piano and sang barbershop quartet. They made the rounds of "third-rate vaudeville circuit," but that was the extent of it.

As a youngster, Fosse had started to smoke the Camels that were to become a lifelong habit, the cigarette dangling from the corner of his mouth, a habit that he borrowed from Weaver. Weaver would put a cigarette on his lip and forget it was there. Fosse, always observant, liked the way it looked. Cigarettes and work went hand in hand. Best of all, he thought, they made him look cool.

Weaver bought the academy in 1934. Its curriculum emphasized tap, toe, and acrobatic dancing. He hired Marguerite Comerford, his common-law wife, to head the dance faculty. She had been a dancer with the Tiller line, a chorus known for their kick line and popular on the Chicago vaudeville circuit as well as in Weimar Berlin. It was Comerford who taught the eight-year old Fosse his first dance steps.

Miss Comerford, as she was known, was "the most elegant woman Bobby had ever known," contends Fosse biographer Sam Wasson. But there were others at the academy that gave Fosse an education the Chicago public schools could not. Jack Halloran, an emcee, showed Fosse how to handle a microphone. There was a clown by the name of Chris who taught his charges how to fall down without getting hurt. Local radio personality Gilbert Ferguson taught the academy students the fine art of proper enunciation. All of these tricks and traits would prove helpful for young Bobby Fosse's future career.

Fosse adored Miss Comerford but he could be stubborn at times, or perhaps it was just his natural dance instincts—even at that young age—coming out. He insisted, for example, on holding his hands straight up when he danced so that his palms faced the audience, in imitation of his heroes Al Jolson and Eddie Cantor. Comerford insisted that he spread his arms wide and keep his fingers together—she scolded him for what she considered a sloppy technique—but instead he kept his elbows in and spread his fingers apart, his elbows tucked closely to his sides. He was adamant about his fingers being open.

One of the academy's best ballet dancers was Charles Grass. Weaver teamed Fosse up with him, and before long they even had a name, the Riff Brothers, an homage to the Nicholas Brothers. Their costumes came from a secondhand clothing store on Maxwell Street: dress suits, white dinner jackets, dress shirts, suspenders, and bow ties with wing collars. Charlie's aunt Rita then custom tailored them to the right fit. They would wear black tails and starched collars or white dinner jackets. They would do entertaining dance tricks. In addition to their dance routines, Fosse also wrote and edited the academy's newsletter, *CATA Gossip*.

At a young age, Bobby Fosse was turning into a perfectionist. He would rehearse his routines every day after school and on weekends. He committed himself to the work, practicing over and over again in front of a mirror. With Weaver, Fosse and Grass also worked on magic tricks: flowers coming out of their sleeve; a chair dance. Fosse practiced dancing on the staircase at the academy, much like one of his other dancing heroes, Bill "Bojangles" Robinson.

Even as an elementary student, Bobby Fosse knew how to separate his public self from his private self. He kept his after-hours training at the academy to himself. None of his friends at Ravenswood Elementary School knew about his secret showbiz life. If they did, they would have belittled him or called him a sissy.

The Riff Brothers also shared bills with strippers. "I still remember the first night we got paid," Fosse told *Chicago Tribune* theater critic Glenna Syse. "We danced in five separate joints in one evening and we walked away with eight bucks." At thirteen, he worked as an emcee at numerous strip joints, "burlesque places," he said, outside Chicago in cities like St. Louis, Des Moines, and Rockford and Springfield, Illinois.

The "brothers" played so many amateur shows in Chicago, notes Fosse biographer Martin Gottfried, that they were invited to appear on the Morris B. Sachs Amateur Hour, a popular show broadcast on WGN Radio. This was a tap-dancing act on radio, not an unusual thing, adds Gottfried, at a time in those pre-television days when the audience had to use their imagination.

Much of the seedy cabaret atmosphere that Fosse captured in his movies and in the theater comes from his real-life experiences in Chicago. He was inspired by the striptease dancers he saw in clubs like the Silver Cloud on

A young Bob Fosse (left) and Charlie Grass (right) as the very dapper Riff Brothers. *Rosemary Tirio collection.*   *Courtesy of Rosemary Tirio*

Milwaukee Avenue, the Gaiety Village on Western Avenue, the Cuban Village on Wabash Avenue, or at the Bijou. Later Fosse would refer to his "strange, schizophrenic childhood" as being "a pull between Sunday School and my wicked underground life."

The Riff Brothers played the local vaudeville circuit, including the Englewood Theatre, the Chicago Theatre, the Regal Theatre, the Milford Theatre, the Portage Theater, and the Oriental Theatre. They also played at American Legion clubs, for the Masons, and at Moose lodges. They played amateur shows too at the Belmont, the Admiral, the Harding, the Terminal, and the Commodore. They even played in the city's smaller nightclubs even though they were underage. They began performing every weekend, doing their homework in the back of a car as they were whisked away to theater after theater. "I played every two-bit beer joint in the Midwest," Fosse once said.

Fosse and Grass took their rehearsals seriously. One routine involved using a derby: juggling it, flipping it onto his head, rolling it down his arm; or practice twirling their canes. They methodically worked on their dance steps. Even at a young age, Fosse fostered the image of a cool, urbane sophisticate, a cigarette dangling from a corner of his mouth.

"Hold Everything! A Streamlined Extravaganza in Two Parts" was possibly the first time Fosse received credit as a choreographer. Held in 1943 at the academy, the dance numbers were credited to Fosse. Among the routines he choreographed was a glitzy rendition, a fan dance, of "That Old Black Magic" performed by the Glamour Girls, consisting of four teenage girls in slinky gowns with oversized, black ostrich feather fans, which he copied from a movie called *Star Spangled Rhythm*. He had seen it six times, but the ostrich fans, says Gottfried, were his own idea. The fans came from striptease dancers that the Riff Brothers met at the various striptease clubs that Weaver had booked for them, places like the Silver Cloud or the Gaiety Village. But Fosse had also seen striptease dancers when he sneaked into Minsky's Burlesque at Lake and Van Buren. His older brother, Buddy, took him to the Rialto, another burlesque house on State Street, which was also run by the Minskys. It was at these types of venues where he first witnessed the broad pratfalls and vulgar slapstick routines that would later inspire him both onstage and on the big screen.

Minsky's
Before *The French Connection*, before *The Exorcist*, William Friedkin directed the musical comedy *The Night They Raided Minsky's* in 1968, a fictional account of the invention of the striptease at Minsky's Burlesque in New York in 1925.

The movie tells the story of a young Amish girl from Pennsylvania named Rachel Schpitendavel played by Britt Ekland (no less), who arrives in the Lower East Side with the intent of becoming a dancer. Rachel's dances. though, are biblically based, which does not go over too well on the burlesque stages of New York. Even so, she auditions at Minsky's.

The plot twist is that the younger Minsky (played by an ebullient Elliott Gould in his film debut) and Minsky's star performer Raymond Paine (Jason Robards) create a plan to fool the movie's moral crusader Vance Fowler (Denholm Elliott), who wants to shut the theater down on moral grounds. Minsky advertises Rachel as the notorious Mademoiselle Fifi who, they promise, will perform the dance "that drove a million Frenchmen wild"—all in an attempt to humiliate Fowler. Basically, it's a publicity stunt to bring in more customers.

During the rehearsals, though, Paine and his sidekick, Chick (the wonderful English comedian Norman Wisdom in his American film debut), fall in love with Rachel as they try to show her the ins and outs of burlesque. The plot thickens when Rachel's father (Harry Andrews) arrives in town, in search of his waylaid daughter. The movie reaches its climax when Rachel goes onstage after her humiliated father has called her a whore and she comes to the realization that the Minskys are using her for their own purposes. As her father tries to drag her offstage, he accidentally tears her dress. The increasingly excited crowd encourages her, and feeling a sense of empowerment for the first time in her life, she

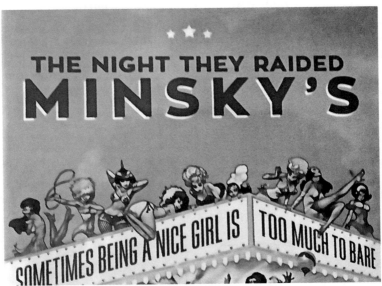

The Night They Raided Minsky's was director William Friedkin's entertaining homage to New York burlesque. The 1968 movie starred Jason Robards, Britt Ekland, Bert Lahr, and the wonderful Norman Wisdom.   *Author collection*

actually begins to strip. When she sees Raymond leaving the theater, she calls out to him and raises her arms, which inadvertently leads to a "wardrobe malfunction." Shocked and alarmed, Fowler blows his whistle. The raid is on.

According to Morton Minsky, a raid actually did take place at one of the Minsky theaters in April 1925, but it was one of many raids on the establishment. Indeed, Minsky's theater had been raided for the first time years earlier, in 1917. But the Mademoiselle Fifi in the movie was an actual person, based on a woman by the name of Mary Dawson, also from Pennsylvania, the daughter of a police officer and a Quaker to boot. Dawson always insisted, however, that she was not a stripper and never did anything risqué.

Regular Minsky patrons during the Prohibition era included John Dos Passos, Robert Benchley, George Jean Nathan, and Hart Crane. Many famous comics were hired by the Minsky brothers, such as Phil Silvers, Zero Mostel, Morey Amsterdam, Red Buttons, Red Skelton, and Abbott and Costello. Stripper Gypsy Rose Lee also performed.

The songs in the movie were written by Charles Strouse, who had won a Tony for *Bye Bye Birdie*. *The Night They Raided Minsky's* was reportedly the first musical shot entirely on location in New York. A block of East 26th Street between First and Second Avenues was changed into the Lower East Side of the 1920s. The actual theater scenes were shot in the Gayety Theater (now a movie theater) on Second Avenue, also on the Lower East Side. It originally presented Yiddish theater and was then a burlesque house until the 1960s. In the late 1960s, it became an off-Broadway theater and presented the musical *Oh! Calcutta!*, which became famous for its full-frontal nudity.

The movie also featured Bert Lahr, the Cowardly Lion himself, in his last role. Lahr was a veteran of burlesque.

Burlesque, a type of cabaret, featured comedy sketches, variety acts, chorus line dancing, and strippers. New York mayor Fiorello LaGuardia closed down the burlesque houses in 1939. The Minsky family, though, also had burlesque venues across the country—in Miami, Chicago, and New Orleans. On Chicago's State Street, Minsky's Burlesque Theatre featured dancers with names like Lili St. Cyr—the kind of places where a young Bob Fosse hung out in his formative years. In fact, there were plenty of vaudeville houses and strip clubs on State Street, especially near the corner of State and Van Buren.

Minsky's, a stage adaptation, opened in February 2009 at the Ahmanson Theatre in Los Angeles. Although quite different from the movie, the score bears a musical resemblance to Kander and Ebb's songs in *Cabaret* and *Chicago*.

Bob Fosse's Chicago

"I'm a Chicago boy," Bob Fosse told Chicago theater critic Glenna Syse. "I am still guided by my early influences and I remember my family and those young days with great affection."

Robert Louis Fosse was born on June 23, 1927, at Chicago's Augustana Hospital, at Lincoln and Armitage in the Lincoln Park neighborhood (the hospital closed in 1989 and has been demolished). Fosse claimed he was named after the Scots writer Robert Louis Stevenson. He was the son of Cyril "Cy" Fosse, whose parents were from Norway, and Sara Alice "Sadie" Stanton, an Irish Catholic. Sara was born in Ireland but brought to America as a child. The family sang Norwegian folk songs at Christmas, and Sadie learned to cook Norwegian dishes, including her husband's favorite, *rasperboller*, a broth with dumplings. Cy Fosse was a song plugger in his youth—he would perform song publishers' songs at various clubs around town—a vaudeville singer, and later a salesman.

Fosse would recall his "strange, schizophrenic childhood . . . a pull between Sunday school and my wicked underground life." Years later, Fosse would describe himself as, "a very religious kid. I mean, I did know all the Bible verses, I really believed that there was a God who was there watching over me all the time, who knew whether I was thinking the bad thoughts, impure thoughts."

Fosse was considered the "good boy" in the family. "My older brother had been in trouble—nothing serious. Stealing cars for a joyride, you know. I was not allowed to get a bad mark or swear around the house. I don't know how much living up to those standards screwed up my personality but I'm sure it did. . . ."

His showbiz childhood left its scars. "I think it's done me a lot of harm, being exposed to things that early that I shouldn't have been exposed to . . . it left some scar that I have not quite been able to figure out."

Numerous buildings associated with Fosse are still standing in Chicago:

4428 North Paulina Street: red stone three-story house. Fosse's childhood home.

666 West Sheridan Road, near the corner of Sheridan and Pine Grove. The Fosses moved from their Paulina Street home to a larger "fifteen-room stone house," according to Martin Gottfried, a short walk from Lake Michigan. The house no longer exists, having been replaced by a garage.

Ravenswood Elementary School, 4332 N. Paulina Avenue. The Fosse family home on Paulina was a short walk away.

Amundsen High School, 5110 N. Damen Avenue. Fosse, a Norwegian American, attended the high school named after the great Norwegian explorer, Roald Amundsen.

Bob Fosse's childhood home, 4428 N. Paulina Street, Chicago.   *Photo by author*

Chicago Academy of Theatre Arts, 4354 N. Ashland Avenue; it later moved to
    1961 W. Lawrence Avenue, which is now a strip mall.
St. Chrysostom's Episcopal Church, 1424 N. Dearborn Parkway in the Gold
    Coast. Fosse married Marian Niles here in 1947. Buddy Hackett served as
    one of the ushers. After the wedding ceremony, the entire cast of the musical
    revue *Call Me Mister* went back to the Fosse homestead for dinner. Fosse's old
    Amundsen High School gang was invited to a reception onstage at the former
    Blackstone Theatre, in downtown Chicago, after the show.
Fosse Way sign. One is down the street from the Fosse family home at the corner
    of Paulina and Sunnyside; the other is outside the Private Bank Theatre (18 W.
    Monroe Street) near the corner of State Street.

Four days after Pearl Harbor was bombed, two of Fosse's brothers
enlisted: Buddy joined the Seabees, Edward the Army. Later, Don was

drafted. Despite his brothers going off to war, his mother desired a bigger place since she wanted all of the military wives and children to stay together. The family moved to 666 Sheridan Road, a fifteen-room stone house.

In 1942, the renowned theater director George Abbott was in Chicago with the national company of the Broadway musical *Best Foot Forward*, a college show choreographed by a young Gene Kelly that had parts for younger performers. Weaver wrote to Abbott and asked for an audition for the Riff Brothers. Abbott's stage manager replied and asked them to appear at the downtown Studebaker Theatre for the audition. They didn't get the parts, but a dozen years later Fosse choreographed *The Pajama Game* for the same George Abbott.

Ambitious

Fosse attended Amundsen High School on Chicago's North Side (Charles Grass was a year behind Fosse at Lakeview High School, also on the North Side). Fosse was a popular figure on campus. He won sports letters for the swimming and track teams, and he played on the football team (for all of a week, according to Gottfried). In October 1943, he was elected president of his senior class. In a mock election, the high school newspaper, the *Amundsen Log*, also voted him as best personality. Ironically, someone else, Wally Hein, was chosen as best dancer.

During his senior year, he joined with a few other friends—George Foutris and Socky Marcos—and imitated the Andrew Sisters' popular recording "Bei Mir Bist du Schoen (Means That You're Grand)." George was Maxine Andrews, Socky Laverne, and Fosse, Patti. While the record played, they lip synched and dressed up in women's clothes. They performed these Andrews Sisters parodies at senior hall shows, eventually even adopting a name, the Three Fakers, and expanded their repertoire to the Mills Brothers' "Up a Lazy River" and Glenn Miller's "Juke Box Saturday Night."

But Fosse was ambitious and driven. He knew the Riff Brothers couldn't last forever. When the act split up, Fosse went on his own and played "in every joint" in Chicago that would take him. "All the terrible theaters," he once told *Variety*. "I remember the first place, the Silver Cloud. They had the strip teasers, the comic and me. I would dance. When the war came along, all the comics had to go. I became the youngest emcee in Chicago. I copied my dance act from anybody I could steal from. Astaire. . . ."

By the time Fosse was ready to graduate from Amundsen, he knew what he wanted to do with his life: to become a professional dancer and enlist

THE AMUNDSEN LOG

Vol. XII. No. 3

Amundsen High School, Chicago, Illinois

October 5, 1944

BOB FOSSE PRESIDENT

Record Pictures Of All Students Taken Oct. 4, 5

All the high and mighty upperclass men know the why and wherefores concerning the school identification pictures, so this is mainly for the newcomers and to remind the absent-minded.

These pictures are made for the records in the main office. They are to be taken October 4 and 5. Now that the date is known, there is no excuse for the girls not coming all slicked up and the boys can at least wear a tie and get a haircut. Students will be taken to the

Mr. Kapsalis Win' 2 Yr. Fellowship

Amundsen will miss Mr. Pet Kapsalis, popular foreign lan teacher, who left the staff S ber 29 af ing her years. I salls ha a two lowsh' searc at Hop sl, pl h'

Mr. P. Kapsalis

line Amundsen to

Right, Standing: Soccy Markos, Helen Klier, Johnny Stewart, Dave and George Foutris. *Seated:* Stanley Carlfeldt, Bob Fosse, Janet Klopfer, George Kutselas and Mrs. Lenore Dolejs, Sponsor.

"Bob Fosse President" proclaims Amundsen High School's newspaper, *The Amundsen Log*. Fosse is in the second row, second from right.

Author collection

in the Navy. Fosse and Grass played military shows at Fort Sheridan, at the USO on Washington Street downtown, and at the Great Lakes Naval Training Center.

After his stint in the navy, he moved to New York, where he took acting and dancing classes with the assistance of the GI Bill. He auditioned for a part in the touring company of ex-GIs doing *Call Me Mister* across the United States. Its cast included a tap dancer by the name of Marian Niles—who would become his first wife—and two up-and-coming comics, Carl Reiner and Buddy Hackett. The ebullient Hackett introduced Fosse to New York's nightclubs and dance halls. In New York, he met Joe Papirofsky, who later changed his name to Joe Papp. He toured the Pacific with Papp's show *Tough Situation*.

He played the lead in a summer stock production of *Pal Joey*. The character was someone that Fosse would have recognized: a second-rate entertainer who doubles as a dancer and emcee in shabby nightclubs. And more to the point, *Pal Joey* was set in Chicago. The original 1940 Broadway production had made Gene Kelly, one of Fosse's heroes, a star. Fosse was hoping for the same. But by the time the Broadway revival opened in early 1952 at the Broadhurst Theatre—the same theater that *Cabaret* would play at in 1966—the lead went to an actor named Harold Lang. Fosse was Lang's understudy.

Lang never missed a show; Fosse couldn't catch a break.

Out West

Fosse had wanted to be the next Gene Kelly. He went out West, trying to make it in the film industry. His screen test was a role also associated with Kelly: Harry in William Saroyan's *The Time of Your Life*. He was offered a seven-year contract with MGM. According to Gottfried, he bought himself a red Chevrolet convertible, "which he named Baby and drove to the Culver City studio each morning." But his experiences as an MGM contract player with small roles in *Give the Girl a Break*, *The Affairs of Dobie Gillis*, and *Kiss Me Kate* led nowhere, and before long he returned to New York.

Even so, *Kiss Me Kate* proved crucial. The *Kiss Me Kate* dance number, Cole Porter's "From This Moment On," involved three couples, Ann Miller and Tommy Rall, Jeanne Coyne and Bobby Van, and Carol Haney and Fosse. Fosse choreographed the Haney segment. If his choreography and signature moves have a creation date, this could be it (although his days as a member of the Riff Brothers could also be considered the starting point).

Haney was a disciple of the Hollywood choreographer Jack Cole, who Denny Martin Flinn has called "America's most influential jazz choreographer." Haney introduced Fosse to Cole's "dance language." With Cole as a foundation, Fosse went his own way by creating his own singular style:

Jackson and Beyoncé

Bob Fosse was one of Michael Jackson's heroes. "You've changed the face of dance," he told him over lunch one day. Jackson took a few tips from the Fosse playbook. Fosse biographer Sam Wasson cites a few examples of the evidence: "the pulled-down Fedora," the "shoulder isolations," the "groinology," as he calls it.

Jackson wanted Fosse to direct the "Thriller" music video, but Fosse turned him down because he thought he was "too weird."

Beyoncé has also channeled Bob Fosse. The singer's popular video "Single Ladies (Put a Ring on It)," for example, was influenced by Fosse's work, specifically "Mexican Breakfast," while her 2007 "Get Me Bodied" video recalls Fosse's "The Rich Man's Frug" from *Sweet Charity*.

shoulders moving in unison, knees slightly bent, inverted toes and knees, a knee slide with arms half outstretched, elbows tucked in, limp wrists, palms out, fingers spread, and, as Gottfried notes, a "Riff Brothers finish."

He left Los Angeles to move to New York and started choreographing. "I was pretty good as a dancer," he told Syse, "but not good enough." Years later, after he was famous as a director, he had a small scene in Stanley Donen's *The Little Prince* as a "dapper snake who dances in the Sahara."

Fosse's first big break was choreographing the stage production of *The Pajama Game* in 1954. "I just remember being scared as hell," he told Syse. "I lied about how much choreography I had done." He was way over his head, and he knew it. But he also liked the challenge of it even when it scared him to death. Fosse also earned his first Tony for *The Pajama Game*.

The Pajama Game was based on the novel *7½ Cents* by Richard Bissell and set in an Iowa pajama factory. The highlight of the production was a number called "Steam Heat," consisting of a trio of dancers dressed in Chaplinesque little tramp clothes: matching short black pipestem trousers that revealed white socks in black shoes, white gloves, and derby hats, their pelvises out, their knees bent, their arms dangling. It was classic Fosse, but nobody knew that yet.

Fosse still made the occasional movie—he is credited as Robert Fosse in the musical version of *My Sister Eileen*—but his heart, and future, lay behind the camera and on Broadway.

Jack Cole

Some argue that Fosse borrowed—stole?—from Jack Cole, or what Fosse himself once described as "a maze of various influences." Although not as well known today, Cole was a major figure in movie choreography during the heyday of the Hollywood musical. He choreographed Rita Hayworth in the 1946 movie *Gilda* and Marilyn Monroe and Jane Russell in *Gentlemen Prefer Blondes* (that's his handiwork in Monroe's "Diamonds Are a Girl's Best Friend"). Cole was the subject of a retrospective in early 2016, *All That Jack (Cole)* at the Museum of Modern Art (MOMA) in New York. He was considered the first choreographer to bring jazz movement to musical theater. Among the other movies he choreographed are *Down to Earth* (1947), *On the Riviera* (1951), and *The I Don't Care Girl* (1953).

In 1955, he choreographed *Damn Yankees* for George Abbott. That's where he met his third wife, Gwen Verdon, who he married in 1960 (a previous marriage to dancer Joan McCracken ended in divorce). Fosse also appeared—briefly—in the film adaptation of *Damn Yankees*. The year he married Verdon was also the year he was both director and choreographer of the musical *Redhead,* and he was the choreographer of the 1961 musical *How to Succeed in Business Without Really Trying,* starring gap-toothed Robert Morse.

Fosse directed and choreographed *Sweet Charity* on Broadway and made his directorial debut in 1969 with the film adaptation, starring Shirley MacLaine. *Cabaret,* in 1972, was only his second film, but the following year it won eight Academy Awards, including best director. That same year, Fosse won a Tony for *Pippin* and an Emmy for directing Liza Minnelli's television concert, *Liza with a Z*—the so-called Triple Crown.

Life After Cabaret

After *Cabaret,* Fosse returned to his show business roots by directing *Lenny* (1974), a biopic of the acerbic comedian Lenny Bruce, starring Dustin Hoffman. *Lenny* was nominated for best picture. Fosse himself was once again nominated for best director. But it's Fosse's musicals that have been his most enduring legacy.

All That Jazz

Fosse's *All That Jazz* (1979) was largely autobiographical. The film, with a script by Robert Alan Aurthur and Fosse, was inspired by Fosse's effort to edit his film *Lenny* while simultaneously staging the Broadway musical *Chicago.*

Roy Scheider plays Joe Gideon, Fosse's alter ego, the unflattering portrait of a womanizing, drug-addicted choreographer-director ("It's showtime, folks!' Gideon likes to say).

Gideon wears the Fosse uniform of black shirt, black boots, and black trousers; a lit cigarette hangs from his lip. The opening song sets the mood: "On Broadway." The movie recalls Fosse's own Chicago childhood with flashbacks to his early vaudeville days at sleazy Chicago strip clubs such as the Silver Cloud and echoes of the Riff Brothers outfit (top hat, white trousers, and white shirt).

"Nothing I ever do is good enough. . . . It's not anything enough," Gideon confides to the angel, his heavenly therapist, played by Jessica Lange, reflecting Fosse's own insecurities. Numerous details—small and large—in the film are taken from Fosse's own life and career—and influences: a poster of Dietrich in *The Blue Angel* poster hangs on the wall in Joe's New York flat; "Everything Old Is New Again" is a dance routine with Joe's ex-wife and dance partner; Fosse's ex-girlfriend Ann Reinking plays the part of Katie Jagger, Joe's girlfriend; the rough treatment of the character of Victoria Porter echoes Fosse's own treatment of dancer Jennifer Nairn Smith during rehearsals of *Pippin*.

Like Fosse, Joe Gideon is Fosse obsessed with music and sex, sex and music. We watch the teenaged Joe tap dancing on sleazy burlesque stages, wearing a top hat and white shirt and trousers. Backstage, strippers come on to him, much like Fosse himself described his Saturday morning-Sunday night teenage years. Fosse, the film's cowriter, even uses the actual name of one of the Chicago clubs where he performed: the Silver Cloud. And like Fosse's own mother, Gideon's mother, insists her Joey is the family good boy, an innocent waif.

All That Jazz also recreates scenes from Fosse's own career. The editing of *Lenny* (called *The Stand-Up* in the film) is over budget and late just as Fosse's *Lenny* was while he was staging *Chicago* on Broadway.

All That Jazz won four Academy Awards, and Fosse received his third Oscar nomination for best director.

The End

Fosse's final film was *Star 80* (1983), a searing, no-holds-barred biopic about slain *Playboy* playmate Dorothy Stratten starring Mariel Hemingway. Three years later, Fosse directed, wrote, and choreographed the Broadway musical *Big Deal*. Despite being nominated for five Tony awards, and winning for best choreography, it closed after only sixty-nine performances.

Fosse died on September 23, 1987, from a heart attack. At the time of his premature death, he was in negotiations to film an adaptation of *Chicago*. Various names were attached to the project, including Madonna and Charlize Theron. Playwright Nicholas Hytner and Wendy Wasserstein even wrote a script and began shopping it around with Theron as the lead. "At one point," Kander told Greg Lawrence, "Liza [Minnelli] and Goldie [Hawn] wanted to do the movie. Liza was going to be Roxie, and Goldie was going to be Velma." They had performed "All That Jazz" on their television special, *Goldie and Liza Together.* Larry Gelbart, of *MASH* fame, had written a screenplay.

Dance Moves

Best Fosse choreography/appearances on stage or screen:

- "Steam Heat" in *The Pajama Game*
- "Lola" in *Damn Yankees*
- "Big Spender" in *Sweet Charity*
- "Rich Man's Frug" in *Sweet Charity*
- "Mein Herr" in *Cabaret*
- "Snake in the Grass" in *The Little Prince*

The Fosse Look

You know it as soon as you see it: the Fosse Look. But just what exactly is the Fosse Look? And how did it come about?

Fosse had a unique style of dancing and numerous signature moves.

His teacher Frederic Weaver particularly liked old vaudeville acts such as Pat Rooney Jr. and Joe Frisco. Rooney was part of a family of dancers. Rooney's dance style was unique, popular, and widely imitated. He shoved his hands into his trouser pockets, hoisted his trouser legs, and danced a soft-shoe across the stage, usually to an Irish tune.

Frisco (1889–1958), born Louis Wilson Joseph in downstate Illinois, was a comedian and a dancer. He was such a famous figure at the time that F. Scott Fitzgerald even mentioned him in *The Great Gatsby*. His trademarks were a derby, a cigar, and "a stutter." He was a regular on the vaudeville circuit during the 1920s and 1930s, dancing a style called the hootchy-kootch, "a sliding, sidewise, slithering kind of shuffle. Many years later, Bob would copy it shamelessly," claims Martin Gottfried. What's more, Frisco was partial to a derby hat, and he usually had a cigar hanging from his mouth. He often performed in front of a bevy of beautiful young women wearing leotards, short jackets, and bowler hats. The women, like Frisco, pretended to puff on big cigars.

The Fosse Look is known for its contradictions: elegant yet funky, sensual yet witty, rhythmic yet lyrical. His influences were Balanchine, Nijinsky, Jerome Robbins, Fred Astaire, Jack Cole, as well as baseball, boxing, and horse racing. Fosse's style was so personal, so singular, so idiosyncratic that it can be described in a very specific way: his choreography was inspired by the way real people moved in daily life.

Even the Chicago weather had its effect on his dancing style. Ann Reinking, for example, once told *Chicago Sun-Times* theater critic Hedy Weiss that Fosse always remembered the brutal Chicago winters of his childhood and youth. "He had this move in which you'd walk slow motion against the wind, your shoulders hunched, your head down, your hands holding your hat."

He had names for his dance moves too: the Slouch, the Zonk, Tea Cup Hands, the Stack, the Amoeba, and, especially, the Drip.

So, here in a nutshell is the essence of the Fosse Look:

- snapping fingers
- bent knees and elbows
- slouching shoulders
- pelvic thrusts
- hitching up trousers
- broken doll step (pigeon toe legs but chest pulled up)
- shoulder roll
- turned-in feet, pigeon-toed
- black bowlers, black derbies
- white gloves
- loose, dangling fingers and hands
- pinky-in-the-air while touching the brim of a hat
- splayed, expressive hands

Other Fosse Productions

Pippin

There have been plenty of strange topics for Broadway musicals. One of the most unusual must be *Pippin*.

Pepin, or Pippin, the Hunchback, was the eldest son of Charlemagne. He had a complex relationship with his father, the king. In 792, Pepin led an unsuccessful revolt against his father with Frankish nobles. Although Charlemagne commuted his son's death sentence, he did have him exiled to a monastery.

The 1972 musical *Pippin* is very loosely based on the life of Pepin. In the stage version, though, Pippin is not a hunchback. More importantly, the revolt against his father actually succeeds. His father is assassinated and Pippin accends to the throne. Finding no meaning in his monarchical status, he practices magic and manages to resurrect his father from the dead. Still not satisfied, he considers suicide until the love of a woman gives him some semblance of happiness.

Lyrics by Stephen Schwartz. Book by Roger O. Hirson. Directed and choreographed by Bob Fosse. The show premiered at the Imperial Theatre on October 23, 1972, and ran for 1,944 performances. It closed on June 12, 1977. Original cast:

Pippin: John Rubinstein

Leading Player: Ben Vereen

Lewis: Christopher Chadman

Charles: Eric Berry

Catherine: Jill Clayburgh

Fastrada: Leland Palmer

Berthe: Irene Ryan

The Broadway revival of *Pippin* opened on April 25, 2013, and closed on January 4, 2015. The revival won four Tony Awards, including best revival of a musical, best performance by a leading actress in a musical for Patina Miller, best performance by a featured actress in a musical for Andrea Martin, and best direction of a musical for Diane Paulus.

Chicago the Musical

Based on the 1926 play of the same name by reporter Maurine Dallas Watkins, *Chicago* is set in Prohibition Chicago. Cynical and ahead of its time, *Chicago* was meant to be a satire on corruption and the rise of the so-called celebrity criminal.

The original Broadway production opened in 1975 at the 46th Street Theatre and closed in 1977. It opened to mixed reviews. The cast starred Gwen Verdon as Roxie Hart, Chita Rivera as Velma Kelly, and Jerry Orbach as Billy Flynn. It made its West End debut in 1979; it was revived on Broadway in 1996 and a year later in the West End.

The Broadway revival holds the record as the longest-running musical revival and the longest-running American musical in Broadway history.

Fred Ebb wrote the book in a "vaudeville style" for a particular reason: the characters were actual performers. What's more, Ebb told Lawrence that "every musical moment in the show was loosely modeled on someone else": Roxie was based on Helen Morgan, Velma on the Chicago moll Texas Guinan, Billy Flynn was Ted Lewis, and Mama Morton was Sophie Tucker.

Murder in Chicago

The musical *Chicago* is based on a real criminal case. Reporter (and playwright) Maurine Dallas Watkins covered the 1924 trials of Beulah Annan and Belva Gaertner, both accused of murder, for the *Chicago Tribune*. The character of Roxie Hart was based on Annan, Velma Kelly on Gaertner.

Annan was just twenty-three when she was accused of murdering Harry Kalstedt in April 1924. She was found not guilty a month later (justice moved swiftly back then). Meanwhile, in a separate case, Gaertner was charged with the murder of her lover and married man Walter Law, who was found slumped over the steering wheel of Gaertner's abandoned car on March 12, 1924. Albert Annan, Beulah's husband, was the inspiration for Amos Hart. But Gaertner, a cabaret singer and divorcée, was also acquitted, three months later. Lawyers William Scott Stewart and W. W. O'Brien were the models for the flamboyant Billy Flynn, a composite character.

Watkins wrote column after column on the trials of the so-called jazz babies. The public loved reading about the sordid details. They were so popular, in fact, that Watkins wrote a play about them. Watkins's *Chicago* made it all the way to Broadway a quick two years later, in 1926, running for 172 performances. Then it toured around the country, including a run in Los Angeles where a little-known actor by the name of Clark Gable played the Amos Hart role. Cecil B. DeMille produced a silent film version of *Chicago* in 1927, which was later remade as *Roxie Hart* in 1942, starring Ginger Rogers.

In the 1960s, Gwen Verdon broached the subject with her then husband Bob Fosse of adapting the *Chicago* material into a musical. Fosse tried numerous times to buy the rights from Watkins, but as a born-again Christian, she refused his offers. It wasn't until her death in 1969 that her estate sold the rights to Verdon, Fosse, and producer Richard Fryer. With the rights in hand, John Kander and Fred Ebb worked on the musical score.

Chicago: A Musical Vaudeville
Original Broadway Production (1975) Musical Selections
Act I

- "Overture": Orchestra
- "All That Jazz": Velma Kelly and Company
- "Funny Honey": Roxie Hart, Amos Hart, and Sergeant Fogarty
- "Cell Block Tango": Velma and the Girls

- "When You're Good to Mama": Matron "Mama" Morton
- "Tap Dance": Roxie, Amos, and the Boys
- "All I Care About": Billy Flynn and the Girls
- "A Little Bit of Good": Mary Sunshine
- "We Both Reached for the Gun": Billy, Roxie, and Mary Sunshine
- "Roxie": Roxie and the Boys
- "I Can't Do It Alone": Velma
- "Chicago After Midnight": Orchestra
- "My Own Best Friend": Roxie and Velma

Act II

- "I Know a Girl": Velma
- "Me and My Baby": Roxie and Company
- "Mr. Cellophane": Amos Hart
- "When Velma Takes the Stand": Velma and the Boys
- "Razzle Dazzle": Billy and Company
- "Class": Velma and Morton
- "Nowadays": Roxie
- Finale: "Nowadays"/"R.S.V.P."/"Keep It Hot": Roxie and Velma

Revival Production (1996)

Act I

- "Overture": Orchestra
- "All That Jazz": Velma Kelly and Company
- "Funny Honey": Roxie Hart
- "Cell Block Tango": Velma and the Murderesses
- "When You're Good to Mama": Matron "Mama" Morton
- "Tap Dance": Roxie, Amos, and the Boys
- "All I Care About": Billy Flynn and the Girls
- "A Little Bit of Good": Mary Sunshine
- "We Both Reached for the Gun": Billy, Roxie, Mary Sunshine, and the Reporters
- "Roxie": Roxie and the Boys
- "I Can't Do It Alone": Velma
- "I Can't Do It Alone (Reprise)": Velma
- "Chicago After Midnight": Orchestra
- "My Own Best Friend": Roxie and Velma
- "Finale Act I: All That Jazz (Reprise)": Velma

Act II

- "Entr'acte": Orchestra

- "I Know a Girl": Velma
- "Me and My Baby": Roxie and Company
- "Mr. Cellophane": Amos Hart
- "When Velma Takes the Stand": Velma and the Boys
- "Razzle Dazzle": Billy and Company
- "Class": Velma and Mama Morton
- "Nowadays/Hot Honey Rag": Velma and Roxie
- "Finale Act II: All That Jazz (Reprise)": Company

Major Characters and Original Performers

Roxie Hart
Gwen Verdon (Broadway)
Antonia Ellis (West End)
Ann Reinking (Broadway Revival)
Ruthie Henshall (West End Revival)

Velma Kelly
Chita Rivera (Broadway)
Jenny Logan (West End)
Bebe Neuwirth (Broadway Revival)
Ute Lemper (West End Revival)

Billy Flynn
Jerry Orbach (Broadway)
Ben Cross (West End)
James Naughton (Broadway Revival)
Henry Goodman (West End Revival)

Amos Hart
Barney Martin (Broadway)
Don Fellows (West End)
Joel Grey (Broadway Revival)
Nigel Planer (West End Revival)

Matron "Mama" Morton
Mary McCarty (Broadway)
Hope Jackman (West End)
Marcia Lewis (Broadway Revival)
Meg Johnson (West End Revival)

Ann Reinking played the role of Roxie Hart in the revival of *Chicago*, which opened in 1996. For the revival, Reinking choreographed the dances "in the style of Bob Fosse."

Among the performers who have appeared in *Chicago* during its Broadway run are Michelle Williams, Usher, Brandy, Michael C. Hall, Jerry Springer, Brooke Shields, Patrick Swayze, Rita Wilson, Alan Thicke, Melanie Griffith, Taye Diggs, Adam Pascal, Marilu Henner, and Sofía Vergara.

Chicago the Movie

Fosse had wanted to make a movie out of *Chicago*. After the funeral of Hugh Wheeler in California, he told John Kander that he had finally figured out how to adapt it into a movie. He said he would talk it over when they all had a chance to meet with Fred Ebb. Fosse died shortly thereafter. "What his version of the movie would have been like we will never know, because he never told anyone," Kander told Greg Lawrence.

Roxie and Velma

The movie version of *Chicago* was finally made and released in 2002, under the direction of Rob Marshall. Marshall completely rechoreographed it for the big screen. Along with screenwriter Bill Condon, he also reconceived and reinvented it. The story is the same—that of would-be chorus girl Roxie Hart (Renée Zellweger), who "bumps off" her caddish and unfaithful lover and then fights the law, and wins, with the help of a cynical lawyer Billy Flynn (Richard Gere) and then teams up with a fellow inmate Velma Kelly (Catherine Zeta-Jones) for fame and fortune. Roxie became a star by murdering someone: a shocking idea when it was first suggested in 1975. But now in Trumpian America, anything is possible.

It makes sense that Marshall reincarnated *Chicago* since Fosse did much the same thing for *Cabaret*. "*Chicago* was conceived as what Fosse called a 'musical vaudeville,'" Marshall told critic Terry Teachout. "Every number is a presentational vaudeville number. The characters aren't signing to each other—they're on stage, singing to an audience. If we'd put those characters in a living room, but still had them singing directly out to you in the theater, it wouldn't have worked. The songs have to take place on *some* sort of stage. You can't change that, or you end up with just another musical."

What Fosse did in *Cabaret*, of course, was ditch all of the book songs and place all the musical numbers on the stage of the Kit Kat Klub with the sole exception of one song in a German beer garden. What Marshall and Condon did was to place the songs in Roxie's imagination. Thus, the movie takes place in two very different places: the gritty, real-world Chicago of 1929 and Roxie's fantasy vaudeville world of the mind.

Chicago: directed by Rob Marshall and written by Bill Condon; released December 27, 2002.

Catherine Zeta-Jones as Velma

Renée Zellweger as Roxie

Richard Gere as Billy Flynn

Queen Latifah as Mama Morton

John C. Reilly as Amos Hart

Chicago won six Academy Awards, including best picture and best supporting actress for Zeta-Jones.

Chicago Goes to Tokyo

Probably one of the most unusual productions of *Chicago* was the all-female Japanese cast that performed at the Lincoln Center Festival in July 2016. Not only was the entire cast Japanese, but so was the dialogue, even as the staging and swagger owe its debt to Fosse. Founded in 1914, the Takarazuka Revue puts on nine hundred shows a year in Tokyo and its original home of Yokohama, according to Jonathan Soble in the *New York Times*.

"Cross-dressing, single-gender theater groups have a long history in Japan," notes Soble. For the women of the cast, assuming male roles is just a form of acting. It is not intended to be rebellious but rather a form of entertainment.

Dancin': 1978

Dancin' was a musical revue originally produced in 1978, a glorious tribute to American dance, featuring a variety of styles from jazz to pop. *Dancin'* was Fosse's idea. He had proposed a show with little dialogue but lots of songs and dances with a score using classical, musical theater tunes, and contemporary music. It was an extension of Fosse's *Pippin* and *Chicago* and Michael Bennett's *A Chorus Line*. It was Fosse's attempt to create a popular dance version of a ballet program. Several numbers from *Dancin'* were re-created for a later Fosse dance revue, *Fosse* (see the next section).

Dancin' opened on Broadway on March 27 1978, at the Broadhurst Theatre before transferring to the Ambassador Theatre. It ran for 1,774 performances. *Dancin'* was directed and choreographed by Bob Fosse with additional choreography by Christopher Chadman.

Act I

* "Hot August Night." Music and lyrics by Neil Diamond
* "Crunchy Granola Suite." Music and lyrics by Neil Diamond
* "Mr. Bojangles." Music and lyrics by Jerry Jeff Walker
* "Chaconne." Music by Johann Sebastian Bach
* "Ionisation." Music by Edgard Varèse

Act II

* "I Wanna Be a Dancin' Man," from the film *The Belle of New York*. Music by Johnny Mercer and Harry Warren
* "If It Feels Good, Let It Ride." Music and lyrics by Carole Bayer Sager and Melissa Manchester
* "Easy." Music and lyrics by Carole Bayer Sager and Melissa Manchester
* "I've Got Them Feelin' Too Good Today Blues." Music and lyrics by Jerry Leiber and Mike Stoller
* "Was Dog a Doughnut." Music by Cat Stevens

Act III

* "Sing, Sing, Sing." Music by Louis Prima
* "Here You Come Again." Music and lyrics by Barry Mann and Cynthia Weil
* "Gary Owen." Traditional
* "Stout Hearted Men" from *The New Moon*. Lyrics by Oscar Hammerstein II, music by Sigmund Romberg
* "Under the Double Eagle"
* "Dixie." Traditional
* "When Johnny Comes Marching Home"
* "Rally Round the Flag"
* "Pack Up Your Troubles in Your Old Kit Bag. " Lyrics by George Asaf, music by Felix Powell
* "The Stars and Stripes Forever." Music by John Philip Sousa
* "Yankee Doodle Disco"
* "Dancin'." Music by Ralph Burns

Dancin': Original Broadway Cast featured Gail Benedict, Sandahl Bergman, Karen G. Burke, René Ceballos, Christopher Chadman, Wayne Cilento, Christine Colby, Jill Cook, Gregory B. Drotar, Vicki Frederick, Linda Haberman, Richard Korthaze, Edward Love, John Mineo, Ann Reinking, Blane Savage, Charles Ward, and William Whitener.

Fosse

After his death, Fosse's colleagues continued his legacy. The dance revue *Fosse* was a compilation of dances created by Bob Fosse, taken from his nightclub days and on to the 1986 production of *Big Deal*. Chet Walker, dance captain on the 1986 revival of *Sweet Charity* and Fosse associate, and his former girlfriend Ann Reinking, re-created the dances.

The original Broadway production of *Fosse* opened at the Broadhurst Theatre on January 14, 1999, and ran for 1,093 performances. It closed on August 25, 2001. The Tony Award-winning revue featured more than two dozen selections from his work. It was directed by Richard Maltby Jr. and Ann Reinking with original choreography by Fosse. The co-choreographer was Ann Reinking with choreography re-creation by Chet Walker and dance reconstructions by Lainie Sakakura and Brad Musgrove. Gwen Verdon served as artistic adviser. In 2002, *Fosse*, featuring Reinking and Fosse veteran Ben Vereen, aired on PBS's *Great Performances* series.

A London production opened at the Prince of Wales Theatre in the West End on February 8, 2000, and ran through January 6, 2001.

Fosse Musical Selections

Act I

- "Life Is Just a Bowl of Cherries," from *Big Deal*
- "Fosse's World"
- "Bye Bye Blackbird," from *Liza with a Z*
- "From the Edge," from *Dancin'*
- "Percussion 4," from *Dancin'*
- "Big Spender," from *Sweet Charity*
- "Crunchy Granola Suite," from *Dancin'*
- "From This Moment On," from *Kiss Me, Kate*
- "Transition," inspired by *Redhead*
- "I Wanna Be a Dancin' Man," from *Dancin'*

Act II

- "Shoeless Joe Ballet," from *Damn Yankees*
- "Dancing in the Dark"
- "Steam Heat," from *The Pajama Game*
- "I Gotcha," from *Liza with a Z*
- "Rich Man's Frug," from *Sweet Charity*
- "Transition: Silky Thoughts"
- "Cool Hand Luke," from a 1968 Bob Hope television special
- "Dancin' Dan (Me and My Shadow)," from *Big Deal*
- "Nowadays/The Hot Honey Rag," from *Chicago*

Act III

- "Glory," from *Pippin*
- "Mansion Trio," from *Pippin*
- "Mein Herr," from *Cabaret*
- "Take Off with Us/Three Pas de Deux," from *All That Jazz*
- "Razzle Dazzle," from *Chicago*
- "Who's Sorry Now?," from *All That Jazz*
- "There'll Be Some Changes Made," from *All That Jazz*
- "Mr. Bojangles," from *Dancin'*
- "Life Is Just a Bowl of Cherries" (Reprise)
- "Sing, Sing, Sing," from *Dancin'*
- Curtain Call: "Beat Me Daddy, Eighth to the Bar," from *Big Deal*

Broadway Original Cast of *Fosse* featured Valarie Pettiford, Jane Lanier, Eugene Fleming, Desmond Richardson, Sergio Trujillo, Scott Wise, Kim Morgan Greene, Mary Ann Lamb, Dana Moore, Elizabeth Parkinson, Julio Agustin, Brad Anderson, Andy Blankenbuehler, Marc Calamia, Holly Cruikshank, Lisa Gajda, Scott Jovovich, Christopher R. Kirby, Dede LaBarre, Shannon Lewis, Mary MacLeod, Brad Musgrove (dance captain), Michael Paternostro, Rachelle Rak, Lainie Sakakura (dance captain), and Alex Sanchez.

Fosse Trilogy

In late 2009, Thodos Dance Chicago presented *Fosse Trilogy*, consisting of three short works choreographed by Bob Fosse for 1960s television variety shows, and mounted by Ann Reinking at the North Shore Center for the Performing Arts in Skokie, Illinois, and at the Harris Theater for Music and Dance in downtown Chicago.

Fosse Trilogy, Thodos Dance Chicago, 2009, at the Harris Theater, Chicago. Ann Reinking revived a trio of short dances by her mentor Fosse, two of which had never before been performed live.   *Author collection. Photo by Theresa Albini*

The pieces were "Mexican Breakfast," an all-female trio created for Gwen Verdon that was first performed on *The Ed Sullivan Show*; "Tijuana Shuffle," for one woman and two men, from a 1968 Bob Hope television special; and "Cool Hand Luke," which Fosse choreographed for Verdon after she gave birth to their daughter.

Liza Minnelli

Liza Minnelli desperately wanted the role of Sally Bowles in the original Broadway production of *Cabaret*. She reportedly auditioned for it twenty times. When it went to someone else—the relatively unknown English singer Jill Haworth—Minnelli didn't hide in a corner and lament her bad luck. Instead, she just incorporated the title song into her regular repertoire. She sang it on television, too: on *The Tonight Show*, on *The Hollywood Palace*.

Cabaret made Liza Minnelli a big star, a superstar, this daughter of a superstar, this offspring of Hollywood royalty. Her life would never be the same. *Cabaret*, in fact, was the high point of her career. Nothing she has done since then has even come close.

Even though Haworth might have won the coveted role, it was Minnelli who quickly became associated with the song. So when movie producer Cy Feuer was looking for someone to play Sally Bowles on the big screen, he must have been aware of Minnelli's performances of it. Either way, when he came to see her show at the Olympia Theater in Paris in December 1969, his mind was made up.

He had found his Sally Bowles.

Minnelli graced the cover of both *Newsweek* and *Time* on the same week, an unusual feat for a pop culture figure (Bruce Springsteen managed the same coup in 1975, after the release of his iconic album *Born to Run*).

Before she snared her career-defining role of Sally Bowles in *Cabaret*, Liza Minnelli was known, to many, as Judy Garland's daughter.

Previous to her star-turning role in *Cabaret*, Minnelli starred in the vastly different *The Sterile Cuckoo* (1969) as the eccentric and needy teenager Pookie Adams, for which she received an Academy Award nomination as best actress; and in Otto Preminger's bleak *Tell Me That You Love Me, Junie Moon* (1970), in which she played a young woman disfigured by burns who must learn how to cope with life and love. Earlier, she had a small part in the Albert Finney movie *Charlie Bubbles* (1967).

But *Cabaret* changed everything.

"Sally was really a tramp and not just another lovable kook," Minnelli told *Newsweek*. "She didn't want to be good, she just wanted to be a star." Sally is tough but also vulnerable with child-like qualities.

"The way Sally sings 'Cabaret'," Minnelli said, "she really is listening to it for the first time, understanding what it means. She makes a breakthrough.

Liza Minnelli as the divine Sally Bowles in *Cabaret*.   *Photofest*

That's what happened to Pookie Adams, a breakthrough to a new understanding. Those kinds of people touch me. I admire their bravery a lot. They're dealing with their own problems and I enjoy seeing their steps forward, with no self-pity."

Newsweek's S. K. Oberbeck aptly describes Minnelli's Sally as "desperately gay, promiscuous, exhibitionist," as "a bruised flower floating between the Lost Generation and the upcoming holocaust. . . . Liza sums up the seductive despair of an era."

A Star Is Born

Born in Cedars of Lebanon Hospital in Los Angeles in 1946 to Judy Garland and film director Vincente Minnelli, Liza made her film debut as a walk-on in one of her mother's films, *In the Good Old Summertime*, at the tender age of two-and-a-half years old. At seven, she danced onstage while her mother sang "Swanee." At fourteen, she starred in a high school production of *The Diary of Anne Frank*, which toured Israel, Greece, and Italy. She attended the Sorbonne at sixteen before dropping out to pursue a career in show business. In 1963, at age seventeen, she was in an off-Broadway revival of *Best Foot Forward*, her first big break. She also performed with her mother during her numerous comebacks, including a stint at the London Palladium.

At nineteen, Minnelli became Broadway's youngest Tony Award winner as best actress in *Flora, the Red Menace*, directed by George Abbott. Although it ran for only eighty-seven performances, Minnelli received the only good reviews. It was also the first time that she worked with John Kander and Fred Ebb. The duo would write other songs for her, including songs that appeared in the scores of *Lucky Lady, A Matter of Time, New York, New York*, and *Stepping Out* (1991). The same year that she appeared on Broadway she also made her nightclub debut at the Shoreham Hotel in Washington, D.C.; a few months later she played the famous Plaza in New York.

Minnelli's other major films include *Lucky Lady* (1975); *A Matter of Time* (1976), which costarred Ingrid Bergman and was directed by her father Vincente Minnelli; Martin Scorsese's *New York, New York* (1977), opposite Robert De Niro; and *Arthur* (1981). *New York, New York* was about the turbulent relationship between sax player Jimmy Doyle (De Niro) and pop singer Francine Evans (Minnelli). Kander and Ebb wrote the title song with Minnelli in mind, but it became a hit for Frank Sinatra in 1980.

Other major Broadway productions/engagements include *The Act* (1977), for which she won a Tony Award; *The Rink* (1984), for which she was nominated for a Tony; and *Liza's at the Palace*, for which she won a Tony in 2009 for best special theatrical event.

Minnelli won the Academy Award for best actress as Sally Bowles. She also won a Golden Globe Award and a BAFTA Award.

Liza with a Z: A Concert for Television

Produced by Fred Ebb and directed and choreographed by Bob Fosse, *Liza with a Z* was a concert film made specifically for television. It was filmed at the Lyceum Theatre in New York after only eight weeks of rehearsals. The film's cinematographer Owen Roizman would later win an Academy Award for his work on *The Exorcist*.

The film was broadcast on NBC on September 10, 1972. It went on to win four Emmys, including a best director nod for Fosse.

A remastered version of the film premiered on Showtime on April 1, 2006. The DVD includes a performance of "Mein Herr," which previously had been cut; and an interview with John Kander conducted by Minnelli herself.

Musical Numbers on the Original Broadcast
- "Yes" (Kander and Ebb)
- "God Bless the Child" (Herzog, Holiday)
- "Say Liza (Liza with a 'Z')" (Kander and Ebb)
- "It Was a Good Time" (Curb, David, Jarre)
- "I Gotcha" (Tex)
- "Son of a Preacher Man" (Hurley, Wilkins)
- "Ring Them Bells" (Kander and Ebb)
- "Bye Bye Blackbird" (Dixon, Henderson)
- "You've Let Yourself Go" (Aznavour)
- "My Mammy" (Donaldson, Lewis, Young)
- Cabaret medley (Kander and Ebb)

Cabaret Film Soundtrack
- "Willkommen"
- "Mein Herr"
- "Two Ladies"
- "Maybe This Time"
- "Sitting Pretty"
- "Tiller Girls"

- "Money, Money"
- "Heiraten (Married)"
- "If You Could See Her (The Gorilla Song)"
- "Tomorrow Belongs to Me"
- "Cabaret"
- "Finale"

Michael York

He heard about the role through the grapevine. Word was out that a film of the Broadway musical *Cabaret* was going to be made and that the producers were looking for a "Michael York type" to play the Christopher Isherwood role. By this time in his career, York already was an established actor. But other actors were also in the running, including Murray Head, who played the young bisexual artist in John Schlesinger's *Sunday Bloody Sunday* (1971), as well as John Hurt and Ian McKellen.

His agent, who had read the screenplay, told him not to get his hopes up. And anyway, the Isherwood character was "straight, dull, square and boring" and existed only to prop up Liza Minnelli's character, Sally Bowles.

Despite his agent's lackluster response, York auditioned for Bob Fosse and producer Cy Feuer. As it happened, he got the part. But he still hadn't read the entire screenplay. When he did, he was, in his own words, "horrified." He read the script over and over again but found no character there—no substance, nothing to base a real human being on. Brian Roberts, the revamped Isherwood, was a cipher, and a passive one at that. "Here was another introspective literate Englishman in the Darley mold, another dull foil to all the brilliant extrovert characters enlivening the story," York laments in his memoir.

He was angry at himself for accepting the role, and yet it was too late to withdraw from the film. He discussed his reservations with Fosse, who, much to York's relief, agreed with his estimation. During the rehearsal process, the characters emerged full-blown from the words written on the page. And from the junk shops along Chelsea's King's Road in London— he returned home to London while the musical numbers were being recorded—York assembled old jackets and "an ancient period raincoat" more appropriate and lived in for the era. Gwen Verdon, Fosse's wife at the time, helped Minnelli put together her own eclectic bohemian wardrobe.

The Kit Kat Klub scenes were re-created in Bavaria Studios in Munich. To York, the German technicians looked as if they themselves stepped out of a George Grosz painting. Joel Grey said much the same thing in his memoir.

Isherwood and York read the reviews of *Cabaret* when it came out in Isherwood's Santa Monica home. "To my undisguised relief he was complimentary about my performance, although less happy with the film's ambiguous sexuality, said York."

Michael York was born in 1942, in Buckinghamshire, England. Unlike Isherwood and his *Cabaret* alter ego Brian Roberts, who attended Cambridge University, York graduated with a degree in English from Oxford. After performing with the Dundee Repertory Theatre and the National Theatre, he worked in British television before making his film debut in Franco Zeffirelli's *The Taming of the Shrew* (1967) and then a year later as Tybalt in Zeffirelli's adaptation of *Romeo and Juliet* (1968). His post-*Cabaret* films included *The Three Musketeers* (1973); *England Made Me* (1973), based on Graham Greene's novel; *Lost Horizon* (1973); *The Four Musketeers* (1974); *Murder on the Orient Express* (1974); *Jesus of Nazareth* (1977); *Logan's Run* (1976); and *The Island of Dr. Moreau* (1977). His Broadway credits include Martin Sherman's *Bent* (1980), Arthur Miller's *The Crucible* (1992), and Frank McGuinness's *Someone Who'll Watch Over Me* (1993).

Marisa Berenson

Born in New York City in 1947, Marisa Berenson was one of the fashion industry's highest-paid models when she won the plum role of Natalia Landauer in *Cabaret*—and she wasn't even German (she is the granddaughter of the famous fashion designer Elsa Schiaparelli and is of Lithuanian, Italian, Swiss, and French ancestry). Other German actresses were considered, including Uschi Glas, Michaela May, Eleonore Weisgerber, and Gila von Weitershausen. Berenson had made her screen debut in Luchino Visconti's *Death in Venice* in 1971.

Berenson's other movies include Stanley Kubrick's *Barry Lyndon* (1975), Blake Edwards's *S.O.B.* (1981), and Clint Eastwood's *White Hunter Black Heart* (1990). She made her Broadway debut in Joe Mantello's 2001 revival of Noël Coward's *Design for Living*, opposite Jennifer Ehle, Dominic West, and Alan Cumming.

For her performance as Natalia Landauer in *Cabaret*, Berenson received two Golden Globe nominations, a BAFTA nomination, and an award from the National Board of Review.

Fritz Wepper and Helmut Griem

The two supporting actors in *Cabaret*, Fritz Wepper and Helmut Griem, were veterans of German television and screen.

Fritz Wepper was born in Munich in 1941. He made his acting debut at the age of eleven as Peter Pan. His breakthrough role, though, was as a young soldier in the antiwar film *Die Brucke* (1959). The movie won the Golden Globe for best foreign language film. He starred in the popular German crime series *Derrick* between 1974 and 1998 and also appeared in the German television series *Um Himmels Willen*.

Born in Hamburg, Helmut Griem performed extensively on the German stage as well as many film and television roles. His other films include *The Damned*, *The McKenzie Break*, and *Ludwig*. He died in Munich in 2004.

Other Cast Members

Other major cast members included two Fosse veterans. Both Louise Quick and Kathryn Doby appeared in the stage and movie versions of *Sweet Charity* and later appeared in Fosse's Broadway musical *Pippin* (1972). Quick had also worked as the assistant choreographer on *Liza with a Z: A Concert for Television* (1972); Doby was an assistant choreographer on Fosse's film *All That Jazz* (1979). She also appeared in the film.

The Technical Team

David Bretherton

David Bretherton (1924–2000) won an Academy Award for his frenetic editing of *Cabaret*, which featured breathtaking cross-cutting and inventive associative montage. His working relationship with Fosse at first was rocky. The dance sequences serve a thematic purpose—to comment on what's going on in Germany and to contrast the insular world of the cabaret with the increasingly violent atmosphere outside. From the start, the Emcee encourages the audience to "leave their troubles outside." As it turns out, one of Fosse's favorite musicals was John Huston's *Moulin Rouge* (1952), which also featured cuts and close-ups to re-create the frenzied dances of the famous Montmartre cabaret.

One of the most effective, and chilling, scenes involves rapid cross-cutting. The comical Bavarian slap dance is intercut, for example, with the "brutal beating" of the Kit Kat Klub owner (in an earlier scene we see him forcibly removing a Nazi from the club). The music, the slapping noises, the stomping of heavy feet choreograph the violent street "dance" as the Nazis punch and kick the owner.

An equally disturbing scene is the cross-cutting of the Emcee in drag and the Kit Kat Girls during the so-called Tiller Girls sequence. Several Nazis leave Natalia's dead dog on her doorstep and write on the sidewalk outside the gate to her building "Juden" in bright yellow letter, while chanting the word, which is a pejorative German slang for "Jews" or "Jewish. At the precise moment when she opens the door and looks down to see the dog, the dancers on the Kit Kat stage transform from a Tiller Girl-like revue into soldiers and start goose-stepping with the Emcee, dressed in drag, as their leader.

Born in Los Angeles, Bretherton served in the Air Force during World War II. After the war, he joined the editing department at Twentieth Century-Fox. His many films include *An Affair to Remember* (1957), *Peyton Place* (1957), *The Diary of Anne Frank* (1959), *The Sandpiper* (1965), *On a Clear Day You Can See Forever* (1970), *Westworld* (1973), *Save the Tiger* (1973), *That's Entertainment, Part II* (1976), *The Best Little Whorehouse in Texas* (1982), *Cannery Row* (1982), *Sea of Love* (1989), and *Malice* (1993).

Geoffrey Unsworth

Geoffrey Unsworth (1914–1978) won an Academy Award for his cinematography of *Cabaret*. Born in Lancashire, England, Unsworth was a veteran craftsman who worked for directors Michael Powell and Emeric Pressburger in Britain as a camera operator before becoming a cinematographer. He received a posthumous Academy Award for his work on Roman Polanski's *Tess* (1979).

Among his many credits are *A Night to Remember* (1958), *Becket* (1964), *Othello* (1965), *2001: A Space Odyssey* (1968), *Cromwell* (1970), *Zardoz* (1974), *Murder on the Orient Express* (1974), *Lucky Lady* (1975), *A Matter of Time* (1976), *A Bridge Too Far* (1977), *Superman* (1978), *The First Great Train Robbery* (1978), and *Superman II* (1980).

Ralph Burns

American pianist, composer, and arranger Ralph Burns (1922–2001) worked extensively with Bob Fosse. In addition to being the music supervisor on *Cabaret*, for which he won an Academy Award for best adapted score, he conducted the orchestra for Fosse's *Sweet Charity* (1969) and the musical *Pippin* (1971) and composed the film scores for Fosse's *Lenny* (1974), *All That Jazz* (1979), and *Star 80* (1983).

He also composed the film scores for *Lucky Lady* (1975), Martin Scorsese's *New York, New York* (1977), *Urban Cowboy* (1980), *Pennies from Heaven* (1981), and *My Favorite Year* (1982).

In addition, he won a second Academy Award for best adapted score for *All That Jazz* in 1979 and a Drama Desk Award in 1986 for outstanding orchestrations for *Sweet Charity* and a Tony Award in 1999 for best orchestrations for *Fosse*.

Cabaret had its world premiere on February 13, 1972, at the Ziegfield Theatre in New York.
- It grossed $41,326,446.
- Allied Artists and ABC Pictures Corp. present an ABC Pictures Corp. production
- Directed by Bob Fosse

Sally Bowles: Liza Minnelli
Brian Roberts: Michael York
Maximilian von Heune: Helmut Griem
Master of Ceremonies: Joel Grey
Fritz Wendel: Fritz Wepper
Natalia Landauer: Marisa Berenson
Fräulein Schneider: Elisabeth Neumann-Viertel
Fräulein Kost: Helen Vita
Fräulein Mayr: Sigrid von Richthofen
Bobby: Gerd Vespermann
Herr Ludwig: Ralf Wolter
Willi: Georg Hartmann
Elke: Ricky Renée
The Cantor: Estrongo Nachama
Kit-Kat Dancers:
    Kathryn Doby
    Inge Jaeger
    Angelia Koch
    Helen Velkovorska
    Gitta Schmidt
    Louise Quick
Hitler Youth Singer: Oliver Collignon

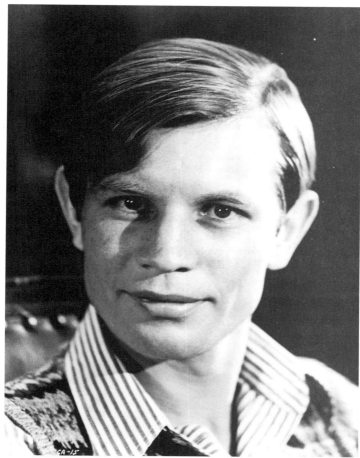

Michael York as Brian Roberts in *Cabaret* and looking very much like a young Christopher Isherwood.　　*Photofest*

Hitler Youth Singer (voice): Mark Lambert
Nazi with Collecting Box: Pierre Franckh
Woman at Party: Ellen Umlauf
Produced by Cy Feuer, Harold Nebenzal, Martin Baum
Music by John Kander and Fred Ebb
Cinematography by Geoffrey Unsworth
Film Editing by David Bretherton
Casting by Renate Neuchl
Production Design by Rolf Zehetbauer
Art Direction by Hans Jürgen Kiebach

Costume Design by Charlotte Flemming
Hair stylist/makeup artist: Susi Krause
Hair stylist/Miss Minnelli: Gus Le Pre
Hair stylist/makeup artist: Raimund Stangl
Production Manager: Pia Arnold
Unit Manager: Wolfram Kohtz
Assistant Director: Wolfgang Glattes
Assistant Director: Douglas Green
Second Assistant Director: Stefan Zürcher
Property Master: Richard Eglseder
Set Dresser: Herbert Strabel
Sound: David Hildyard
Dubbing: Robert Knudson
Dubbing: Arthur Piantadosi
Sound Editor: Doug Grindstaff
Supervising Sound Editor: James Nelson
Gaffer: Herbert Fischer
Stills: Lars Looschen
Camera Operator: Peter MacDonald
Assistant Camera: John Campbell
Wardrobe: Ille Sievers
Costume Assistant: Ute Meyer-Martin
Assistant Editor: David Ramirez
Conductor/Music Arranger/Music Supervisor: Ralph Burns
Music Editor: Illo Endrulat
Musical numbers staged by Bob Fosse
Composer/additional songs: John Kander
Music Coordinator: Raoul Kraushaar
Music Editor: Karola Storr
Music Editor: Robert N. Tracy
Choreographic Music Associate: Fred Werner
Dance Coordinator: Jutta Bell
Dances staged by Bob Fosse
Unit Publicist: Vic Heutschy
Auditor: Jane Meagher
Produced on the New York stage by Harold Prince
Dialogue Coach: Osman Ragheb
Choreographic Assistant: John Sharpe

Script Supervisor: Trudi Von Trotha
Research Consultant: Hugh Wheeler
Publicists: Michael Alpert, Virginia Lord, Myrna Post
Double for Liza Minnelli: Stephanie Daniel

What the Critics Said About the Movie

Beyond Ordinary

The world premiere of *Cabaret* was held at the Ziegfeld Theater in Manhattan on February 13, 1972. The movie received mostly excellent reviews.

Roger Ebert of the *Chicago Sun-Times* found it to be the opposite of ordinary, partly because it didn't fall for the old clichés that musicals are supposed to make the audience happy. Instead, he claimed that director Bob Fosse had gone "right to the bleak heart" of Christopher Isherwood's original source material.

Stanley Kauffmann in the *New Republic* also praised Isherwood's original stories, which he called "incomparably the best," but he insisted that the film was much better than the Broadway musical and was much better cast too, using the political atmosphere of Weimar Berlin for much more than a "first-act curtain."

Hollis Alpert in the *Saturday Review* acknowledged its groundbreaking status since the only actors allowed to sing in the film were those who could sing—"clearly an innovation in musicals."

Variety also commented on the film's inventiveness, praising it for being literate and bawdy, sophisticated and sensual, cynical and heartwarming and "disturbingly thought-provoking."

Perhaps the most famous review of the film was by Pauline Kael in the *New Yorker*. *Cabaret*, she wrote, "is a great movie musical, made, miraculously, without compromises." She admired it for being unsentimental, for before *Cabaret*, she insisted, there had never been a "diamond-hard big American movie musical."

She found it to be "everything one hopes for and more." If it is not a commercial success—for there was no guarantee that it would be—she maintained it would still make movie history. How? "By defying the traditional breaking-out-into-song."

The Man Who Fell to Berlin

Bowie in Berlin

> Visions of swastikas in my head
> Plans for everyone
>
> —*David Bowie, "China Girl"*

C abaret—the musical, the film, and its various reincarnations—had an effect on many artists, either directly or indirectly.

Some people were influenced by seeing the play or the movie. Others, such as David Bowie, were affected not only by the movie but also by the literature, by the artwork, of the period—by the city of Berlin itself.

Don't Go to Berlin

"Don't go to Berlin," Christopher Isherwood told Bowie during the last night of the singer's three-night stand at the Forum in Inglewood, just outside Los Angeles as part of the 1976 *Station to Station* tour. Isherwood even jotted down the encounter in his diary that he met Bowie and his wife at the time, Angie Bowie, along with the English painter David Hockney backstage at the Forum.

Celebrities in attendance at the Forum during his run included Alice Cooper, Carole King, Elton John, Ray Bradbury, and Patti Smith. It was David Hockney who introduced Bowie to Isherwood on the third and final night of the tour. Shortly before Isherwood met Bowie, a compilation of his Berlin stories had been reissued.

Bowie and Isherwood spoke at length. At the time, the singer, tired of the LA music scene, was considering a new location: Berlin was among the top sites on his list. Isherwood, though, tried to discourage Bowie from resettling there, maintaining that Berlin was no longer the exciting place it had been during its Weimar heyday. But Bowie seemed insistent upon moving there. He felt Berlin was the center of everything. Ironically, Brecht, Lang, Schoenberg, Mann, and other German exiles had sought refuge in Los Angeles, the city he was now so desperately trying to escape from.

Thus, despite admiring Isherwood and his work, he went anyway. As it turns out, Bowie's relatively short time in Berlin turned out to be one of the most creative periods in his career. While there he created his so-called Berlin trilogy of albums: *Low* and *"Heroes,"* both released in 1977, and *Lodger* in 1979. The city had a major effect on Bowie, allowing him to create among the most influential work of his career.

Berlin was an altogether different kind of place from the City of Angels. Berlin in the 1970s was a city of faded glamour, a city steeped in economic anxiety, a city that was melancholy and yet somehow defiant that appealed to Bowie's own melancholy spirit; and a city that was remarkably similar to the Berlin of the Weimar era. In Berlin, Bowie went in and out of cafés and restaurants. He visited galleries and, according to Thomas Jerome Seabrook, drank himself "into oblivion in working men's clubs and transvestite cabaret bars." Nobody knew, or cared, who he was.

The Berlin sound, the Berlin milieu, but most of all, the Berlin myth fascinated him, whether Fritz Lang, George Grosz, Marlene Dietrich, or Christopher Isherwood. He also admired the so-called Krautrock of Kraftwerk, Can, Neu!, and others, of which he became a part of when he moved to Berlin.

"It was one of the few cities where I could move around in virtual anonymity. I was going broke; it was cheap to live," Bowie told a reporter in the magazine *Uncut.*

Here Bowie read Nietzsche and painted. He turned to painting when he moved to Berlin in 1976, as a deliberate, but ultimately unsuccessful, distraction from the rock 'n' roll lifestyle. He went to the Brücke Museum to look at the works of German painters—George Grosz, Egon Schiele, and Otto Mueller. He was especially fond of Erich Heckel's *Roquairol,* which became the inspiration for the cover of Iggy Pop's *The Idiot,* which Bowie produced. He also studied the work of other German artists of the Weimar and other periods.

Since he was a teenager in England, Bowie had been obsessed with the work of the German Expressionists, in particular the work of Max Reinhardt and Bertolt Brecht, but he was also taken with the vivid imagery in the films *Metropolis* and *The Cabinet of Dr. Caligari.* By the 1970s, he felt pulled once again to Berlin, to the *idea* of Berlin. One of the German bands that Bowie most admired was Kraftwerk, especially their album *The Man-Machine*, which had its roots in German cabaret but also in the music of Marlene Dietrich and in the film *Metropolis*.

Bowie's work combined elements of cabaret, cinema, modern dance, musical comedy, music hall, vaudeville, as well as blues, folk, rock, and soul. Growing up, he might have idolized Little Richard, but as the creator of so many inventive and original pop songs, he actually was the heir of Dada and Surrealism. Being in Berlin made creative sense. He had even met his own Sally Bowles in Romy Haag, a monologuist from West Berlin. She had a nightclub, Chez Romy, on the Fuggerstrasse, a 1970s Kit Kat Klub.

"I think in the '70s . . . there was a general feeling of chaos, a feeling that the idea of the '60s as 'ideal' was a misnomer. Nothing seemed ideal anymore. Everything seemed in-between," Bowie told Michael Kimmelman in 1998.

The Berlin Trilogy

The so-called Berlin trilogy consisted of *Low,* "*Heroes,*" and *Lodger.*

With selections like "Art Decade" and "Subterraneans," the modern pop minimalism of *Low* evoked the spirit of a Berlin cut off from the rest of the Western world. "Subterraneans," the last track, according to Bowie, is about "people caught in East Berlin after the division of the city." *Low,* in fact, had two personalities: one side consisted of short songs with cut-up music and lyrics; the other side had longer, synthesizer-based instrumentals. A number of the cuts were originally intended for the movie soundtrack of *The Man Who Fell to Earth*. Its pessimistic tone reflected the film's themes of isolation and the consequences of greed. The cover of *Low* was inspired by imagery from the movie: Bowie's flaming orange hair is the same color as the cover's orange background.

When *Low* was completed, Bowie moved, with Iggy Pop, from the Hotel Gehrus into a modest flat above an auto parts store in the Schöneberg district at 155 Hauptstrasse, a ten-minute walk from where Isherwood lived. The location was a poor section of West Berlin, mostly populated by Turkish immigrants but within easy walking distance of the Hansa studio and the Wall. Bowie producer Tony Visconti once described Bowie's Berlin as "a stark, scary place" but with a "very exciting" if "bizarre" nightlife as well as "reminders of Hitler's not-too-distant presence. As it happens, Schöneberg was also where Dietrich had been born.

Bowie had long admired Dietrich—perhaps even channeled her in some profound, mysterious way. Mark Kermode, film critic and broadcaster, once noted: "He always thought of himself as Marlene Dietrich—and on the cover of *Hunky Dory*, he is being Dietrich, he does look like her."

Others have acknowledged the Bowie-Dietrich connections. During the fourth season premiere of Ryan Murphy's popular *American Horror Story: Freak Show*, Jessica Lange played the role of Elsa Mars, the owner of a troupe of freak show performers called Fraulein Elsa's Cabinet of Curiosities, perhaps a pun on Robert Wiene's *The Cabinet of Dr. Caligari*. In it, Lange sings with a strong German accent Bowie's "Life on Mars," wearing a powder-blue pantsuit with matching blue eye shadow, rouge cheeks, bright red lipstick, and Dietrich-like blonde curls. Although the show is set in 1952 Florida, Murphy has said it was meant to be a homage to Baz Luhrmann and his 2001 musical *Moulin Rouge*.

"*Heroes*," the second album in the Berlin trilogy, was recorded during the summer of 1977 at Berlin's Hansa studio, only several hundred yards away from the Berlin Wall. From the studio, Bowie could see armed border guards patrolling the area. Hansa was a Weimar-era former ballroom, reportedly used by the Nazis for their various functions. Hansa was also within walking distance of the cabaret clubs and low-rent theaters that had inspired Weill and Brecht's music theater collaborations in 1920s and '30s Weimar Germany.

In interviews, Bowie initially said the song really was about a pair of lovers he saw standing by the Wall, but he later admitted that the idea was really inspired by his producer Tony Visconti and Antonia Maaß, Visconti's German girlfriend at the time. From the studio control room Bowie reportedly saw them kiss—by the Wall.

Bowie Album Covers and the German Influence

The striking black-and-white photograph on the cover of "*Heroes*" was by Masayoshi Sukita and reveals Bowie's ongoing obsession with German culture, from the cabaret scene of the 1930s evoked in Christopher Isherwood's *Goodbye to Berlin* through the rise of fascism. Inspired by Erich Heckel's (1883–1970) painting *Roquiarol* (1917), it references the angular gestures of various *Die Brücke* paintings and even strikes a similar pose—a left arm raised with the thumb jutting out—*Roquiarol*. But Bowie also intended the *Heroes*' cover to playfully echo punk, which was then very much in vogue, from his leather jacket to the design's overall black and white moodiness.

The cover art of the final Berlin album, *Lodger,* was taken by photographer Brian Duffy. According to Peter Doggett, *Lodger* "represented a deliberate step into a world in which [German painter] Egon Schiele became the art director for a futuristic horror movie, directed perhaps by David Cronenberg. Bowie's body was depicted across the gatefold sleeve, prone like Schiele's portrait of Friederike Maria Beer, distorted like the same artist's lacerated self-portraits." Shot in low resolution, Bowie appears to have been beaten up, complete with a broken nose. The entire concept is reminiscent of Weegee's black-and-white photographs of the gritty Lower East Side of the 1940s in a strange combination of Berlin meets New York.

In interviews, Bowie talked about being involved in a biopic of Schiele, an artist he admired. The movie did, in fact, move forward under the title of *Excess and Punishment* (1981), but by the time it had received the greenlight, Bowie was not involved. Another biopic, *Egon Schiele: Death and the Maiden,* was released in 2016.

Of the Berlin trilogy of *Low,* "*Heroes,*" and *Lodger* only "*Heroes*" was actually recorded at Hansa in its entirety. The creative chemistry of Bowie, producers Brian Eno and Tony Visconti working in a milieu of electronic-acoustic experimentation under often tense working conditions—Bowie was trying to shake off his drug habit—created three distinct but intertwining works. The trilogy and Bowie's dystopian Berlin-etched vision influenced the New Romantics of the early 1980s and later such popular bands as Franz Ferdinand, Coldplay, Depeche Mode, and Radiohead.

Other German Influences

Bowie was influenced by Weimar-era Berlin in other ways. The set for his 1974 *Diamond Dogs* tour, which reportedly cost $250,000, was inspired by German Expressionist cinema of the silent era; in particular, Robert Wiene's *The Cabinet of Dr. Caligari* and Fritz Lang's *Metropolis.* The backdrop was called Hunger City, and based on Wiene's angular and otherworldly set design in *Caligari.* The cover art of his 1971 album *Hunky Dory* was influenced by a Marlene Dietrich photography book.

The shadows of Brecht and Weill have followed Bowie throughout his career. Kurt Weill-like chords even started permeating his vocal delivery. During his 1978 world tour he used Brecht's and Weill's "Alabama Song" from Brecht's and Weill's *Rise and Fall of the City of Mahagonny* as background music. In early 1982, he released *Baal,* songs written for Brecht's first full-length 1923 play of the same name.

In 2013, a list of his one hundred favorite books was featured during the traveling exhibit *David Bowie Is* at the Art Gallery of Ontario in Toronto. Several prominent books on Germany were on the list, including *Berlin Alexanderplatz* by Alfred Döblin, *Before the Deluge* by Otto Friedrich, and Isherwood's *Mr. Norris Changes Trains*.

Just a Gigolo, Aliens, and His Final Days

In 1978, Bowie agreed to appear in the movie *Just a Gigolo*, an inferior knock-off of *Cabaret*, mostly because of his friendship with director (and actor) David Hemmings but also because he wanted to work with Marlene Dietrich. In retrospect, he said he should have known better. Bowie once described the movie as "my 32 Elvis films rolled into one."

Bowie played a shell-shocked Prussian officer who returns home to Berlin after the end of World War I. Unable to find work in postwar Germany, he works as a gigolo in a brothel run by Baroness von Semering, played by the seventy-seven-year-old Marlene Dietrich in her last role.

Toward the end of the movie, Dietrich performs "Just a Gigolo," which she sings in her own inimitable world-weary way about life going on without her. "Dancing, music, champagne," she says to Bowie's character. "The best way to forget until you find something you want to remember."

Ironically, Bowie and Dietrich never actually met on the set: Dietrich shot her brief scenes in Paris. The scenes between her and Bowie were later edited together. But Bowie did sing the Weill and Brecht homage "Revolutionary Song" on the soundtrack, which was later released as a single in Japan.

Bowie's character of Thomas Jerome Newton, the alien who lands on earth to bring water back to his drought-stricken planet, in Nicolas Roeg's classic 1975 film *The Man Who Fell to Earth*, owed much to Berlin cabaret of the Weimar era, with a touch of Dietrich.

In 2015, Bowie and director Ivo van Hove collaborated on a new work, *Lazarus*, cowritten by Bowie and Irish playwright Enda Walsh. *Blackstar*, Bowie's final album, was released two days before his death. A few months before his death, the New York Theatre Workshop's production of

Nicholas Roeg considered Peter O'Toole for the role of Thomas Jerome Newton, as well as the novelist Michael Crichton.

Lazarus premiered off-Broadway. Directed by Enda Walsh, it was a sequel, of sorts, to Bowie's 1976 movie *The Man Who Fell to Earth* and featured Michael C. Hall in the role of Thomas Jerome Newton, Bowie's alien. The musical's dark theme—a lonely outsider pondering his last days—echoed Bowie's own obsession with death. The soundtrack, which was released in late 2016, was reportedly recorded the morning when the cast learned of Bowie's death.

Of course, the world didn't know that just as the play was receiving its New York premiere, Bowie was dying from cancer. He succumbed to the disease at the age of sixty-nine in January 2016.

I Am Everyone

Major Tom. Ziggy Stardust. Aladdin Sane. The Man Who Fell to Earth. The Thin White Duke. Like "Christopher Isherwood" in *Goodbye to Berlin*, the personas were all variations of himself.

On Monday, August 22, 2016, Michael Mueller, the mayor of Berlin, unveiled a plaque commemorating David Bowie "special relationship" with the city at the building where he lived from 1976 to 1978 on Hauptstrasse, 155 in the Schöneberg district. The plaque, in German, reads:

In diesem Haus wohnte von 1976 bis 1978

DAVID BOWIE

8.1. 1947-10.1. 2016

In dieser Zeit entstanden die Alben "Low," "Heroes," und "Lodger." Sie gingen als Berliner Trilogie in die Musikgeschichte ein

It states that Bowie lived in this house from 1976 to 1978. During this time he created the albums Low, "Heroes," and Lodger, which were known in musical history as the Berlin Trilogy.

It ends with a line from "Heroes":

"We can be heroes, just for one day."

And it contains a quote, in English, from *"Heroes."*

Berlin Songs

David Bowie was not the only contemporary musician inspired by the music and culture of Berlin. Here are other contemporary songs with Berlin as the theme:

"Berlin"

Lou Reed from *Berlin* (1973)
Lou Reed's controversial album was a commercial dud when it was first released. A ten-song concept album, it chronicled the disintegration of a dissolute, drug-addicted couple in West Berlin before the Wall came down. In late 2006, Reed presented, with a thirty-piece ensemble, a series of concerts of the album at St. Ann's Warehouse in Brooklyn. Two years later, *Lou Reed's Berlin*, a movie version of the performances, directed by Julian Schnabel, was released.

"Weeping Wall" (instrumental)

David Bowie from *Low* (1977)
Bowie has said this moody piece was meant to evoke the misery of the Berlin Wall.

"Heroes"

David Bowie from *"Heroes"* (1977)
Bowie's melancholy song about how the Wall divided two lovers, it is also a paean to the ordinary Germans who lived along the Wall and, through their normal activities, gave it meaning. An anthem for Berlin.

"Holidays in the Sun"

Sex Pistols from *Never Mind the Bollocks, Here's the Sex Pistols* (1977)
Only the Sex Pistols could come up with this holiday nightmare to see the Berlin Wall. It even includes the sound of goose-stepping Nazi storm troopers. "Berlin and its decadence was a good idea," said John Lydon (aka Johnny Rotten), the lead singer. "I loved Berlin. I loved the wall and the insanity of the place."

"Heroes," one of David Bowie's Berlin trio of albums.   *Author collection*

"The Passenger"

Iggy Pop from *Lust for Life* (1977)

Reportedly Iggy wrote the song while on a Berlin train in the late 1970s; said to be loosely based on a poem by Jim Morrison. Bowie sings backup on the chorus.

"Another Brick in the Wall"

Pink Floyd from *The Wall* (1979)

The Wall was a concept album inspired by the fall of the Berlin Wall. "Another Brick in the Wall" is based on the so-called 412th brick used in the Wall's construction. As Richard Jobs has noted, from the earliest days of the Wall, East German officials "sought not only to halt the drain of young workers . . . but also to stop the influx of West Europeans and especially American cultural products." In 1959, for example, he writes that adolescents in Leipzig and Dresden marched through the streets shouting, "Long live Elvis Presley!" Years later, on July 21, 1990, Roger Waters of Pink Floyd performed *The Wall* in front of a crowd of 350,000 people at what was once Potsdamer Platz. Before it was destroyed by Allied bombing during World War II, the plaza was considered the transportation hub of Berlin. In Cold War-era Berlin, though, it became more of a no-man's-land of barbed wire and minefields. The massive stage for *The Wall* was six hundred feet long and sixty feet high. The "wall" of the title consisted of more than two thousand plastic foam bricks. The production featured the Marching Band of the Combined Soviet Forces and the East Berlin Rundfunk Symphony Orchestra as well as a fifty-foot-high inflatable pig. Guest musicians included Sinead O'Connor, Joni Mitchell, Bryan Adams, Cyndi Lauper, and Van Morrison.

"99 Luftballons"

Nena from *Nena* (1983)

Hard to believe, but Nena, the German singer (born Gabriele Susanne Kerner) waited until October 2016 to make her American debut, some thirty-plus years after her initial fame. Despite its bouncy and irresistible melody, the song is actually about the aftereffects of nuclear war. Written before the fall of the Berlin Wall and the unification of Germany in 1990, the song is about a "bunch" of balloons that float over the border between West Germany and East Germany that inadvertently trigger each country's defense systems and lead to nuclear war. But the lyrics do have some basis in fact. Nena's guitarist Carlo Karges wrote the lyrics, which were reportedly inspired by the Rolling Stones concert that took place in West Berlin in 1982. At the end of the performance, Mick Jagger released thousands of helium balloons, but the wind blew them toward East Berlin.

"Nikita"

Elton John from *Ice on Fire* (1985)

Set during the Cold War, the song is about a man in love with an East German guard named Nikita.

"Zoo Station"

U2 from *Achtung Baby* (1991)

The song was inspired by a story that Bono heard about Berlin during World War II, when Allied bombing damaged the zoo, allowing the terrified animals to escape and wander around the debris. Bono has also said he was inspired by Berlin's Zoologischer Garten railway station. He used it as a metaphor to encourage a reunited Germany.

Symphony No. 2 "Low" (1992) and Symphony No. 4 "Heroes" (1996)

Philip Glass
Glass composed two symphonies based on material from *Low* and *"Heroes"*; the latter was also adapted into a contemporary dance piece by Twyla Tharp.

"A Great Day for Freedom"

Pink Floyd from *The Division Bell* (1994)
Written a few years after the fall of the Berlin Wall, the song is about the crushing disappointment of the German population when its collapse did not create the utopia they had expected or at least anticipated. On the day the Wall came down, the singer raises a glass to the freedom that they had anticipated for so long but never really came.

"Tear Me Down"

John Cameron Mitchell from *Hedwig and the Angry Inch* (1999)
Hedwig is a rock musical about a fictional rock band fronted by a transgender East German singer, with music strongly influenced by Bowie, Lou Reed, and Iggy Pop. In the song, written by Stephen Trask, Hedwig compares her desperate situation to the Berlin Wall. Like the Wall, she is also "split in two." The collapse of the Wall is the movie's central metaphor and a symbol of the various paradoxes in the story: male vs. female, gay vs. straight; the ambiguity of gender. "Try and tear me down," Hedwig taunts anyone within crying distance.

"1961"

The Fray from *Scars & Stories* (2012)
The title refers to the year the Berlin Wall was built.

"Where Are We Now?"

David Bowie from *The Next Day* (2013)
The singer recalls memories from the time he spent—and wasted—in Berlin as a young man and mentions famous Berlin spots such as the Potsdamer Plaza.

Berlin Cabaret Songs

A sampling of popular cabaret songs from Berlin:

- "Veronika, Der Lenz Ist Da." The Comedian Harmonists
- "Night and Day." The Comedian Harmonists
- "Der Onkel Bumba aus Kalumb." The Comedian Harmonists
- "Du, schliess dein Herz nicht zu." Egon Kaiser
- "Caravan." Erhard Bauschke and His Dance Orchestra
- "Pinguin Swing." Fritz Weber and His Dance Orchestra
- "Once in a While." Greta Keller
- "Thanks for the Memory." Greta Keller
- "Der alte Schwede." Jack Hylton Und Seine B
- "Ich bin die fesche Lola (I Am the Naughty Lola)." Marlene Dietrich
- "Ich bin vom Kopf bis Fuss auf Liebe eingest (Falling in Love Again)." Marlene Dietrich
- "Sei lieb zu mir (Mean to Me)." Marlene Dietrich
- "Lili Marlene." Marlene Dietrich
- "Taglich Musik." Theo Mackeben Jazz Band

16

Modern Cabarets

Beyond the Margins

abaret, the art form, is alive and well around the world. But for practitioners of the "lost" art, it is, and always has been, a struggle. It will never be part of mainstream society in the way of, say, cinema or television. It probably will always be "beyond the margins," as *Chicago Tribune* music critic Howard Reich says. This "glorious art is still very fringe." The audience may be small, but it is devoted, and the art of cabaret, he maintains, is thriving and vital.

As is evident from this book, there are many different kinds of cabarets. Theater revues. Political cabaret. Even burlesque. It can be subversive, silly, and sublime. To some it's the "Little Sparrow," Edith Piaf and her story-songs about the downtrodden and the desperate, still somehow clinging to life. To others it still means Sally Bowles in that black bowler hat belting out "Mein Herr" at the top of her lungs. And to more than a few it is an intimate evening spent listening to exquisite interpreters of song.

Cabaret is all this, and more.

What Makes Cabaret Unique?

Specific qualities set cabaret apart from other types of music.

Intimacy is the lifeblood of cabaret. The intimacy of the setting is paramount—the singer alone on the stage. The intimacy of the voice. The intimacy behind the emotions expressed in the lyrics of a song. That is, the best cabaret singers emphasize phrasing and other delicate details that bring out a song's hidden emotions by digging deep down within them in order to truly learn what a song is all about.

Another quality is audience expectations. Audiences expect the singer to reveal his or her emotional self through the performance of a song because what makes cabaret such a cathartic experience, such an unfettered emotional experience, are personal revelations. The essence of modern cabaret is "the art of confession," says Reich. For this reason, a cabaret singer needs to be a strong interpreter. "There's no room for fakery," he says. "Either you can sing or you can't."

The songs must be strong both lyrically and musically. The lyric takes precedence. The lyric is of primary importance: the music must help tell the story of the song.

The song should be pared down to human size so it is approachable. Cabaret is never about the voice, practitioners of the form say. It is about the lyric and making the lyric personal. It is about *owning* the song in the way that, say, Liza Minnelli owned "Maybe This Time," in the way that the lyrics of that song and how she, the singer, carried herself, told the audience—the moviegoing audience—what it meant to be her at that particular moment in time—when, in the lyrics of the song at least, anything was possible.

The cabaret repertoire consists of jazz material, musical theater, and songs culled from the Great American Songbook (1910–1950). But humor has always been a big part of the cabaret story too. Dark humor. Satire. Slapstick. Humor is always welcome here—and pathos. "It's music reshaped by virtue of being in that setting," says Reich.

Cabaret Singers

Although the cabaret world is a fairly small one, it is blessed with its share of gifted singers and interpreters. A few of them have a deep knowledge of the cabarets of Weimar Germany or have a sincere interest in perpetuating the music, keeping it alive for the next generation.

Early in her career, German singer and actress Ute Lemper was renowned for her singular interpretation of the songs of Weimar Germany, especially the work of Kurt Weill (she has recorded two volumes of Weill's music), but also German cabaret music in general.

Born in Munster, she attended the Max Reinhardt seminary in Vienna. Her career soared when Andrew Lloyd Webber offered her a part in the Austrian production of *Cats*.

In addition to Weill, her repertoire has consisted of selections by Mischa Spoliansky, Kurt Tucholsky, and Friedrich Hollaender, as well as songs made famous by Marlene Dietrich. But she also has a *Cabaret* connection, too. She played Sally Bowles in the original Paris production, for which she won the 1987 Molière Award—the French equivalent of the Tonys—for best newcomer. A year later in New York, she sang and acted in a show based on the life and work of Kurt Weill. She has also portrayed Velma Kelly in the revival of *Chicago* in both London and New York. Her recording of *Berlin Cabaret Songs* (Decca) in 1996 features songs suppressed by the Third Reich, including songs by Marcellus Schiffer, Friedrich Hollaender, and Kurt Tucholsky (also known as Theobold Tiger) and features some of the most important songs of the Weimar-era cabaret scene.

Karen Kohler is another modern interpreter of German cabaret. Born in Frankfurt and raised in New York, Kohler has recorded albums dedicated to Kurt Weill, *Jam and Spice: The Songs of Kurt Weill* (1999) and Marlene Dietrich, *The Moons of Venus: Romancing Marlene Dietrich* (2005). In 2003, she formed the Kabarett Kollektit, dedicated to preserving the European cabaret tradition. In early 2017, she gave a two-part lecture on the history of cabaret, "The Tenth Muse: Cabaret from Montmartre to Manhattan," at the C. W. Post campus of Long Island University in Nassau County, New York.

Recently, her repertoire has extended beyond cabaret classics by Kurt Weill to embrace Middle Eastern, Indian, and South American music, but she remains one of the finest interpreters of the German cabaret tradition.

Karen Kohler in Marlene Dietrich mode at the New York cabaret Don't Tell Mama.
Photo by Theresa Albini

In 2013, she presented the show *Last Tango in Berlin* at 54 Below in New York in which she sang in German, English, and French—and in her best German cabaret fashion—interwove songs, fragments of song, personal stories, social commentary—all the while channeling her inner Marlene Dietrich. The year prior she put on a show, *Berlin Nights/Paris Days*, at New York's Zankel Hall and sang what Anthony Tommasini called "bleakly beautiful" songs about prostitutes, criminals, and other denizens of the dark.

Lenya. Dietrich. Lemper. They all had—have—that same Teutonic metallic quality: their voice is a unique instrument and, for some, an acquired taste—there's nothing pretty about it, just real. And sharp. Acidic. World-weary. Unsentimental. The English singer Marianne Faithfull has this quality too. It's perhaps no accident that she recorded Weill and Brecht's *Seven Deadly Sins* a few decades ago and heard in their compositions something of herself.

The Other Cabaret

Another type of cabaret is an informal hodge-podge. The former punk photographer Patty Hefflet created what she called the Renegade Cabaret from her fourth-floor New York apartment overlooking the High Line that consisted of comedy routines, musical numbers, and various other pieces (including, reportedly, science lectures). Nowadays she holds her cabarets on the lower deck of the High Line. In 2016, it was a part of the Out of Line summer series of free performances in the park.

The Boston-based Dresden Dolls perform what they call "Brechtian punk cabaret," part of the so-called underground dark cabaret movement that started during the early years of the twenty-first century that draws on the aesthetics of Weimar-era cabaret with elements of post-1970s goth and punk.

Still another type of cabaret is called alt.cabaret, similar in terminology to, say, alt-country or alt-rock. The term refers to cabaret that defies categories, a free-spirited style that transcends the type of cabaret songs usually affiliated with the Great American Songbook and that typically fuses performance art, music, and stand-up comedy. *New York Times* music critic Stephen Holden has called fashion designer-entertainer Isaac Mizrahi the founding father of the genre. Thus, in Mizrahi's version of cabaret no subject is off-limits; his cabaret looks to the future instead of wallowing in the past.

Return to Weimar

Berlin cabaret was known for its dissonant lyricism and sardonic sophistication. The music found in such clubs as Kabarett der Komiker was beautiful and brutal. Songs such as Friedrich Hollaender's "Munchhausen" possessed, to borrow the words of W. B. Yeats, "a terrible beauty." Admittedly, the cabaret of Weimar Berlin is a far cry from the cabaret of upscale New York: the cabaret shows associated with, say, Café Carlyle, where two tickets and dinner can cost almost as much as airfare to Europe. It is intended for people with deep pockets or those pretending to have them. But the German cabaret was more than just entertainment. The great German cabaret performers (Hesterberg, Valetti, Gerron, Dietrich, and Ute Lemper in our own day) and writers (Tucholsky, Mehring, Kästner, and Spoliansky) were activists. Probably the best contemporary equivalent of Berlin's cabarets is a venue like Pangea in the East Village (for more on Pangea, see the description below) or poetry slams or even stand-up comic routines.

In recent years, several contemporary cabaret singers have produced shows, and made recordings, that recreate, or at least recall, the cabarets of Weimar Germany. Mark Nadler and Kim David Smith have presented programs in various cabarets showcasing these songs and these artists. Several years ago, Eric Dax, a former political activist, created *Weimar, New York*, a cabaret revue that presented shows at the Spiegeltent, near the South Street Seaport. In typical Weimar fashion, the shows had a political edge, mixing art and politics and sex, very similar to the type of shows in Berlin between the wars. Jenny Lee Mitchell, a native New Yorker who has lived in Berlin, Hamburg, Munich, and Vienna, has presented her program *Mad Jenny's Love und Greed* at various cabarets and burlesque houses in New York. It features songs from 1920s and 1930s Berlin, specifically by or associated with Mischa Spoliansky, Brecht and Weill, Brecht and Eisler, and Claire Waldoff.

In 2013, Mark Nadler presented *I'm a Stranger Here Myself* at the York Theater Company in New York. Appropriately, the show began as a cabaret piece a year earlier at one of the city's premier cabarets, 54 Below. For this new production, Nadler added details about the songs and anecdotes about the composers and his own life. The York production also included projections of vintage photographs and film clips depicting life as lived by Germany's marginalized people—including Jews and gays—in Weimar Germany put together by Justin West. Like *Cabaret*, Nadler's play/performance piece saluted outsiders while being true to himself.

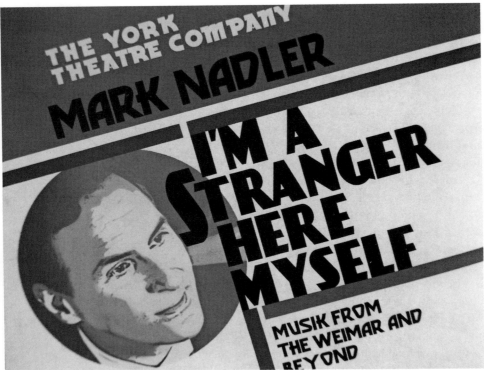

Mark Nadler, one of the premier interpreters of Weimar-era songs. His show—and his album of the same name—is *I'm a Stranger Here Myself: Music from the Weimar and Beyond.*
Author collection. Photo by Theresa Albini

On the recording of the same name, Nadler included the crème of the Weimar composers: Hollaender's humorous "Oh, How We Wish That We Were Kids Again" and "Oh, Just Suppose" and his "Eine Kleine Sehnsucht" (with its doleful line "a little bit of yearning that won't be fulfilled"); Weill and Brecht's "Bilbao Song"; Weill and Ogden Nash's title cut, "I'm a Stranger Here Myself"; and Spoliansky and Schwabach's "The Lavender Song": songs of deep romanticism but also deep pessimism ("This is the end of romance"; "Love is only a dance").

Similarly, Kim David Smith, an Australian transplant, merges music with performance art, political satire, and gender and genre bending, much in the vein of Weimar cabaret. Some critics have said he resembles a male Marlene Dietrich in both style and presentation (he usually performs "Illusions," Dietrich's signature song from the film *A Foreign Affair*). He has also been called the "David Bowie of cabaret." His cabaret show, "Morphium Kabarett," features the Weimar-era music of Hollaender, Weill, and Spoliansky along with modern touches, including his iconic version of "Over the Rainbow," in German, or pairing "Pirate Jenny" with "What Shall We Do with the Drunken Sailors"—and all part of what has been called a "neo-Weimar cabaret fantasia."

Smith has portrayed the Emcee in Hunter Foster's production of *Cabaret* at the Cape Playhouse in Florida. He is a member of the Kabarett Kolletif, a group of New York-based artists dedicated to preserving the European cabaret tradition. Meanwhile, Chicago-based Scott Gryder has presented *Life Is a Cabaret! The Words and Music of Kander & Ebb* around town, which included songs from *Flora the Red Menace; Woman of the Year; Chicago; 70 Girls 70; Kiss of the Spider Woman; New York, New York;* and, of course, *Cabaret.*

Actor and writer Jeremy Lawrence wrote and performed "Lavender Songs: A Queer Weimar Berlin Cabaret," which consists of seventeen songs written between 1920 and 1937. (It has played several times at Pangea.) In the show, Lawrence portrays Tante Fritzy, a former "rent boy"—similar to the rent boys that Christopher Isherwood met when he first came to Berlin—who served in the German army during World War I and, ulti-mately, became a popular cabaret singer in Weimar Berlin. Now he (or she, since Lawrence is in drag during the performance) is an aging cabaret star. The premise behind the show is that the audience is gathered to watch her last performance as Nazism looms on the horizon.

"Lavender Songs" is based on a program created by Alan Lareau, a professor of German at the University of Wisconsin, for the US Holocaust Museum in Washington, D.C., in conjunction with the exhibition *Nazi Persecution of Homosexuals 1933–1945*. But Lawrence's interest in the cabaret culture of Weimar Berlin dates back to the early 1990s when he developed *Cabaret Verboten: Songs and Sketches of the Cabarets of Weimar Germany*, which had its premiere at the Mark Taper Forum theater in Los Angeles. After its LA run, it enjoyed subsequent productions in New York; Pittsburgh; Baltimore; West Palm Beach; Boston; Ashland, Oregon; London; and Stockholm. Lawrence also wrote the English lyrics for Ute Lemper's CD *Berlin Cabaret Songs*.

The songs—all originally written or performed by gay artists in Weimar Berlin—include the music of Friedrich Hollaender, Rudolf Nelson, and Mischa Spoliansky and lyrics by Hollaender and Kurt Tucholsky, among others. While singing Hollaender's "I Don't Know Who I Belong To," Fritzy concludes, much like Sally Bowles, that she belongs to herself. Like Mark Nadler's *I'm a Stranger Here Myself,* Lawrence peppers the show with personal anecdotes and historical references, such as Paragraph 175, which refers to a

Ute Lemper sings *Berlin Cabaret Songs*, at the Athenaeum Theatre, Chicago.

provision of the German criminal code that existed from 1871 to as recently as 1994, which made homosexual acts between males a crime.

Lawrence has also performed one-man shows on Tennessee Williams and Albert Einstein.

In Berlin itself, the German singer Max Raabe is one of the few contemporary cabaret singers who has been able to fill large halls, both in his native

Germany and in the United States, as he did in 2005 when he performed in New York and Philadelphia. If you want to hear cabaret in German in Berlin, Tipi Am Kanzleramt has been presenting *Cabaret Das Musical* for several years now.

Cabaret Venues

Although most cabarets are in New York, there are scattered cabaret communities throughout the United States, including Chicago, Boston, Las Vegas, Los Angeles, Palm Springs, and San Francisco. For the most part, these are not cabarets in the style of Weimar Germany (with the exception of Pangea). Rather, they are nightclubs in an intimate setting specializing in the Great American Songbook. Sometimes they are intimate piano bars. Here's a national sampling:

New York

Café Carlyle, the Carlyle, 35 E. 76th Street (212-744-1600); www.thecarlyle.com

The Carlyle books the biggest names in contemporary cabaret (Christine Ebersole, Ana Gesteyer, Judy Collins, John Pizzarelli, Steve Tyrell, and others).

The space is intimate: it seats up to ninety for dinner and a show. The atmosphere at the Carlyle is elegant: waiters in black jackets and trousers, white shirts, and black bowties along with resin gold chairs, white tablecloths, and upholstered seating. The wall murals by Marcel Vertes depict ballet dancers, dogs, and horses. Vertes (1895–1961) was a French costume designer who won two Academy Awards for his work on John Huston's 1952 film *Moulin Rouge*. In a recent show, Ebersole wedded a narrative theme of empty nesters, life on the road, and Hurricane Sandy with songs such as "Autumn Leaves," "Tootsie Goodbye," "'S Wonderful," and "Paper Moon." All this talent and ambiance comes at a price, though.

Pangea, 178 2nd Avenue (212) 995-0900; www.pangeanyc.com

A downtown cabaret in the East Village; Italian/Mediterranean restaurant-bar and cabaret; dinner, drink, or a show.

Twenty small tables in the back room. With its funky vibe, small stage, and intimate setting, it is probably the closest thing to the Kit Kat Klub in the United States. The twenty-dollar cover charge (plus a twenty-dollar food/drink minimum) makes it the affordable choice for anyone who is curious about the cabaret experience. Several artists have presented

The upscale New York cabaret Café Carlyle on the Upper East Side.

Photo by Theresa Albini

Weimar-inspired shows there, including Mark Nadler, Kim David Smith, and Jeremy Lawrence.

Other Weimar-themed programs at Pangea have included Mad Jenny's *Love Und Greed*, which featured songs from Weimar Berlin by Mischa Spoliansky, Brecht and Weill, Brecht and Eisler, Claire Waldoff, and others. The Jenny of the title is Jenny Lee Mitchell, a native New Yorker who has performed in Vienna, Munich, Hamburg, and Berlin. What also sets this venue apart is the Pangea Mural in the bar/lounge area by artist Judy

The downtown New York cabaret Pangea often features music inspired by the Weimar Republic, by such artists as Kim David Smith, Mark Nadler, and Jeremy Lawrence.   *Photo by author*

Don't Tell Mama in Midtown Manhattan takes its name from the song of the same name in *Cabaret*.
Photo by author

Morlock, a playful blend of geometric shapes and colors that echoes the work of Jean-Michel Basquiat.

Don't Tell Mama, 343 W. 46th Street (212-757-0788)

Dark, cozy room; black tables and chairs; banquettes and full back bar. It features a piano bar (with singing waitresses/bartenders), a restaurant, and two cabaret rooms. Typical programs range from *Judy Garland and Liza Minnelli Live!* to Karen Kohler's Marlene Dietrich show. (The Frankfurt-born Kohler has also recorded *Jam and Spice: The Songs of Kurt Weill*). The club takes its name from *Cabaret*'s "Don't Tell Mama."

Feinstein's/54 Below, 254 West 54th Street (646-476-3551); www.54below.com

Elegant supper club/restaurant. Up to three shows nightly; late-night lounge. Presents new musicals, tribute shows, Greatest Songs of the American Songbook.

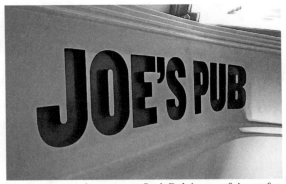

Music venue and restaurant Joe's Pub is one of six performance spaces at the Public Theater and is named after Joseph Papp, the producer who established the New York Shakespeare Festival and the free Shakespeare in the Park held each summer at the Delacorte Theater in Central Park. Shows have included tributes to Fleetwood Mac, literary salons, John Kelly singing the songs of Joni Mitchell, literary cabaret series, Mandy Gonzalez from *Hamilton* and *In the Heights*, Kentucky singer-songwriter and guitarist Joan Shelley, the acclaimed English jazz and cabaret singer Barb Jungr (best known perhaps for her distinctive interpretations of the songs of Bob Dylan), and a program by the Bearded Ladies, *Marlene and the Machine: A German Expressionist Cabaret*, which combined the music of Marlene Dietrich, Fiona Apple, and Regina Spektor with the visual and musical language of German Expressionism and the Weimar era.

Photo by author

Other New York venues include

- The Cutting Room, 44 East 32nd Street (212-691-1900); www.thecut-tingroomnyc.com
- The Duplex, 61 Christopher Street (212-255-5438); www.theduplex.com
- Marie's Crisis, 59 Grove Street (212-243-9323). New York's premier piano bar.
- Metropolitan Room, 34 West 22nd Street (212-206-0440); www.metro-politanroom.com
- Joe's Pub, Public Theatre, 425 Lafayette Street (212-539-8778)

Chicago

Davenport's Piano Bar and Cabaret, 1383 N. Milwaukee Avenue

When Bill Davenport, Sue Berry, and Donna Kirchman opened Davenport's in 1998 in the Wicker Park neighborhood on the Northwest Side, they knew it would be a struggle (Davenport has since relocated to Palm Springs; Berry and Kirchman bought him out). Indeed, since it opened, some of the city's other venues have closed, such as the Gold Star Sardine Bar or the Toulouse Cognac Bar. But through ups and downs it has survived. Now it is considered the city's premier cabaret. It has two rooms: the bigger lounge in the back accommodates seventy-five; the piano bar upfront, fifty. Located on a commercial strip in a funky neighborhood, the view from the window is far from glamorous—a pharmacy is located directly across the street—but it presents the best of local and national talent, from Karen Mason to Andrea Marcovicci. Best, in the piano bar you can hear singers for free, singers with voices that really belong on Broadway.

Monday Night Live at Petterino's Restaurant, 150 N. Dearborn Street

On Monday nights this swanky Italian steakhouse located next door to the Goodman Theatre presents cabaret/open mic performances. Co-hosted by Denise McGowan Tracy and Beckie Menzie.

Other Chicago and Chicago-area Venues

The Drifter, 676 N. Orleans Street (312-631-3887); www.thedrifterchicago.com

The Drifter is housed in the basement of the Green Door Tavern, reportedly Chicago's oldest pub and a former speakeasy ("green door" was said to be a euphemism for speakeasy during the Prohibition era). The Drifter features an old-fashioned cocktail bar with a drink list printed on tarot cards. In true cabaret fashion and in keeping with the Coney Island-style carnival sideshow ambiance, the tiny stage presents burlesque acts, magicians, short films, and other surprises. Think of it as a cross between Weimar Germany and *American Horror Story*.

Bordel, 1721 W. Division Street (773-227-8600); www.bordelchicago.com
Located above a tapas restaurant and behind an unmarked door, this cocktail bar/speakeasy in trendy Wicker Park features jazz, burlesque/vaudeville, and cabaret nights.

Theo Ubique, which presented exquisite shows in its tiny storefront space on Chicago's North Side, describes itself as 'cabaret theatre' and rightly so. Past productions have included "A Kurt Weill Cabaret," "A Jacques Brel Revue," a rotating series of weekend-only cabaret acts as well as Kander and Ebb's *Flora, the Red Menace* and, during the 2007–8 season, a well-received production of *Cabaret*. In 2017, the company announced they were moving to new quarters in the nearby suburb of Evanston.

Skokie Theatre, 7924 N. Lincoln Avenue, Skokie (847-677-7761)
www.skokietheatre.org
Cabaret, tribute shows, some live theater too.

Boston

- Club Café, 209 Columbus Avenue (617-536-0966); www.clubcafe.com
- Sculler's Jazz Club, Double Tree Guest Suites Hotel, 400 Soldiers Field Road (617-562-4111); www.scullers-jazz.com

Florida

Royal Room, the Colony Hotel, 155 Hammon Avenue, Palm Beach (561-655-5430); www.thecolonypalmbeach.com

Las Vegas

Cabaret Jazz at the Smith Center for the Performing Arts,
361 Symphony Park Avenue (702-749-2012); www.thesmithcenter.com

Los Angeles

- Sterling's Upstairs at the Federal, 5303 Lankershim Boulevard, North Hollywood (818-980-2555); www.msapr.net/Sterlings-at-the-Federal.html
- Tom Rolla's Gardenia, 7066 Santa Monica Boulevard, Los Angeles (323-467-7444)

Palm Springs

- Georgie's Alibi Azul, 369 N. Palm Canyon Drive (760-325-5533); www.alibi-azul.com
- The Purple Room Restaurant & Stage, 1900 E. Palm Canyon Drive (760-322-4422); www.purpleroompalmsprings.com
- Three Sixty North, 360 N. Palm Canyon Drive (760-327-1773); www.three-sixtynorth.com
- The Tropicale Restaurant & Coral Seas Lounge, 330 E. Amado (760-866-1952); www.thetropicale.com

San Francisco

- Feinstein's at the Nikko, 222 Mason Street (415-394-1111); www.hotelnikkosf.com
- Society Cabaret in the Hotel Rex, 562 Sutter Street (415-857-1896); www.societycabaret.com

St. Louis

The Gaslight Theater, 358 N. Boyle Avenue (314-458-2978); www.gaslighttheater.net

Texas

- Austin Cabaret Theatre, Shoal Crossing, 8611 N. Mopac, Austin (512-786-6121); www.austincabaret.org
- Sammons Cabaret, 3630 Harry Hines Boulevard, Dallas (214-520-7789); www.sammoncenter.org

Washington, DC

Blues Alley, 1073 Wisconsin Avenue NW (212-337-4141); www.bluesalley.com

What is the Great American Songbook?

The Great American Songbook refers to the canon of largely pre-rock songs from the 1920s to 1950s that were created for musical theater and Hollywood musicals. Prominent contributors to the songbook include:

Rosemary Clooney	Billie Holiday
Nat King Cole	Lena Horne
Ella Fitzgerald	Al Jolson
Judy Garland	Frank Sinatra

Contemporary masters: a short list would include Jason Robert Brown, Michael Bublé, Betty Buckley, Ann Hampton Callaway, Liz Callaway, Joan Curto, Christine Ebersole, Michael Feinstein, Sutton Foster, Megan Hilty, Malcolm Gets, Cheyenne Jackson, Jeremy Jordan, Barb Jungr, Karen Kohler, Diana Krall, Andrea Marcovicci, Karen Mason, Nellie McKay, Amanda McBroom, Maureen McGovern, Brian Stokes Mitchell, Matthew Morrison, Mark Nadler, Kim David Smith, Spider Saloff, and KT Sullivan.

Organizations, Foundations, and Annual Events

Mabel Mercer Foundation, 160 East 48th Street, #1P, New York; (212) 980-3026; www.mabelmercer.org; info@mabelmercer.org.
Mabel Mercer Foundation, an organization founded by Donald F. Smith; Mabel Mercer Award at New York Cabaret Convention; "it has flourished since singer and actress KT Sullivan took over" (Stephen Holden, *New York Times*).

Manhattan Association of Cabarets & Clubs (MAC)

Founded in 1983, the trade organization's mission is to advance the art and business of live entertainment; to heighten public awareness of the field's contributions; to honor its creativity; to build on its current and future audiences; and to speak out on behalf of its members and the industry at large. The MAC honorary board has included Joan Rivers, Kaye Ballard, Phyllis Diller, Jerry Herman, Rex Reed, Julie Wilson, and Liza Minnelli.

Chicago Cabaret Professionals (CCP)

Co-founded by Claudia Hommel in 1998, CCP promotes the art of cabaret by educating performers, the media, and the public at large through meetings, benefits, workshops, seminars, and networking. Each October CCP presents an annual gala show that brings together the best of Chicago cabaret performers. In addition, Hommel sponsors annual tours to Parisian cabarets and, along with her colleagues Elizabeth Doyle and Lynne Jordan, in 2017 she started the Chicago Paris Cabaret Connexion, in which Chicago cabaret artists join performers from France to meet, jam, and perform in historic Parisian cabarets.

Great American Songbook

In 2007, Michael Feinstein, Emmy- and Grammy-winning singer, founded the Great American Songbook Foundation. Feinstein, often dubbed "the Ambassador of the Great American Songbook," is considered one of the best interpreters of American standards. The foundation is dedicated to celebrating and preserving these songs through educational programs, master classes, and the annual High School Vocal Academy and Competition, which awards scholarships and prizes to students.

Feinstein also serves as artistic director of the Center for the Performing Arts, a theater based in Carmel, Indiana, which opened in 2011. The center presents an annual international Great American Arts Festival, offers live programming, and houses a museum of Feinstein's rare memorabilia and manuscripts.

Conventions

• New York Cabaret Convention. Every October.

What Makes a Great Cabaret Song?

You don't have to engage in histrionics to make your point or prove your mettle. In cabaret, in the art of cabaret anyway, subtlety goes a long way. The best cabaret singers are not only storytellers but also truth tellers.

A great cabaret song is a marriage of lyrics and melody so intertwined that you can't imagine one without the other. It allows the melody to capture the emotional content of the words. It can tell a story, but it also can just paint a mood. A great cabaret song is open to ambiguity. "A lot of different subtexts that can be brought out," says Howard Reich.

What the Singers Say

I interviewed several cabaret singers on what makes a great cabaret song, a great cabaret singer.

Karen Mason, singer

"A great cabaret song is a great story. A story that is from the heart, and sent to another heart. The cabaret singer finds what makes the song a personal journey, and then tells this story to the people in the audience. To me, cabaret is a way of sharing our humanity. We share stories about our lives.

"And in that same definition, what makes a great cabaret singer, to me, is someone who shares their experiences and stories with me, the audience. I want to feel like I am listening to a friend tell me about life and all the crazy complexities in it. And somehow, we all survive! A great cabaret singer to me is a great story-teller, using words and music to let me know I am not alone."

Singer, songwriter, actress, cabaret performer extraordinaire Ann Hampton Callaway. Callaway is the daughter of journalist and broadcaster John Callaway and the sister of singer Liz Callaway. Her music and lyrics have been recorded and performed by Barbra Streisand, Blossom Dearie, Michael Feinstein, Carole King, Patti LuPone, Amanda McBroom, Donna McKechnie, and Liza Minnelli, to name more than a few.
Courtesy Ann Hampton Callaway

Ann Hampton Callaway, singer

"A great cabaret song is something that creates an experience of stopping time and inviting a listener into a world, a memory, or an emotional revelation. It can be almost any style of music, but it has to create a space where all you can think about is what is happening in the song. I'm a lyric girl, so for me the words have to sweep me off my feet and make me think and feel and wake up to some part of myself.

"A great cabaret singer is someone who connects with your heart and mind in a powerful way through music, stories, and even simply their stage presence. Usually this person is an open-hearted person who sings from his or her heart and welcomes the audience in a way that creates exquisite intimacy. It's nice if they have a great voice, but it's not essential. They need to communicate things that wake up people's senses, inspire their souls, tickle their funny bone, and make them fall in love with life all over again.

Beckie Menzie, singer, pianist, musical director for Michael Feinstein's Songbook Academy

"I think the best of us remember our responsibility is to entertain, amuse, and to affect the audience. You can accomplish this with your own unique vantage point in terms of selecting and understanding the songs you choose and communicating that.

"Cabaret songs used to draw from the Great American Songbook. The old masters like Berlin, Gershwin, Cole Porter . . . songs written before the 1960s. But some think the Great American Songbook is still being written. Think of Carole King, Barry Manilow, and such.

"First, cabaret singers should know their way around a song. You don't need to have a great voice. Great cabaret singers make do with what they are given; with what they have. Great cabaret singers also need to have the ability to connect with an audience."

As far as the future is concerned, the *Tribune*'s Reich is sanguine. "Cabaret is always hanging by its fingernails but it keeps on hanging," he says.

> Cabaret is music and theatre. It is satire and revolution. What makes the art form unique is the proximity between artist and audience and the resulting intimacy. For me, a great cabaret song is one whose lyric penetrates deeply into the arc of human experience—the light, the dark, and the in-between. It transcends language and culture . . . Apart from her powerful instrument, what makes a cabaret singer great is the total willingness to lay herself bare.
>
> — *Karen Kohler*

17

Why *Cabaret* Still Matters

Ongoing Influences

> To sum it all up, I must say that I regret nothing.
> —*SS officer Adolf Eichmann*

In 1995, *Cabaret* was added to the National Film Registry. In 2004, the American Film Institute (AFI) ranked the title song #18 in its list of the top 100 songs in American cinema. And two years later, the movie was ranked number 5 on the AFI's list of top 100 musicals; in 2007, it was #63 on the AFI's list of the 100 greatest American movies ever made.

Cabaret has been called the first adult musical. It's also been called the first concept musical. In a concept musical, the story is central to its over-arching metaphor. Others would follow: *Company, Follies, Pacific Overtures,* and *Kiss of the Spider Woman.*

What made *Cabaret* so innovative? Several things:

- its double score (one for the book scenes, one for the cabaret scenes)
- music as social commentary
- its expressionistic motifs (tilted mirror, black box setting, spiral staircase)

Its structure is that of a parallel musical that, as some critics have noted, almost functions like a Teutonic Greek chorus. The stage design accentuates this, indicating that a large mirror should hang from the stage so that the audience could see itself; in essence, breaking through the Brechtian fourth wall.

But the idea of mixing realistic book scenes with cabaret scenes is among its most innovative features. The songs in *Cabaret* grow out of the dialogue. The rise of fascism is seen through the perspective of the cabaret and its denizens. "[T]he show's mixture of lowbrow and middlebrow music captures something that was in vogue in Brecht's and Weill's day," asserts Keith Garebian.

Cabaret reinvented the moribund Hollywood movie musical. The 1960s effectively killed off the old-fashioned musical, the big bloated musicals of the time. *Cabaret* was the opposite of *Camelot, Paint Your Wagon, Funny Girl,* and similar-style musicals—and gave the genre new life.

Other Musicals

There have been many innovative stage and movie musicals since *Cabaret.* Some, like *Hair, The Rocky Horror Picture Show, Rent, Hedwig and the Angry Inch, American Idiot,* and, most recently, *Hamilton* have been just as distinctive, and just as revolutionary in their own way. The anti-Vietnam War rock musical *Hair,* for example, celebrated its fiftieth anniversary in January 2017 at La MaMa in New York, as part of the venue's Coffeehouse Chronicles series. It was controversial for several reasons: for its profanity, its depiction of illegal drugs, and its nude scene, to mention a few, as well as for its exploration of racism, poverty, sexism, pacifism, political corruption, and environmentalism. And several of its songs—including "Aquarius," "Easy to Be Hard," and "Good Morning Starshine"—became popular anthems of both the antiwar movement and the peace movement. It broke new ground too by using a racially integrated cast. Unusual subject matter is not an uncommon thing in musical theater. Just think of the work of Stephen Sondheim, from his *Sweeney Todd* (1979), about that psychopathic barber of Fleet Street to his *Assassins* (1990) in which multiple presidents are shot or killed, from Garfield to Ford to Reagan.

Hedwig, in particular, shares similar traits with *Cabaret.* One could even make a strong case that the characters of Hedwig and Sally Bowles have a lot in common: Sally, the coked-up heroine of the Kit Kat Klub, and Hedwig, the East German transgender rock singer with an, uh, problem.

John Cameron Mitchell has been influenced by many artists, including the film directors Todd Haynes and Gus Van Sant, and such earlier generations of directors as Jean Genet, Derek Jarman, and George Cukor. What's more, the work—and very sensibility—of Bob Fosse has had a considerable impact on Mitchell, especially on the evolution of *Hedwig.*

Hedwig and the Angry Inch is a rock musical about the adventures of a transsexual rock singer and her often poignant—and defiantly angry— search for love and acceptance on her own terms. Hedwig, the character, transcends gender. Like the Emcee—and even Cliff Bradshaw/Christopher

Isherwood—Hedwig's sexuality is fluid. Hedwig not only plays with her sexuality but also with her nationality (Is she German? Is she American?) as well as with musical genres and styles, from heavy metal to power ballads. The film version of *Hedwig* is fluid too, combining elements of hard rock, glam rock, drag, performance art, video art, and stand-up theater.

Euan Morton as Hedwig in the 2017 national touring production of *Hedwig and the Angry Inch.*   *Courtesy Margie Korshak, Inc.*

Cabaret, Hedwig, and the Curious Scottish Connection

What is it about *Cabaret, Hedwig,* and the curious Scottish connection? Consider: Alan Cumming, the quintessential post-Joel Grey Emcee, was born in the small Scottish market town of Aberfeldy but grew up in a country estate near the town of Carnoustie in northeast Scotland. John Cameron Mitchell, the creator of *Hedwig and the Angry Inch,* also has strong Scottish roots. His mother is a native of Glasgow, and he spent a few of his formative years attending a Scottish boarding school. And Euan Morton, who played Hedwig in the 2016–2017 national tour, hails from Falkirk in the Central Lowlands. In addition to his many musical theater roles, most famously as Boy George in the West End musical *Taboo* in 2002 and on Broadway in 2003, Morton also is a fine cabaret performer in his own right, playing sold-out shows at such New York City venues as the Oak Room in the Algonquin Hotel, Joe's Pub, and the Town Hall.

Mitchell has said that he is an admirer of Bob Fosse—and nontraditional musicals. Growing up, Fosse was for a time his muse. In particular, in developing and visualizing the structure of both the play and film, Mitchell was influenced by the give-and-take, stream-of-consciousness style of Fosse's autobiographical film *All That Jazz*.

Based on Mitchell's 1998 off-Broadway musical, *Hedwig* is the story of Hansel, an East German boy who loves rock 'n' roll and yearns to see life beyond the confines of his native Germany and beyond, in particular, the Berlin Wall. He meets a handsome American soldier. They agree to marry and leave Germany. But just dressing as a bride won't allow him to leave the country. So Hansel agrees to undergo a sex change operation. But the operation is less than successful and leaves the patient, now renamed Hedwig, with scar tissue, the eponymous "angry inch." Thus, confined to a state of sexual limbo, Hedwig decides to make the best of a dire situation by transforming herself into an "internationally ignored" rock singer. But instead of touring stadiums, she makes the run of dive restaurants in generic strip malls.

Sally and Hedwig and the Emcee

The characters of Sally Bowles and Hedwig Robinson have much in common. The obvious connection is Berlin. Sally, the tawdry English rose, sang in a seedy cabaret during the Weimar years; Hedwig, the sexually compromised, gender-bending German, performs in second-rate rock clubs in the American hinterlands.

Hedwig Robinson made her first appearance at a New York gay club called Squeezebox in the Soho neighborhood in 1994, during the waning years of the AIDS crisis. It was here that actor-writer John Cameron Mitchell and composer Stephen Trask brought the unconventional character to life. Hedwig was based on a real person, a German-born babysitter and part-time prostitute that Army brat Mitchell knew.

The mid-1990s was a period, Mitchell told *Chicago Tribune* theater critic Chris Jones, when it was "suddenly cool to be queer for the first time ever." There was a punk revival on the charts (Nirvana and Sonic Youth, to name a few) and artists such as Courtney Love and the members of Green Day hung out "with the drag queens," said Mitchell, at the Squeezebox.

Although influenced by *Cabaret*, Hedwig was meant to be much raunchier, much rougher. "We were performing in a flophouse where junkies were being carried out in stretchers," Mitchell told Jones.

In fact, the character of Hedwig is part Marlene Dietrich, part Dr. Frank N. Furter from the *Rocky Horror Picture Show*, and part David Bowie. Like the Berlin Wall, she is neither East nor West, man nor woman, but rather something altogether new and different. On the other hand, a comparison could also be made between Hedwig and the Emcee even though we don't get to know the Emcee on a personal level. Still, their public personas sometimes overlap. Like Hedwig, the Emcee can be funny (bits of stand-up routines), does some slapstick, and engages in audience participation. And both are sardonic, sad, and, at times, tragic figures. Hedwig carries within the spirit of the cabaret.

On the other hand, and unlike the Emcee whose fate seems doomed, Sally and Hedwig are born survivors. Both are bruised and battered (especially the Sally as embodied by Natasha Richardson and, later, Sienna Miller). Both characters learned at a young age to rely on no one but themselves. And both are pragmatists, doing whatever it takes to come out on top. Both demand that you pay attention to them. That they count.

Beyond Cabaret

In recent years, the musical has received new life on television shows such as *Glee* and *Smash*. But among the most significant thing to happen to musicals was the release of Damien Chazelle's film *La La Land* in 2016.

Chazelle's *La La Land* is the opposite of *Cabaret* in that it is an old-fashioned movie musical—Chazelle knows his history--with big numbers but with a twenty-first-century sensibility. An exercise in pure cinema, it has long takes reminiscent of the work of Vincente Minnelli and Stanley Donen and culminating in a gorgeous musical fantasy pastiche that echoes elements such as the "Girl Hunt" sequence from Minnelli's *The Band Wagon*, the "Broadway Ballet" from *Singin' in the Rain*, and the dream ballet from *An American in Paris*.

Nothing is ironic or camp here. On the contrary, Chazelle accepts, embraces, and indeed respects musical traditions. In Chazelle's world, it is perfectly natural for characters to break out into song. Song is, in fact, a form of expression. It is a fully realized MGM-style musical in a modern setting; in this case, traffic-clogged Los Angeles. It has the bold colors—the bright primary colors of red, yellow, blue, and green of Vincente Minnelli musicals—and elaborate studio sets of Old Hollywood but is deeply rooted in naturalism. Chazelle wears his influences on his sleeve: Fred Astaire and Ginger Rogers, Cyd Charisse, Jerome Robbins, Jacques Demy, Gene Kelly, choreographer Michael Kidd. Even Fosse is here. When Mia (Emma Stone) and her roommates arrive at a typical Hollywood party, at one point, dancers remain stationary just as in Fosse's "Rich Man's Frug" in *Sweet Charity*. The dances were shot in single takes, using natural light. Set in the ultimate fantasy land, the film celebrates the big dreams of big dreamers in a land where hope is not a four-letter word.

Still Relevant

Cabaret remains just as relevant—perhaps even more relevant—since it was released in 1972. It reinvented and reinvigorated the stage and movie musical. The true genius behind *Cabaret* lies in its tripartite nature: the figure of the Emcee acts as a three-way mirror reflecting the Bowles-Isherwood relationship, the rise of Nazi Germany, and the acquiescence of the audience itself. It is also the only big American musical that takes its form from political cabaret.

The show must go on. "Life Is a Cabaret, Old Chum," Sally Bowles' anthemic rallying cry. *Author collection. Photo by Theresa Albini*

Cabaret and the team of John Kander and Fred Ebb have influenced subsequent generations of musical theater artists. When he was writing *In the Heights* and *Hamilton*, Lin-Manuel Miranda listened to the old Broadway masters, including the scores of Kander and Ebb. As Miranda and Jeremy McCarter mention in their book on the creation of *Hamilton*, when John Kander saw *In the Heights* in 2007, he went backstage to meet Miranda. They became fast friends. During the development stages of *Hamilton*, Kander even attended early workshops. The two men spent some quality time together.

But what in particular makes *Cabaret* so relevant today? Let's reconsider some of the details and characters.

In the play, Ernst Ludwig is likable and friendly. He introduces Cliff to the underground world of the Kit Kat Klub. So when the audience, and Cliff, learns that he is a Nazi, the shock is palpable. The intent is clear—the Nazis were people just like you and me. The moment epitomizes what Hannah Arendt has called "the banality of evil," a reference to Lieutenant Colonel Adolf Eichmann, one of the masterminds behind the Holocaust, from when she covered the Eichmann trial for the *New Yorker* in 1961. At the trial, Eichmann, being a Good German, protested that he was only following orders. Ludwig, and others like him, were also being just Good Germans, rallying around the Nazis because they promised prosperity, jobs, and the redemption of Germany. They considered themselves and the Nazis patriots, not murderers.

And then there is the Emcee.

The Emcee serves as the thematic narrator—the thread that holds the play and, later, the movie together. He symbolizes the liberal lifestyle of Sally Bowles as well as reflecting the growing strength of Nazism. And he embodies the lascivious nature of the Berlin cabarets, on the one hand, and their sardonic undercurrent, on the other. After all, the Berlin cabarets often satirized and mocked politics and popular culture in the vein of, say, today's *Saturday Night Live* and Second City. In songs such as "If You Could See Her," the Emcee dances with a gorilla, a ridiculous idea on its face until at its conclusion—in the last line—he whispers in a confessional voice, "she wouldn't look Jewish at all!" That is, everyone agrees that a man cannot fall in love with a gorilla just like an increasing number of Germans at the time—especially when the Nazis began to wield power—believed that a gentile could not marry a Jew, an outcome that Fräulein Schneider (and Natalia Landauer in the movie), seeing the writing on the wall, regretfully concluded.

The environment of the stage of the Kit Kat Klub, as well as the backstage ambiance, serves as a metaphor for human nature, and German society specifically, writ large. Both the stage play and the movie address Nazism on various levels. In the early scenes, the patrons of the Kit Kat Klub make light of the Nazis. In the movie, we see the club's owner even kicking them out of the venue at one point. But it is clear by the end of the first act in the play that the Nazis need to be taken seriously, as when Fräulein Kost sings the Nazi anthem "Tomorrow Belongs to Me" to Ernst Ludwig. In the film, Brian Roberts (the Christopher Isherwood/Clifford Bradshaw character) and Max, Brian and Sally's bisexual lover, listen in an outdoor beer garden as a German youth passionately sings the song along with the rest of the patrons (with the possible exception of a grumpy old man who, from the looks of him, would rather just be drinking his beer). And what is also made clear here is that the Nazis can no longer be easily controlled. Earlier in the scene leading up to the beer garden, Max definitively dismisses the Nazis as "just a gang of stupid barbarians." But as they leave the beer garden, Brian asks him, "Do you still think you can control them?" In the final shots of the movie, Nazis now frequent the club, their tan uniforms and swastika bands in plain sight. In the 2017 Roosevelt University production of *Cabaret*, the director/choreographer Jane Lanier, inspired by the movie, intentionally planted Nazis in the small tables in front of the stage to indicate the sinister turn of events.

Sally herself is the ultimate hedonist, the child-woman (in *Goodbye to Berlin*, she is, after all, only nineteen when she arrives in Berlin) who purports to be more sophisticated and shocking than she actually is. She is the ostrich who plants her head in the sand, pretending that everything is fine. She seeks instant gratification and freedom from adult responsibility. "You

In March 2017, white nationalist Richard Spencer referenced "Tomorrow Belongs to Me" on his Twitter feed during a particularly heated exchange with Talking Points Memo editor Josh Marshall. When Marshall told Spencer to "take your trash philosophy back to the 1930s, chump," Spencer replied, "1930s? No, tomorrow belongs to us." In turn, Spencer's tweet prompted Jason Kander, nephew of John Kander and former secretary of state of Missouri, to respond, "Hey buddy, that song you love was written by my uncle. He's been married to my other uncle for 40 years. And he's a Jew. Sing it proud."

mean—politics? But what has *that* to do with us?" she asks Cliff at one point. By the time she wakes up to the reality surrounding her—and it is worth asking if she in fact ever really does wake up—it is too late. Sally and Cliff/ Brian belong to the past, Hitler and the Nazis to the future.

The character of Cliff Bradshaw has historically been the blandest figure in the cast. There have been exceptions (Bill Heck in the Mendes revival, for example, offered a nuanced performance that was lacking in other productions). But it's important to acknowledge that Cliff Bradshaw/Brian Roberts is like Christopher Isherwood, an outsider. From the moment he steps off the train platform he is a stranger in a strange land. Significantly, he is the narrator. There is a reason why he is the narrator. We see Berlin from his point of view. Initially, he is a passive observer before he becomes actively involved and, indeed, wakes up from his sleepwalking state. But, ultimately, he decides to leave Berlin—and its deadly fate—behind by returning home, either to the United States or to Britain.

But the Isherwood character is not the only outsider in *Cabaret*. From Berlin to Los Angeles, Christopher Isherwood himself was, by choice, an outsider, a perennial exile. Sally, too—whether being portrayed as a decadent English rose or a flamboyant American émigré—was also an outsider, as were all the denizens of the Kit Kat Klub. Misfits.

Which leads us back once again to the Emcee. Perhaps no one is more of an outsider than the Emcee, one of the most enigmatic figures in musical theater. He is an archetype. In the Mendes revivals, he appears onstage during many of the book scenes, observing the action of his fellow characters, a theatrical device that Hal Prince used elsewhere in such shows as *Company* and *Sweeney Todd*. He makes paradoxical statements. "Even the orchestra is beautiful," he announces, although the orchestra is clearly the exact opposite: garish and vulgar. He is charming but shallow, likable but dangerous. And, ultimately, he is also a tragic figure as we, the audience, learn of his sad fate: being both gay and Jewish in Nazi Germany can only mean one thing.

In 1966, *Cabaret*'s frank subject matter was controversial—Nazis, anti-Semitism, and abortion were atypical themes for Broadway musicals. But the world has changed considerably since then. Consequently, later productions grew bolder—Cliff Bradshaw went from heterosexual to bisexual to gay— while Sam Mendes's revivals featured simulated sex acts (behind a sheet) and even a flash of nudity at the end of the first act (the Emcee baring his swastika-tattooed buttocks). The film pushed the envelope at the time of its release. Even its love story was unconventional: a promiscuous woman and two bisexual males in a ménage a trois.

The original Broadway production was Hal Prince's first attempt at making a concept musical, where the story is secondary to a central metaphor. Prince would later continue the concept musical with *Company, Follies, Pacific Overtures*, and *Kiss of the Spider Woman*. And still other musicals also experimented with the concept musical idea, including *A Chorus Line* or *Nine*.

Dominic Fontana as the Emcee in concentration camp garb in Roosevelt University's 2017 production of *Cabaret*. Note the pink triangle, the Third Reich's symbol for gay people.   *Photo by Nic Mains. Courtesy Roosevelt University*

It's often been said that *Cabaret* was a musical for people who did not like musicals. Whether this is true is neither here nor there. What is important is that *Cabaret* was intended to make people uncomfortable—to make people think—in the best Brechtian tradition. And yet despite the unconventional subject matter, and unconventional approach, when *Cabaret* first appeared on the Great White Way, it was still 1966 and Broadway audiences were accustomed to seeing a romantic couple as the main characters and a secondary couple in a subplot. *Cabaret* was groundbreaking but certain Broadway conventions were maintained. Prince got around the usual plot conventions by creating two shows: Masteroff's book with its traditional musical comedy songs, and songs that also commented on the action and the central metaphor that he wanted to get across. In essence, the original *Cabaret*—his *Cabaret*—combined the best of two different worlds: show business as metaphor of mass delusion.

It's easy to forget that *Cabaret* was created during a time of crisis—the Vietnam War era of the 1960s. But as other critics have noted, its earlier incarnations also appeared during turbulent or uncertain eras: Christopher Isherwood's *Goodbye to Berlin* near the end of World War II, John Van Druten's *I Am a Camera* during the turmoil of McCarthyism, and Fosse's movie just as the Watergate scandal was erupting. And now Sam Mendes's revival is especially relevant as the Trump era begins with its disturbing claims of the media being the opposition party and the "enemy of the people." The phrase is historically associated with Joseph Stalin, although it was also used during the French Revolution and is the title of Henrik Ibsen's 1882 play.

Cabaret addresses prejudice (specifically, anti-Semitism) and the danger of political complacency. Since the 2016 election, there has been a tremendous increase in the number of hate crimes as well as a backlash (American activist and commentator Van Jones has called it a "whitelash") against progressive values and political liberalism, with increasingly strong xenophobic, racist, and sexist rhetoric. As of this writing, the world is seeing a rise in incidents of anti-Semitism. According to the Anti-Defamation League, sixty-five episodes of white supremacist activity took place on American college campuses in more than thirty states from January to March 2017, including the distribution of anti-Semitic flyers; vendors selling items with swastika symbols; and, perhaps the most egregious example, an Adolf Hitler–themed Valentine's Day card. White supremacist and other alt-right groups seem to be emboldened by what they interpret to be a general level of acceptance in mainstream society since the "election" of Donald Trump.

Cabaret continues to resonate on many levels. The Nazis demonized minorities, using Jews as scapegoats for the economic turmoil that engulfed Weimar Germany (even though Jews accounted for less than 1 percent of the German population, which prompted Chicago lawyer William Choslovsky to call them "the original '1-percenters.'").

They promised a return to simpler days when Germany was at its height of power, which today has echoes of Trump's "Make America Great Again" slogan. Ernst Ludwig in the stage production promises Cliff that the Nazis will be the builders of a new and stronger and better Germany. The clear parallels between Weimar Berlin and the political climate today with the rise of so-called populism around the globe makes *Cabaret* as relevant as ever, perhaps more so.

What's more, *Cabaret* continues to make people think and feel.

Director and choreographer Jane Lanier had planned to mount a production of *Cabaret* at Chicago's Roosevelt University in the fall of 2016, when Hillary Clinton was expected to win the presidency. But when Lanier finally obtained the rights to do the play in early 2017, the political climate had

Cabaret through the decades.   *Photo by Theresa Albini. Courtesy Playbill*

changed considerably. In the program notes, she writes, "As artists we have a responsibility, not only to provide entertainment, but to use our art as reminders of social injustice and the horrifying acts by man upon man. We must never forget, lest it should happen again. Unfortunately, the timing of this show couldn't be more perfect." Set designer Michael Lasswell agrees. "There is simply no better time in history to be doing this play."

And yet *Cabaret* takes place right before the Nazis assumed power. In other words, theoretically at least, it is still not too late for the country to go down another road. That should be remembered too. The audiences of the Kit Kat Klub, unlike the people watching in theaters or the big screen, don't know what we know. They could not predict the future. *Cabaret* is thus a cautionary morality tale for the ages.

In the end, the central conceit of *Cabaret* revolves around a simple but chilling question: How could a society allow Hitler to happen? And will it happen again? Let us give Sam Mendes the last word as he issues a cautionary warning to the world: "It's really about the central mystery of the twentieth century—how Hitler could have happened. And it's important that we go on asking the question whether or not we can find some sort of answer."

Can it happen again? Or has it already happened?

Appendix One
Cabaret Timeline

1918

Kaiser Wilhelm abdicates.

1919

Treaty of Versailles signed.

1920

German Workers' Party changes its name to National Socialist German Workers' Party (Nazi Party).

1921

Adolf Hitler becomes leader, or Der Führer, of the Nazi Party.

1922

Benito Mussolini establishes a fascist dictatorship in Italy.

1924

Hitler imprisoned for rioting (the famous Munich Beer Hall Putsch). He is sentenced to five years in prison but serves only nine months.

Kadeko (Kabarett der Komiker), one of the most popular Weimar cabarets, opens.

1925

Hitler's *Mein Kampf* (My Struggle) is published.

1929

The Great Depression.

Christopher Isherwood arrives in Berlin.

1931

Four million unemployed in Germany. Membership in Nazi Party soars.

Tingel-Tangel Cabaret opens in Berlin.

1932

Nazis gain majority in German elections.

1933

Nazi Party wins a majority in the Reichstag; Hitler assumes position of Chancellor.

Germany and Japan withdraw from League of Nations.

Hitler establishes the Third Reich.

First concentration camp opens outside Berlin.

Nazi boycott of Jewish-owned shops.

Nazis open Dachau concentration camp.

Isherwood leaves Berlin.

1934

Christopher Isherwood publishes *Mr. Norris Changes Trains*, a novella about double agents.

1937

Isherwood publishes "Sally Bowles"; it eventually appears as part of a longer collection of stories, *The Berlin Stories*.

Isherwood publishes *Goodbye to Berlin*.

1938

Kristallnacht (Night of Broken Glass), an organized Nazi campaign to persecute and massacre Jews throughout Germany. The name refers to shards of broken glass of Jewish-owned shops and synagogues.

1939

World War II begins.

1941

Hermann Goering announces "the final solution" (the murder of European Jews). Wannsee Conference takes place outside Berlin wherein senior officials of Nazi Germany and SS leaders meet to coordinate the implementation of the Final Solution.

1942

Wannsee Conference takes place outside Berlin wherein senior officials of Nazi Germany and SS leaders meet to coordinate the implementation of the Final Solution.

1945

Auschwitz, Buchenwald, and Dachau are liberated by Allied forces; Germany and Japan surrender; World War II ends.

1945–1946

The Nuremberg trials took place in Germany. Judges from the Allied powers—Great Britain, France, the United States, and the Soviet Union—presided over the hearings of twenty-two Nazi criminals; twelve were sentenced to death.

1946

Isherwood reissues *The Berlin Stories*.

1951

I Am a Camera, John Van Druten's stage adaptation of Isherwood's *Berlin Stories*, opens on Broadway.

1952

John Van Druten's stage play *I Am a Camera*, based on Isherwood's *Berlin Stories*, opens on Broadway starring Julie Harris as Sally Bowles.

1955

The film *I Am a Camera* opens, starring Julie Harris as Sally Bowles and Laurence Harvey as Cliff.

1961

The trial of Nazi SS officer Adolf Eichmann begins in April in Jerusalem. Eichmann was convicted and hanged the following year. Hannah Arendt covered the trial for the *New Yorker*.

The film *Judgment at Nuremberg* is released in December. Directed by Stanley Kramer, it featured an all-star cast, including Spencer Tracy, Burt Lancaster, Richard Widmark, Maximilian Schell, Werner Klemperer, Montgomery Clift, Judy Garland, and Marlene Dietrich as the widow of a German general.

1966

Cabaret opens on Broadway.

1972

The film adaptation of *Cabaret* is released.

1987

The revival of *Cabaret* appears on Broadway, directed by Harold Prince with Joel Grey reprising his role as the Emcee. The play receives mostly negative reviews and closes after a short run.

1989

The fall of the Berlin Wall on November 9.

1990

East and West Germany reunite on October 3.

1993

Cabaret is staged by English director Sam Mendes at the Donmar Warehouse in London, starring Alan Cumming as the Master of Ceremonies and Jane Horrocks as Sally Bowles. It receives rave reviews.

1998

Cabaret is revived once again on Broadway in a critically acclaimed production starring Natasha Richardson as Sally Bowles and Alan Cumming reprising his role as the Master of Ceremonies.

2014

A revival of *Cabaret*, starring Alan Cumming and Michelle Williams, opens on Broadway.

2016–2017

Cabaret national tour in honor of the fiftieth anniversary of the Roundabout Theatre Company.

Appendix Two
Awards

Tony Awards

Cabaret, 1966–1967

Best Musical
Best Featured Actor in a Musical: Joel Grey as the Emcee
Best Featured Actress in a Musical: Peg Murray as Fräulein Kost
Best Director of a Musical: Hal Prince
Set Design: Boris Aronson
Costume Design: Patricia Zipprodt
Composer and Lyricist: John Kander and Fred Ebb
Choreography: Ronald Field

Cabaret, 1998

Best Performance by a Leading Actor in a Musical: Alan Cumming as the
    Emcee
Best Performance by a Leading Actress in a Musical: Natasha Richardson
    as Sally Bowles
Best Performance by a Featured Actor in a Musical: Ron Rifkin as Herr
    Schultz
Best Revival of a Musical

Cabaret (film, 1972) Awards/Nominations

The 45th Academy Awards

The 45th Academy Awards were presented March 27, 1973, at the Dorothy Chandler Pavilion in Los Angeles.

Cabaret was nominated ten times and won eight awards:

Best Actress: Liza Minnelli as Sally Bowles
Supporting Actor: Joel Grey as the Emcee
Director: Bob Fosse
Cinematography: Geoffrey Unsworth
Art and Set Direction: Rolf Zehetbauer and Jurgen Kiebach and Herbert Strabel
Sound: Robert Knudson and David Hildyard
Scoring: Ralph Burns
Film Editing: David Bretherton

Cabaret at the Academy Awards
Best Picture Nominees:
> *The Godfather*
> *Cabaret*
> *Deliverance*
> *The Emigrants*
> *Sounder*

> *The Godfather* won.

Best Director
> Winner: Bob Fosse
> Presenters: Diana Ross and James Coburn
> Presenters: George Stevens and Julie Andrews

Other Best Director Nominees:
> John Boorman for *Deliverance*
> Jan Troell for *The Emigrants*
> Francis Ford Coppola for *The Godfather*
> Joseph Mankiewicz for *Sleuth*

Best Actress:
> Winner: Liza Minnelli
> Presenters: Raquel Welch and Gene Hackman

Other Best Actress Nominees:
    Diana Ross, *Lady Sings the Blues*
    Maggie Smith, *Travels with My Aunt*
    Cicely Tyson, *Sounder*
    Liv Ullmann, *The Emigrants*
Actor in a Supporting Role:
    Winner: Joel Grey
    Presenters: Diana Ross and James Coburn
Other Best Supporting Actor Nominees:
    Eddie Albert, *The Heartbreak Kid*
    James Caan, *The Godfather*
    Robert Duvall, *The Godfather*
    Al Pacino, *The Godfather*

Additional Academy Awards

Best Art Direction/Set Direction: Rolf Zehetbauer, Hans Jurgen Kiebach, Herbert Strabel
Best Cinematography: Geoffrey Unsworth
Best Film Editing: David Bretherton
Best Music, Scoring Original Song Score and/or Adaptation: Ralph Burns
Best Sound: Robert Knudson, David Hildyard

BAFTA

Best Film
Best Director: Bob Fosse
Best Screenplay: Jay Allen (nominee)
Best Actress: Liza Minnelli
Best Supporting Actress: Marisa Berenson (nominee)
Best Art Direction: Rolf Zehetbauer
Best Sound: David Hildyard, Robert Knudson, Arthur Piantadosi
Most Promising Newcomer: Joel Grey
Best Film Editing: David Bretherton (nominee)
Best Costume Design: Charlotte Flemming (nominee)

Golden Globes

Best Motion Picture—Music/Comedy
Best Motion Picture Actress—Music/Comedy: Liza Minnelli

Best Supporting Actor—Motion Picture: Joel Grey
Best Original Song, "Mein Herr" and "Money, Money": John Kander and
    Fred Ebb (nominees)
Best Screenplay: Jay Allen (nominee)
Best Supporting Actress—Motion Picture: Marisa Berenson (nominee)
Most Promising Newcomer—Female: Marisa Berenson (nominee)

National Board of Review

Best Director: Bob Fosse
Best Film
Best Supporting Actor: Joel Grey (tied with Al Pacino, *The Godfather*)
Best Supporting Actress: Marisa Berenson

National Society of Film Critics

Best Supporting Actor: Joel Grey (tied with Eddie Albert, *The Heartbreak Kid*)

Tony Awards and Nominations

Cabaret, 1966–1967

Best Musical
Best Original Score: John Kander and Fred Ebb
Best Performance by a Leading Actor in a Musical: Jack Gilford (nominee)
Best Performance by a Leading Actress in a Musical: Lotte Lenya (nominee)
Best Performance by a Featured Actor in a Musical: Joel Grey
Best Performance by a Featured Actress in a Musical: Peg Murray
Best Direction of a Musical: Hal Prince
Best Choreography: Ron Field
Best Set Design: Boris Aronson
Best Costume Design: Patricia Zipprodt
Best Composer and Lyricist: John Kander and Fred Ebb

1987 Broadway Revival

Best Revival of a Musical (nominee)
Best Performance by a Featured Actor in a Musical: Werner Klemperer
    (nominee)

Best Performance by a Featured Actress in a Musical: Alyson Reed (nominee)
Best Performance by a Featured Actress in a Musical: Regina Resnik (nominee)

1998 Broadway Revival

Best Revival of a Musical
Best Performance by a Leading Actor in a Musical: Alan Cumming
Best Performance by a Leading Actress in a Musical: Natasha Richardson
Best Performance by a Featured Actor in a Musical: Ron Rifkin
Best Performance by a Featured Actress in a Musical: Mary Louise Wilson (nominee)
Best Direction of a Musical: Sam Mendes and Rob Marshall (nominee)
Best Choreography: Rob Marshall (nominee)
Best Orchestrations: Michael Gibson (nominee)
Best Costume Design: William Ivey Long (nominee)
Best Lighting Design: Peggy Eisenhauer and Mike Baldassari (nominee)

2014 Broadway Revival

Best Featured Actor in a Musical: Danny Burstein (nominee)
Best Featured Actress in a Musical: Linda Emond (nominee)

Other Theater Awards
1987 Broadway Revival

Drama Desk Award
Outstanding Revival of a Musical: (nominee)
Outstanding Actor in a Musical: Joel Grey (nominee)
Outstanding Director of a Musical: Hal Prince (nominee)

1993 London Revival

Laurence Olivier Award
Best Musical Revival: (nominee)
Best Actor in a Musical: Alan Cumming (nominee)
Best Performance in a Supporting Role in a Musical: Sara Kestelman
Best Director of a Musical: Sam Mendes (nominee)

1998 Revival

Drama Desk Award
Outstanding Revival of a Musical: Won
Outstanding Actor in a Musical: Alan Cumming
Outstanding Actress in a Musical: Natasha Richardson
Outstanding Featured Actress in a Musical: Michele Pawk (nominee)
Outstanding Director: Sam Mendes and Rob Marshall (nominee)
Outstanding Choreography: Rob Marshall (nominee)
Outstanding Orchestrations: Michael Gibson (nominee)
Outstanding Set Design: Robert Brill (nominee)
Outstanding Costume Design: William Ivey Long (nominee)
Outstanding Lighting Design: Peggy Eisenhauer and Mike Baldassari
(nominee)

2006 London Revival

Laurence Olivier Award
Best Musical Revival: (nominee)
Best Performance in a Supporting Role in a Musical: Sheila Hancock
Best Theatre Choreographer: Javier de Frutos

2012 London Revival

Laurence Olivier Award
Best Musical Revival: (nominee)
Best Actor in a Musical: Will Young (nominee)
Best Performance in a Supporting Role in a Musical: Siân Phillips (nominee)

Appendix Three
Cabaret Cast Recordings

From Broadway to London to Madrid to Düsseldorf to Israel, *Cabaret* cast recordings span the world.

- *Cabaret*: Original Broadway Cast Recording (Sony, 1966). Featuring Jill Haworth, Joel Grey, Bert Convy, Lotte Lenya, Jack Gilford.
- *Cabaret*: Original London Cast (Masterworks Broadway, 1968). Featuring Kevin Colson, Judi Dench, Barry Dennen, Lila Kedrova, Richard Owens, Peter Sallis, Pamela Strong. At the Palace Theatre.
- *Cabaret*: Original Oslo Cast (NorDisc, 1968). Featuring Kjersti Dovigen, Wenche Foss, Toralv Maurstad, Georg Richter, Kari Laila Thorsen.
- *Cabaret*: Original Vienna Cast (Preiser, 1970). Featuring Blanche Aubry, Lya Dulizkaya, Violetta Ferrari, Harry Fuss, Klaus Gerboth, Ingeborg Knopf, Heide Steinwachs, Klaus Wildbolz.
- *Cabaret:* Original Film Soundtrack (ABC Records, 1972). Featuring Liza Minnelli, Joel Grey.
- *Cabaret*: Greek Cast (Philips, 1978). Featuring Despo Diamantidou, Danis Katranidis, George Michalakopoulos, Efi Strati, Aliki Vougiouklaki.
- *Kabape*: Bulgarian Cast (Balkanton, 1982). Featuring Kalina Angelova, Nikolaj Borisov.
- *Cabaret*: London Cast (First Night, 1986). Featuring Rodney Cottam, Grazina Frame, Kelly Hunter, Peter Land, Vivienne Martin, Oscar Quitak, Wayne Sleep. At Strand Theatre.
- *Cabaret*: Dutch Cast (Disky, 1989). Featuring Lia Dorana, Alexandra van Marken, Willem Nijholt, Theo Nijland, Guus Verstraete.
- *Cabaret*: Israeli Cast (Honda Music International, 1989). Featuring Moscu Alkalai, Moshe Becker, Rivka Gur, Micki Kam, Yotam Silberman.

- *Cabaret*: Hungarian Cast (Media, 1992). Featuring Juli Básti, Dezsö Garas, Anna Györgi, István Hirtling, Aladár Laklóth, Béla Paudits, Irén Psota, Klára Varga, Tímea Vertig.
- *Cabaret*: Italian Cast (Carisch, 1993). Featuring Maria Laura Baccarini, Gennaro Cannavacciuolo, Giorgio Carosi, Michela D'Alessio, Gabriele Eleonori, Giovanni Moschella, Carlo Reali.
- *Cabaret*: London Studio Cast (Jay, 1993). Featuring Judi Dench, Jonathan Pryce. Two-CD set.
- *Cabaret:* Vienna Cast (Reverso, 1996). Featuring Carl Achleitner, Karl Markovics, Otto Pichler, Nina Proll, Heidi Stahl, Marius Sverrisson, Nicole Weber.
- *Cabaret*: New Broadway Cast Recording (RCA Victor, 1998). Featuring Alan Cumming, Natasha Richardson, John Benjamin Hickey, Denis O'Hare, Mary Louise Wilson, Ron Rifkin, Michele Pawk.
- *Cabaret*: Düsseldorf Cast (Freetime, 1999). Featuring Marc Bollmeier, Natacza Soozie Boon.
- *Cabaret*: Bremer Cast (Bremer Theater, 2002). Featuring Helmut Baumann, Ruth Brauer, Eva Gilhofer, Jon Andrew Kemna, Thomas Kylau, Stefanie Ribitzki, Susanne Riegger.
- *Cabaret*: Madrid Cast (CIE/Stage Entertainment España, 2004). Featuring Asier Etxeandia, Natalía Millán, Manuel Rodríguez, Emilio Alonso, Manuel Bandera, María Blanco, Patricia Clark.
- *Cabaret*: Mexican Cast (Retrolab, 2004). Featuring Itati Cantoral, Patricio Castillo, Carlos De la Mota, Lorena Glinz, Luis Roberto Guzman, Heidy Infante, Raquel Olmedo.
- *Cabaret:* London Cast (Bk Records, 2006). Featuring James Dreyfus, Sheila Hancock, Michael Hayden, Anna Maxwell Martin.
- *Cabaret*: Paris Cast (EMI, 2007). Featuring Catherine Arditi, Geoffrey Guerrier, Patrick Mazet, Claire Pérot, Pierre Reggiani, Fabian Richard.

Bibliography

Alleman, Richard. "Back to the Cabaret." *Playbill*, November 1987.

Allen, Jay Presson. *Cabaret*. Hollywood: Script City, 1970.

Als, Hilton. "Dear Heart: A Stern Take on 'Sweet Charity.'" *New Yorker*, December 5, 2016.

———. "I, Me, Mine: A New Biography of Christopher Isherwood." *New Yorker*, January 17, 2005.

———. "Stars: Michelle Williams and Neil Patrick Harris Play Performers on Broadway." *New Yorker*, May 5, 2014.

———. "Static: David Bowie and 'Lazarus.'" *New Yorker*, December 21 & 28, 2015.

Appignanesi, Lisa. *The Cabaret*. Revised and expanded. New Haven, CT: Yale University Press, 2004.

Arendt, Hannah. *Eichmann in Jerusalem: A Report on the Banality of Evil*. New York: Viking Press, 1963.

———. *The Origins of Totalitarianism*. New York: Schocken Books, 1951.

Bailey, Hilary. *After the Cabaret*. London: Little, Brown, 1998.

Barone, Joshua. "Unearthing a National Treasure. Finally: A Festival Helps Restore Kurt Weill's Legacy in Germany." *New York Times*, March 12, 2017.

Beachy, Robert. *Gay Berlin: Birthplace of a Modern Identity*. New York: Alfred A. Knopf, 2014.

Berg, James J., and Chris Freeman, eds. *The American Isherwood*. Minneapolis: University of Minnesota Press, 2015.

———. *The Isherwood Century: Essays on the Life and Work of Christopher Isherwood*. Madison: University of Wisconsin Press, 2000.

Berger, Joseph. "You'll Laugh, You'll Cry, You'll Kibitz." *New York Times*, March 11, 2016.

Bernstein, Arnie. *Swastika Nation: Fritz Kuhn and the Rise and Fall of the German-American Bund*. New York: St. Martin's Press, 2013.

Best, Tamara. "White Supremacists Step Up Recruiting on Campus in Over 30 States, Report Says." *New York Times*, March 7, 2017.

Bittner, Jochen. "The West's Weimar Moment." *New York Times*, May 31, 2016.

Blades, Joe. "The Evolution of *Cabaret*." *Literature/Film Quarterly* 1 (1973): 226–38.

Bloom, Ken. *The American Songbook: The Singers, the Songwriters, and the Songs.* New York: Black Dog & Leventhal, 2005.

Bloom, Ken, and Frank Vlastnik. *Broadway Musicals: The 101 Greatest Shows of All Time.* New York: Black Dog & Leventhal, 2004.

"Bob Fosse: Steam Heat." *Great Performances: Dance in America.* PBS; first aired February 23, 1990.

Brantley, Ben. "Hedwig and Sally: New Faces, New Ideas." *New York Times*, March 14, 2015.

———. "Old Chums Return, Where Club Is Home." *New York Times*, April 25, 2014.

Brantley, Ben. "Saucy Sally, Desperately Imbibing Your Gaze." *New York Times*, December 5, 2014.

Brendel, Alfred. "The Growing Charm of Dada." *New York Review of Books*, October 27, 2016.

Broackes, Victoria, and Geoffrey Marsh, eds. *David Bowie Is.* London: V&A Publishing, 2013.

Brooks, David. "The Coming Incompetence Crisis." *New York Times*, April 7, 2017.

Browning, Christopher R. "Lessons from Hitler's Rise." *New York Review of Books*, April 20, 2017.

Buckley, David, in collaboration with Nigel Forrest. *Kraftwerk Publikation.* London: Omnibus Press, 2015.

Caldwell, Christopher. "What the Alt-Right Really Means." *New York Times*, December 4, 2016.

Canby, Victor. "At the Heart of a Spellbinding 'Cabaret,' a Star." *New York Times*, March 29, 1998.

Choslovsky, William. "Anti-Semitic Fliers at UIC Evoke Old Nazi Tactic." *Chicago Tribune*, March 19, 2017.

Citron, Stephen. *The Musical from the Inside Out.* Chicago: Ivan R. Dee, 1997.

Clurman, Harold. Review of *Cabaret* by Joe Masteroff. *The Nation*, December 12, 1966.

Clurman, Harold. Review of *I Am a Camera* by John Van Druten. *The New Republic*, December 24, 1951.

"Code Denies Seal to 'I Am a Camera'; DCA May Balk at Cuts Demanded." *Variety Daily*, July 27, 1955.

Cohen, Roger. "How Dictatorships Are Born." *New York Times*, October 15, 2016.

Copeland, Roger. "Cabaret at the End of the World." *American Theatre*, January 1999.

Crowther, Bosley. Review of *I Am a Camera* by Henry Cornelius. *New York Times*, August 9, 1955.

Cumming, Alan. *Goodbye to Berlin*. Introduction. New York: New Directions, 2012.

———. *Not My Father's Son: A Memoir*. New York: Dey St./William Morrow Publishers, 2014.

da Fonseca-Wollheim, Corinna. "Dada Is 100 Years Old. So What?" *New York Times*, July 10, 2016.

Dargis, Manohla. "Making Musicals Matter Again." *New York Times*, November 27, 2016.

Doggett, Peter. *The Man Who Sold the World: David Bowie and the 1970s*. London: Vintage, 2012.

Doyle, Rachel B. "Looking for Isherwood's Berlin." *New York Times*, April 12, 2013.

Dylan, Bob. *Chronicles, Volume One*. New York: Simon & Schuster, 2004.

Eddy, Melissa. "Annotated 'Mein Kampf' Is Best-seller in Germany." *New York Times*, January 4, 2017.

Edwards, Gavin. "'99 Luftballons,' Bouquet to the '80s, Alights Live in U.S." *New York Times*, October 3, 2016.

Egan, Sean, ed. *Bowie on Bowie: Interviews and Encounters with David Bowie*. Chicago: Chicago Review Press, 2015.

Farago, Jason. "A Most-wanted Nazi in His Glass Cage: Eichmann's Abduction and Trial Are the Subject of a New Show." *New York Times*, August 4, 2017.

Feuer, Cy, with Ken Gross. *I Got the Show Right Here*. New York: Simon & Schuster, 2003.

Finney, Brian. *Christopher Isherwood: A Critical Biography*. New York: Oxford University Press, 1979.

Flinn, Denny Martin. *The Great American Book Musical: A Manifesto, a Monograph, a Manual*. Limelight Editions/Hal Leonard, 2008.

Franklin, Nancy. "The Gathering Storm." *New Yorker*, April 6, 1998.

Friedrich, Thomas. *Berlin Between the Wars*. New York: Vendome Press, 1991.

Fryer, Jonathan. *Eye of the Camera: A Life of Christopher Isherwood*. London: Allison & Busby, 1993.

Garebian, Keith. *The Making of Cabaret*. Second edition. New York: Oxford University Press, 2011.

Gay, Peter. *Weimar Culture: The Outsider as Insider.* New York: W. W. Norton, 2001.

Genesis Dada: 100 Years of Dada Zurich (catalogue). Arp Museum Bahnhof Rolandseck. Zurich: Scheidegger & Spiess, 2016.

Genzlinger, Neil. "Sally Bowles Wasn't Alone." Review of *I'm a Stranger Here Myself: Musik from the Weimar and Beyond. New York Times,* May 4, 2013.

Gibbs, Wollcott. Review of *I Am a Camera* by John Van Druten. *New Yorker,* December 8, 1951.

Gillmor, Alan M. *Erik Satie.* New York: W. W. Norton, 1992.

Gilman, Richard. "I Am a Musical." *Newsweek,* December 5, 1966.

Gottfried, Martin. *All His Jazz: The Life and Death of Bob Fosse.* Second edition. New York: Da Capo Press, 2003.

———. Review of *Cabaret* by Joe Masteroff. *Women's Wear Daily,* November 21, 1966.

Gray, Margaret. "50 Years of 'Cabaret;' How the 1966 Musical Keeps Sharpening Its Edges for Modern Times." *Los Angeles Times,* July 20, 2016.

Grode, Eric. "Two Generations, One Golden Age: A Composer Helps Celebrate Hal Prince's Broadway." *New York Times,* August 6, 2017.

Grubb, Kevin Boyd. *Razzle Dazzle: The Life and Work of Bob Fosse.* New York: St. Martin's Press, 1989.

Guernsey, Otis L. Jr., ed. *Broadway Song & Story: Playwrights/Lyricists/ Composers Discuss Their Hits.* New York: Dodd, Mead, 1985.

Guzmán, Isaac. "David Bowie 1947–2016: Appreciation." *Time,* January 25, 2016.

Haber, Joyce. "Joel Grey Talks About the Good Old, Bad Old Days." *Los Angeles Times,* March 4, 1973.

Hannaham, James. "Transformation: The Straight Sex Symbol Taye Diggs Prepares to Take on the Most Gender-Bending Role on Broadway." *New York Times Magazine,* July 26, 2015.

Hartung, Philip. Review of *I Am a Camera* by Henry Cornelius. *Commonweal,* September 9, 1955.

Haslett, Adam. "In Flight." *New York Times,* February 7, 2016.

Heilbrun, Carolyn. "Christopher Isherwood: An Interview." *Twentieth Century Literature* 22 (1976): 253–63.

Henderson, Eric. "Cabaret." *Slant* magazine, February 8, 2013. Accessed January 2, 2016.

Hess, Amanda. "Identity Theft." *New York Times Magazine,* April 2, 2017.

Hirsch, Foster. *Harold Prince and the American Musical Theatre*. Expanded edition. New York: Applause, 2005.

Hodgson, Moira. "When Bob Fosse's Art Imitates Life, It's Just 'All That Jazz.'" *New York Times*, December 30, 1979.

Holden, Stephen. "Pushing Cabaret into a Brash New Age of Candor." *New York Times*, February 7, 2017.

———. "Tales from Divided Berlin, Where Angst Ate the Soul." *New York Times*, July 18, 2008.

Holley, Eugene Jr. "Berlin Story." *Publishers Weekly*, February 15, 2016.

Isherwood, Charles. "The Gaiety and Sorrows of His Nights." *New York Times*, May 14, 2016.

———. "Here and Now, Life Is (Finally) Beautiful." *New York Times*, February 14, 2016.

———. "One Mad Power Grab, Many Dramatic Roles: Macbeth, with Alan Cumming at the Barrymore Theater." *New York Times*, April 21, 2013.

Isherwood, Christopher. *Berlin Stories: The Last of Mr. Norris and Goodbye to Berlin*. New York: New Directions, 1954.

———. *Christopher and His Kind, 1929–1939*. New York: Farrar, Straus & Giroux, 1976.

———. *Diaries, Volume One: 1939–1960*. Edited and introduced by Katherine Bucknell. London: Methuen, 1996.

———. *Goodbye to Berlin*. New York: Random House, 1939.

———. *Lost Years: A Memoir, 1945–1951*. Edited by Katherine Bucknell. New York: HarperCollins, 2000.

Jacobs, Alexandra. "The M.C. and I: Joel Grey's Memoir Recounts His Conflicts and Struggles." *New York Times*, March 6, 2016.

Jelavich, Peter. *Berlin Cabaret*. Cambridge, MA: Harvard University Press, 1993.

Jennings, C. Robert. "Divine Decadence Provides the Theme for German 'Cabaret.'" *Los Angeles Times*, June 27, 1971.

Jobs, Richard Ivan. *Backpack Ambassadors: How Youth Travel Integrated Europe*. Chicago: University of Chicago Press, 2017.

Johnstone, Iain. "The Real Sally Bowles." *Folio* (Autumn 1975): 32–38.

Jones, Chris. "Edgy 'Hedwig' Is Our Litmus Test." *Chicago Tribune*, March 3, 2017.

———. "We're Once Again in Hands of the Emcee in 'Cabaret.'" *Chicago Tribune*, April 25, 2014.

Jones, Dylan. *David Bowie: A Life*. New York: Crown Archetype, 2017.

Kael, Pauline. "Grinning." *New Yorker*, February 19, 1972.

Kakutani, Michiko. "Window on the World." *New York Times*, April 26, 1998.

Kander, John, and Fred Ebb, as told to Greg Lawrence. *Colored Lights: Forty Years of Words and Music, Show Biz, Collaboration, and All That Jazz*. New York: Faber and Faber, 2003.

Kauffmann, Stanley. Review of Fosse's *Cabaret*. *New Republic*, March 4, 1972.

Kelly, Kevin. "*Cabaret* Has the Makings of a Rare Musical." *Boston Globe*, October 11, 1966.

Kerr, Walter. "The Theater: 'Cabaret' Opens at the Broadhurst." *New York Times*, November 21, 1966.

Kimmelman, Michael. "At Heart, an Artist with Many Muses." *New York Times*, January 15, 2016.

Kinser, Jeremy. "John Cameron Mitchell on Justin Timberlake and Gaga as Hedwig, Cultural Assimilation, and His Own Remarkable Career," Queerty, July 8, 2015.

Kirsch, Adam. "The Führer Without Myth: A New Biography Focuses on Hitler the Man." *New York Times*, October 16, 2016

Kourlas, Gia. "Shall We Dance? Making 'La La Land' Move." *New York Times*, December 18, 2016.

Lehmann, John. *Christopher Isherwood: A Personal Memoir*. New York: Henry Holt, 1987.

Leve, James. *Kander and Ebb*. New Haven, CT: Yale University Press, 2009.

Levine, Robert. "Keeping the Old Cabaret Alive in the Land of 'Cabaret.'" *New York Times*, November 29, 2005.

Lewis, Sinclair. *It Can't Happen Here*. New York: Signet Classics/Penguin, 2014.

Loney, Glenn. "The Many Facets of Bob Fosse." *After Dark*, June 1972.

MacLean, Rory. *Berlin: Portrait of a City Through the Centuries*. New York: Picador, 2015.

Marcus, Greil. *Lipstick Traces: A Secret History of the Twentieth Century*. Cambridge, MA: Harvard University Press, 1990.

Mast, Gerald. *Can't Help Singin': The American Musical on Stage and Screen*. Woodstock, NY: Overlook Press, 1987.

Masteroff, Joe. *Cabaret*. New York: Random House, 1967.

Masteroff, Joe, John Kander, and Fred Ebb. *Cabaret: The Illustrated Book and Lyrics*. Roundabout Theatre Company Production. Edited by Linda Sunshine. New York: Newmarket, 1999.

McGrath, Charles. "Life Is an Audition: Michelle Williams May Not Be a Natural Singer-Dancer, But Neither Is Sally Bowles." *New York Times*, March 30, 2014.

McNeil, Liz. "Joel Grey's Odyssey." *Entertainment Weekly*, February 19/26, 2016.

Miller, Scott. *From Assassins to West Side Story: The Director's Guide to Musical Theatre*. New York: Heinemann Publishing, 1996.

Miranda, Lin-Manuel, and Jeremy McCarter. *Hamilton the Revolution*. New York: Grand Central Publishing, 2016.

Mizejewski, Linda. *Divine Decadence: Fascism, Female Spectacle, and the Makings of Sally Bowles*. Princeton, NJ: Princeton University Press, 1992.

Mordden, Ethan. *The Happiest Corpse I've Ever Seen: The Last 25 Years of the Broadway Musical*. New York: Palgrave, 2004.

———. *Open a New Window: The Broadway Musical in the 1960s*. New York: St. Martin's Griffin, 2002.

Niarchos, Nicolas. "Berlin." *New Yorker*, February 8 & 15, 2016.

Oberbeck, S. K. "Movies." A review of Fosse's *Cabaret. Newsweek*, February 28, 1972.

Oberthur, Mariel. *Cafés and Cabarets of Montmartre*. Salt Lake City: Gibbs M. Smith/Peregrine Smith Books, 1984.

O'Toole, Fintan. "Under the Spell of a Stark 'Cabaret.'" *New York Daily News*, March 20, 1998.

Page, Norman. *Auden and Isherwood: The Berlin Years*. New York: St. Martin's Press, 1998.

Parker, James. "The Resurrections of David Bowie." *Atlantic*, April 2016.

Parker, Peter. *Isherwood: A Life Revealed*. New York: Random House, 2005.

Parnell, Sean. *Historic Bars of Chicago*. Chicago: Lake Claremont Press, 2010.

Philip, Richard. "Bob Fosse's 'Chicago': Roxie's Razzle Dazzle and All That Jazz." *Dance Magazine*, November 1975.

Phillips, Michael. "Bob Fosse's Chicago Story, Long before 'Chicago.'" *Chicago Tribune*, October 25, 2013.

Picard, Lil. "Interview with Bob Fosse." *Inter/View*, March 1972.

Pugh, Megan. *America Dancing: From the Cakewalk to the Moonwalk*. New Haven, CT: Yale University Press, 2015.

Rehfeld, Barry. "Bob Fosse's Follies." *Rolling Stone*, January 19, 1984.

Rich, Frank. "*Cabaret* and Joel Grey Return." *New York Times*, October 23, 1987.

Richter, Hans. *Dada: Art and Anti-Art*. London: Thames & Hudson, 1965.

Riedel, Michael. *Razzle Dazzle: The Battle for Broadway*. New York: Simon & Schuster, 2015.

Rizzo, Frank. "His First American Musical Has Broadway Hopes and a French Soul." *New York Times*, May 10, 2016.

Roe, Sue. *In Montmartre: Picasso, Matisse, and the Birth of Modernist Art*. New York: Penguin, 2016.

Rothstein, Mervyn. "A Life in the Theatre: Come Hear the Music Play." *Playbill*, August 2014.

Rudorff, Raymond. *The Belle Epoque: Paris in the Nineties*. New York: Saturday Review Press, 1973.

Ruether, Tobias. "The Man Who Came from Hell." *Exile on Main*, Issue #12. Winter 2006/2007. Accessed November 29, 2015.

Ryzik, Melena. "Life Is a Weimar Dream, Old Chum, and Downtown Loves a Nouveau Cabaret." *New York Times*, July 17, 2007.

Sanders, Ronald. *The Days Grow Short: The Life and Music of Kurt Weill*. New York: Holt Rinehart Winston, 1980.

Schulman, Michael. "For Alan Cumming, Life Isn't Always a Cabaret." *New York Times*, October 3, 2014.

Seabrook, Thomas Jerome. *Bowie in Berlin: A New Career in a New Town*. London: Jawbone Press, 2008.

Segel, Harold B. *Turn-of-the-Century Cabaret: Paris, Barcelona, Berlin, Munich, Vienna, Cracow, Moscow, St. Petersburg, Zurich*. New York: Columbia University Press, 1987.

Seigel, Jerrold. *Bohemian Paris: Culture, Politics, and the Boundaries of Bourgeois Life, 1830–1930*. New York: Penguin, 1987.

Shteir, Rachel. *Striptease: The Untold Story of the Girlie Show*. New York: Oxford University Press, 2004.

Simonson, Robert. "Channeling Fosse: Beyoncé and Beyond." *Playbill*, February 20, 2009.

Singer, Barry. "When Cabaret Had an Edge." *New York Times*, February 27, 2000.

Smith, Sid. "The Fosse Look: It's All about Underlying Images." *Chicago Tribune*, September 5, 1999.

———. "Heart of Darkness: 'Cabaret' Is Racier and Raunchier—and More True to the Spirit of the Times." *Chicago Tribune*, June 6, 1999.

———. "Thodos Dance Chicago to Show Off Bob Fosse's Endless Possibilities," *Chicago Tribune*, November 6, 1999.

Snyder, Robert W. *The Voice of the City: Vaudeville and Popular Culture in New York*. Chicago: Ivan R. Dee, 2000.

Soble, Jonathan. "You Haven't Seen This 'Chicago': A Japanese Troupe Brings Its All-Female Cast to New York." *New York Times*, July 17, 2016.

Solway, Diana. "The Odyssey of Joel Grey." *New York Times*, October 18, 1987.

Spencer, Charles. "A Dark and Decadent Sally." *Telegraph*, October 11, 2006.

Spoto, Donald. *Lenya: A Life*. New York: Little, Brown, 1989.

Spender, Stephen. *Letters to Christopher*. Santa Barbara, CA: Black Sparrow, 1980.

———. "On Being a Ghost in Isherwood's Berlin." *Mademoiselle*, September 1974.

Stasio, Marilyn. "A Tough 'Chicago' Is Where Bob Fosse Lives." *Cue*, July 7, 1975.

Stempel, Larry. *Showtime: A History of Broadway*. New York: W. W. Norton, 2016.

Stoop, Norma McLain. "Christopher Isherwood: A Meeting by another River." *After Dark* 7 (1975): 60–65.

Sullivan, Dan. "Welcome to 'Cabaret'—For a New Generation." *Los Angeles Times*, June 22, 1987.

Taubeneck, Anne. "A Fraulein of All Trades." *Chicago Tribune*, July 6, 1999.

Teachout, Terry. "It's a Noisy Hall with a Nightly Brawl, but No Fosse." *New York Times*, December 22, 2002.

———. "Seamy and Steamy: *Fosse* Makes Broadway Dance the Way It Used To." *Time*, January 25, 1999.

Terry, Clifford. "Home Town Boy Bob Fosse Makes Good." *Chicago Tribune*, April 20, 1969.

Tropiano, Stephen. *Music on Film: Cabaret*. Milwaukee: Limelight Editions/ Hal Leonard, 2011.

Ullrich, Volker. *Hitler: Ascent 1889–1939*. Translated by Jefferson Chase. New York: Knopf, 2016.

Van Druten, John. *I Am a Camera: A Play in Three Acts*. New York: Dramatists Play Service, 1951.

Viertel, Jack. *The Secret Life of the American Musical: How Broadway Shows Are Built*. New York: Sarah Crichton Books/Farrar, Straus & Giroux, 2016.

Visconti, Tony. *Bowie, Bolan, and the Brooklyn Boy: The Autobiography*. New York: HarperCollins, 2007.

Von Rhein, John. "Singer Revives 'Subversive' Songs Suppressed by the Nazis." *Chicago Tribune*, April 23, 1998.

Wasson, Sam. *Fosse*. New York: Mariner/Houghton Mifflin Harcourt, 2014.

Weisberg, Gabriel P., ed. *Montmartre and the Making of Mass Culture*. New Brunswick, NJ: Rutgers University Press, 2001.

Weiss, Hedy. "The Fosse Lexicon." *Chicago Sun-Times*, September 19, 1999.

Westerbeck, Colin L. Review of Fosse's *Cabaret*. *Commonweal*, April 21, 1972.

Wieland, Karin. *Dietrich & Riefenstahl: Hollywood, Berlin, and a Century in Two Lives*. New York: Liveright, 2015.

Wilder, Charly. "On the Bauhaus Trail: Much of What We Associate with Modernism Has Roots in a Small German Design School That Existed for Only 14 Years." *New York Times*, August 14, 2016.

Williamson, Bruce. "All That Fosse." *Playboy*, March 1980.

Winer, Linda. "Shade of Bob Fosse Raised by 'Chicago.'" *Newsday*, November 22, 1996.

Wolfe, Tom. *From Bauhaus to Our House*. Farrar, Straus, and Giroux, New York, 1981.

Wolf, Matt. *Sam Mendes at the Donmar: Stepping into Freedom*. London: Nick Hern Books, 2002.

York, Michael. *Accidentally on Purpose: An Autobiography*. New York: Simon & Schuster, 1991.

Zoglin, Richard. "Springtime for Sally: Weimar Germany Goes '90s Hip in a Bold New Staging of Cabaret." *Time*, March 30, 1998.

Index

THE FAQ SERIES

AC/DC FAQ
by Susan Masino
Backbeat Books
9781480394506.................$24.99

Armageddon Films FAQ
by Dale Sherman
Applause Books
9781617131196........................$24.99

The Band FAQ
by Peter Aaron
Backbeat Books
9781617136139.........................$19.99

Baseball FAQ
by Tom DeMichael
Backbeat Books
9781617136061.........................$24.99

The Beach Boys FAQ
by Jon Stebbins
Backbeat Books
9780879309879.................$22.99

The Beat Generation FAQ
by Rich Weidman
Backbeat Books
9781617136016 ....$19.99

Beer FAQ
by Jeff Cioletti
Backbeat Books
9781617136115 ....$24.99

Black Sabbath FAQ
by Martin Popoff
Backbeat Books
9780879309572....................$19.99

Bob Dylan FAQ
by Bruce Pollock
Backbeat Books
9781617136078....................$19.99

Britcoms FAQ
by Dave Thompson
Applause Books
9781495018992 ....$19.99

Bruce Springsteen FAQ
by John D. Luerssen
Backbeat Books
9781617130939.....................$22.99

A Chorus Line FAQ
by Tom Rowan
Applause Books
9781480367548 ....$19.99

The Clash FAQ
by Gary J. Jucha
Backbeat Books
9781480364509 ....$19.99

Doctor Who FAQ
by Dave Thompson
Applause Books
9781557838544.....................$22.99

The Doors FAQ
by Rich Weidman
Backbeat Books
9781617130175 ....$24.99

Dracula FAQ
by Bruce Scivally
Backbeat Books
9781617136009 ....$19.99

The Eagles FAQ
by Andrew Vaughan
Backbeat Books
9781480385412......................$24.99

Elvis Films FAQ
by Paul Simpson
Applause Books
9781557838582......................$24.99

Elvis Music FAQ
by Mike Eder
Backbeat Books
9781617130496......................$24.99

Eric Clapton FAQ
by David Bowling
Backbeat Books
9781617134548 ....$22.99

Fab Four FAQ
*by Stuart Shea and
Robert Rodriguez*
Hal Leonard Books
9781423421382.......................$19.99

Fab Four FAQ 2.0
by Robert Rodriguez
Backbeat Books
9780879309688....................$19.99

Film Noir FAQ
by David J. Hogan
Applause Books
9781557838551......................$22.99

Football FAQ
by Dave Thompson
Backbeat Books
9781495007484 ....$24.99

Frank Zappa FAQ
by John Corcelli
Backbeat Books
9781617136030.....................$19.99

Godzilla FAQ
by Brian Solomon
Applause Books
9781495045684 ....$19.99

The Grateful Dead FAQ
by Tony Sclafani
Backbeat Books
9781617130861........................$24.99

Guns N' Roses FAQ
by Rich Weidman
Backbeat Books
9781495025884 ....$19.99

Haunted America FAQ
by Dave Thompson
Backbeat Books
9781480392625....................$19.99

Horror Films FAQ
by John Kenneth Muir
Applause Books
9781557839503 ....$22.99

James Bond FAQ
by Tom DeMichael
Applause Books
9781557838568...................$22.99

Jimi Hendrix FAQ
by Gary J. Jucha
Backbeat Books
9781617130953.....................$22.99

Prices, contents, and availability
subject to change without notice.

Johnny Cash FAQ
by C. Eric Banister
Backbeat Books
9781480385405.................. $24.99

KISS FAQ
by Dale Sherman
Backbeat Books
9781617130915...................... $24.99

Led Zeppelin FAQ
by George Case
Backbeat Books
9781617130250 ....$22.99

Lucille Ball FAQ
*by James Sheridan
and Barry Monush*
Applause Books
9781617740824.......................$19.99

M.A.S.H. FAQ
by Dale Sherman
Applause Books
9781480355897.......................$19.99

Michael Jackson FAQ
by Kit O'Toole
Backbeat Books
9781480371064.......................$19.99

Modern Sci-Fi Films FAQ
by Tom DeMichael
Applause Books
9781480350618 .... $24.99

Monty Python FAQ
*by Chris Barsanti, Brian Cogan,
and Jeff Massey*
Applause Books
9781495049439 ....$19.99

Morrissey FAQ
by D. McKinney
Backbeat Books
9781480394483................. $24.99

Neil Young FAQ
by Glen Boyd
Backbeat Books
9781617130373.......................$19.99

Nirvana FAQ
by John D. Luerssen
Backbeat Books
9781617134500...................... $24.99

Pearl Jam FAQ
*by Bernard M. Corbett and
Thomas Edward Harkins*
Backbeat Books
9781617136122 ....$19.99

Pink Floyd FAQ
by Stuart Shea
Backbeat Books
9780879309503...................$19.99

Pro Wrestling FAQ
by Brian Solomon
Backbeat Books
9781617135996...................... $29.99

Prog Rock FAQ
by Will Romano
Backbeat Books
9781617135873...................... $24.99

Quentin Tarantino FAQ
by Dale Sherman
Applause Books
9781480355880 .... $24.99

Robin Hood FAQ
by Dave Thompson
Applause Books
9781495048227 ....$19.99

**The Rocky Horror
Picture Show FAQ**
by Dave Thompson
Applause Books
9781495007477 ....$19.99

Rush FAQ
by Max Mobley
Backbeat Books
9781617134517 ....$19.99

Saturday Night Live FAQ
by Stephen Tropiano
Applause Books
9781557839510...................... $24.99

Seinfeld FAQ
by Nicholas Nigro
Applause Books
9781557838575...................... $24.99

Sherlock Holmes FAQ
by Dave Thompson
Applause Books
9781480331495...................... $24.99

The Smiths FAQ
by John D. Luerssen
Backbeat Books
9781480394490.................... $24.99

Soccer FAQ
by Dave Thompson
Backbeat Books
9781617135989...................... $24.99

The Sound of Music FAQ
by Barry Monush
Applause Books
9781480360433................... $27.99

South Park FAQ
by Dave Thompson
Applause Books
9781480350649................... $24.99

Star Trek FAQ
(Unofficial and Unauthorized)
by Mark Clark
Applause Books
9781557837929.......................$19.99

Star Trek FAQ 2.0
(Unofficial and Unauthorized)
by Mark Clark
Applause Books
9781557837936....................$22.99

Star Wars FAQ
by Mark Clark
Applause Books
9781480360181...................... $24.99

Steely Dan FAQ
by Anthony Robustelli
Backbeat Books
9781495025129 ....$19.99

Stephen King Films FAQ
by Scott Von Doviak
Applause Books
9781480355514.................... $24.99

Three Stooges FAQ
by David J. Hogan
Applause Books
9781557837882......................$22.99

TV Finales FAQ
*by Stephen Tropiano and
Holly Van Buren*
Applause Books
9781480391444.......................$19.99

The Twilight Zone FAQ
by Dave Thompson
Applause Books
9781480396180 ....$19.99

Twin Peaks FAQ
*by David Bushman and
Arthur Smith*
Applause Books
9781495015861.......................$19.99

UFO FAQ
by David J. Hogan
Backbeat Books
9781480393851.......................$19.99

Video Games FAQ
by Mark J.P. Wolf
Backbeat Books
9781617136306 ....$19.99

The Who FAQ
by Mike Segretto
Backbeat Books
9781480361034 .... $24.99

The Wizard of Oz FAQ
by David J. Hogan
Applause Books
9781480350625 .... $24.99

The X-Files FAQ
by John Kenneth Muir
Applause Books
9781480369740................... $24.99

HAL•LEONARD®
PERFORMING ARTS
PUBLISHING GROUP

FAQ.halleonardbooks.com